SHAKESPEARE AT WAR

Presenting engaging, thought-provoking stories across centuries of military activity, this book demonstrates just how extensively Shakespeare's cultural capital has been deployed at times of national conflict. Drawing upon scholarly expertise in Shakespeare and war studies, first-hand experience from public military figures and insights from world-renowned theatre directors, this is the first material history of how Shakespeare has been used in wartime. Addressing home fronts and battle fronts, the collection's broad chronological coverage encompasses the Seven Years' War, the American Revolutionary War, the Napoleonic Wars, the Russian War, the First and Second World Wars, and the Iraq War. Each chapter reveals an archival object that tells us something about who 'recruited' Shakespeare, what they did with him, and to what effect. Richly illustrated throughout, the collection uniquely uncovers the agendas that Shakespeare has been enlisted to support (and critique) at times of great national crisis and loss.

AMY LIDSTER is a departmental lecturer in English language and literature at the University of Oxford. She is the author of *Publishing the History Play in the Time of Shakespeare: Stationers Shaping a Genre* (Cambridge University Press, 2022), *Authorships and Authority in Early Modern Dramatic Paratexts* (Routledge, forthcoming), and *Wartime Shakespeare: Performing Narratives of Conflict* (Cambridge University Press, 2023), a companion monograph linked to this edited collection. Her work has appeared widely in books and journals, including *Old St Paul's and Culture* (Palgrave, 2021), *Shakespeare Survey*, and *Renaissance Drama*. She is currently preparing the introduction for the Oxford World's Classics edition of *1 Henry VI*.

SONIA MASSAI is a professor of Shakespeare studies at King's College London. Her publications include *Shakespeare's Accents* (Cambridge University Press, 2020), which was a CHOICE Best Academic Book 2021, and *Shakespeare and the Rise of the Editor* (Cambridge University Press, 2007). She has edited collections of essays about *Hamlet* (Bloomsbury, 2021), *Ivo van Hove* (Bloomsbury, 2018), *Shakespeare and Textual Studies* (Cambridge University Press, 2015) and on *World-Wide Shakespeares* (Routledge, 2005), and critical editions of *Paratexts in English Printed Drama to 1642* (Cambridge University Press, 2014) and John Ford's *'Tis Pity She's a Whore* (Bloomsbury, 2011). She is currently editing a new edition of *Richard III* for the Arden Shakespeare, 4th series, and has been appointed General Editor of the Cambridge Shakespeare Editions series.

SHAKESPEARE AT WAR

A Material History

EDITED BY

AMY LIDSTER

University of Oxford

SONIA MASSAI

King's College London

CAMBRIDGE
UNIVERSITY PRESS

Shaftesbury Road, Cambridge CB2 8EA, United Kingdom

One Liberty Plaza, 20th Floor, New York, NY 10006, USA

477 Williamstown Road, Port Melbourne, VIC 3207, Australia

314–321, 3rd Floor, Plot 3, Splendor Forum, Jasola District Centre, New Delhi – 110025, India

103 Penang Road, #05–06/07, Visioncrest Commercial, Singapore 238467

Cambridge University Press is part of Cambridge University Press & Assessment,
a department of the University of Cambridge.

We share the University's mission to contribute to society through the pursuit of
education, learning and research at the highest international levels of excellence.

www.cambridge.org
Information on this title: www.cambridge.org/9781316517482

DOI: 10.1017/9781009042383

First published 2023

Printed in the United Kingdom by TJ Books Limited, Padstow Cornwall

A catalogue record for this publication is available from the British Library.

Library of Congress Cataloging-in-Publication Data
NAMES: Lidster, Amy, editor. | Massai, Sonia, editor.
TITLE: Shakespeare at war : a material history / edited by Amy Lidster, Sonia Massai.
DESCRIPTION: Cambridge ; New York, NY : Cambridge University Press, 2023. |
Includes bibliographical references and index.
IDENTIFIERS: LCCN 2023004183 | ISBN 9781316517482 (hardback) |
ISBN 9781009042383 (ebook)
SUBJECTS: LCSH: Shakespeare, William, 1564–1616 – Criticism and interpretation. |
War and literature. | LCGFT: Literary criticism.
CLASSIFICATION: LCC PR3069.W37 S43 2023 | DDC 822.3/3–dc23/eng/20230316
LC record available at https://lccn.loc.gov/2023004183

ISBN 978-1-316-51748-2 Hardback

Contents

Figures

Notes on Contributors

MARIA ABERG is a theatre director. She started her career at the Royal Court Theatre and has directed at all of the major theatres in the UK. Maria is the artistic director of PROJEKT EUROPA and an associate artist at the Royal Shakespeare Company.

CLARA CALVO is Professor of English Studies at the University of Murcia (Spain). Her research interests include Shakespeare and the First World War, literary adaptation, and cultural memory. She has recently edited, with Coppélia Kahn, *Celebrating Shakespeare: Commemoration and Cultural Memory* (Cambridge University Press, 2015).

TIM COLLINS is an Irish-born Army Colonel who served with the Royal Irish Regiment and the Special Air Service Regiment. Since leaving the army, he has been an author, broadcaster, and public speaker as well as established several successful companies.

EDWARD CORSE is an Honorary Research Fellow at the University of Kent and at the University of Hamburg and author of *A Battle for Neutral Europe* (Bloomsbury, 2012). He specializes in the history of propaganda, particularly relating to neutrality and cultural relations.

JONATHAN CRIMMINS is Associate Professor at the University of Virginia's College at Wise. His first book, *The Romanticism to Come*, was published by Bloomsbury Press in 2018. He is currently at work on a project about British harlequinades.

AILSA GRANT FERGUSON is Principal Lecturer in Literature at the University of Brighton. Her books include *Shakespeare, Cinema, Counterculture* (Routledge, 2016), *The Shakespeare Hut* (Bloomsbury, 2018), and *Shakespeare and Gender* (Bloomsbury, 2020). She is widely published on the literature and afterlives of Shakespeare and his contemporaries.

KATHERINE HENNESSEY researches Shakespeare and global literature, particularly Irish and Arab drama. She is an NEH Research Fellowship recipient (2020–21), author of *Shakespeare on the Arabian Peninsula* (Palgrave Macmillan, 2018), and co-organizer of Princeton's *Ireland and Shakespeare* symposium (2016).

NICHOLAS HYTNER is an English theatre director, film director, and film producer. In 2017, he co-founded the London Theatre Company at the newly built Bridge Theatre. He was previously the Artistic Director of London's National Theatre.

IQBAL KHAN is Associate Director of Birmingham Rep and Associate Artist of Box Clever Theatre Company. He has directed productions for the RSC, the National Theatre, Shakespeare's Globe, and many other London and regional theatres.

ROS KING is Professor Emeritus at the University of Southampton and has written and edited many books and articles on Shakespeare, including *Shakespeare and War* with Paul Franssen (Palgrave Macmillan, 2008) and *Shakespeare: A Beginner's Guide* (Oneworld, 2011).

RICHARD NED LEBOW is Professor Emeritus of International Political Theory at King's College London. His most recent books are *The Quest for Knowledge in International Relations: How Do We Know?* (Cambridge University Press, 2021) and, co-authored with Feng Zhang, *Justice East and West and International Order* (Oxford University Press, 2022).

AMY LIDSTER is Departmental Lecturer in English at Jesus College, University of Oxford. Her recent books include *Publishing the History Play in the Time of Shakespeare: Stationers Shaping a Genre* (Cambridge University Press, 2022), and *Wartime Shakespeare: Performing Narratives of Conflict* (Cambridge University Press, 2023).

IRENA R. MAKARYK is Distinguished University Professor, Department of English, University of Ottawa. She is the author of numerous books and articles on Shakespeare in times of great upheaval, including revolution, civil and world wars, and their aftermath.

SONIA MASSAI is Professor of Shakespeare Studies at King's College London. She is General Editor of the Cambridge Shakespeare Editions series and editor of the forthcoming Arden 4 *Richard III*. Her recent books include *Shakespeare's Accents* (Cambridge University Press, 2020).

ANDREW MURPHY is 1867 Professor of English at Trinity College Dublin. His books include *Shakespeare in Print: A History and Chronology of Shakespeare Publishing* (Cambridge University Press, second edition 2021) and *Ireland, Reading and Cultural Nationalism* (Cambridge University Press, 2018).

MARIUS S. OSTROWSKI is a Research Fellow in the history of ideas and social theory at the University of Nottingham and the European University Institute. He is Co-Editor of the Journal of Political Ideologies and author of Left Unity (Rowman & Littlefield, 2020) and Ideology (Polity, 2022).

REIKO OYA is English Professor at Keio University, Tokyo. Her research focuses on Shakespeare's artistic afterlives, and her publications include 'The Comedy of *Hamlet* in Nazi-Occupied Warsaw: An Exploration of Lubitsch's *To Be or Not To Be* (1942)' (*Shakespeare Survey*).

JULIA PASCAL is a playwright, theatre director, and scholar. Her dramatic works are published by Bloomsbury Publishing, and her productions have been staged in the UK, Europe, and the USA. She is a research fellow at King's College London. Her plays include *Crossing Jerusalem* and *The Holocaust Trilogy.*

ANNE SOPHIE REFSKOU teaches comparative literature at Aarhus University, Denmark, and researches early modern drama and Shakespearean afterlives. She is currently completing a monograph on Shakespeare and compassion in early modern culture.

ROBERT SAWYER is Professor of English at East Tennessee State University. Author of *Marlowe and Shakespeare: The Critical Rivalry* (Palgrave Macmillan, 2017) and *Shakespeare between the World Wars* (Palgrave Macmillan, 2019), he recently co-edited an issue of *Multicultural Shakespeare* on the topic of 'Shakespeare Our Posthumanist' (2022).

ESTHER B. SCHUPAK is a faculty member in the Department of English Literature and Linguistics at Bar-Ilan University. Her research focuses on Shakespeare, rhetoric, performance, and pedagogy.

JONATHAN SHAW was commander of allied forces in southern Iraq in 2007. He was appointed Companion of the Order of the Bath (CB) in 2012. He is the author of *Britain in a Perilous World* (Haus, 2014) and is chairman of Optima Group.

STUART SILLARS is Emeritus Professor at the University of Bergen, Norway. He has written extensively on literature and visual culture in Shakespeare, the Victorians, and the two world wars.

MAGGIE SMALES is a theatre maker in York. After a career teaching drama during which she was able to 'play' with texts and ideas in an educational context, she has enjoyed continuing the practice. She is also a performer and Director at Theatre@41.

MONIKA SMIALKOWSKA is Assistant Professor in English Literature at Northumbria University. Having published book chapters and articles about the celebrations of the 1916 Shakespeare Tercentenary, she is finalizing a monograph exploring the Tercentenary's local and global dimensions.

EMMA SMITH is Professor of Shakespeare Studies at Hertford College, University of Oxford. The second edition of her book *Shakespeare's First Folio: Four Centuries of an Iconic Book* was published in April 2023 by Oxford University Press, and she is working on an edition of *Twelfth Night*.

RAMONA WRAY is Professor of English at Queen's University Belfast. She is the co-author of *Great Shakespeareans: Welles, Kozintsev, Kurosawa, Zeffirelli* (Bloomsbury Arden, 2013). Recent essays on Shakespeare film and television have appeared in *Cahiers Élisabéthains*, *Shakespeare Bulletin*, and *Shakespeare Survey*.

Acknowledgements

We are very grateful to the Leverhulme Trust for funding 'Wartime Shakespeare' (2018–21), the research project within which this collection of essays was originally conceived. We are also thankful to Jane Holmes, Ian Maine, and Glyn Prysor at the National Army Museum for inviting us to curate the forthcoming 'Shakespeare at War' exhibition (October 2023 to May 2024), for which this collection doubles as an exhibition book, and to Emily Hockley and George Laver at Cambridge University Press for commissioning *Shakespeare at War* and for supporting us with their advice and expertise throughout the contracting and production process. Last but not least, we want to take this opportunity to thank all our contributors for writing such an exciting range of essays and for agreeing to take part in the interviews included in this collection. We have thoroughly enjoyed working with you all!

AMY LIDSTER AND SONIA MASSAI

Note on the Text

All quotations from Shakespeare's plays and poems refer to the single-volume editions of the works included in The New Cambridge Shakespeare series, published by Cambridge University Press.

Introduction
A Material History

Amy Lidster and Sonia Massai

War is an abiding concern in many of Shakespeare's plays, and memorable lines from them are routinely used in international-relations parlance or by political leaders either to caution against military action or to garner public support for conflict. Rousing reminders that 'the valiant never taste of death but once' (*Julius Caesar*, 2.2.33) are balanced by sobering admonitions that 'few die well that die in a battle' (*Henry V*, 4.1.129). But war is never simply eulogized or critiqued in Shakespeare, as these lines seem to suggest when extracted from the context within which they were originally written and performed. Shortly after speaking the first line, Julius Caesar gets himself assassinated out of vanity rather than valour; and few would guess that the second line comes from a play often associated with national pride and military prowess. Views about war, like much else in Shakespeare, are not only multiple and varied across the canon, they are also nuanced through complexity of characterization or dramatic irony within a fictive world.

While sustained attention has been devoted to the rich and multiple perspectives on war in Shakespeare, our emphasis is on the use and reception of Shakespeare during wartime, a topic that is attracting increasing critical interest.[1] Indeed, the way in which we use Shakespeare and his plays reveals their meaning for us. Conditions of war are sometimes assumed to prompt clear-cut, didactic, or propagandistic engagement with the arts, including Shakespeare; but this collection shows how even ostensible propaganda involving the mobilization of Shakespeare's works – or his cultural capital – has in fact proven invariably complex or complicated by the variety of uses and interpretations that they have produced. This collection featuring essays and interviews from a wide range of contributors, including Shakespeare scholars, theatre practitioners, military figures, and political and wartime historians, explores how Shakespeare – in performance, text, and quotation – has been used over the past two-and-a-half centuries. We strive to offer an expansive historical perspective, while concentrating

on conflicts that directly involved Britain, including the Seven Years'
War and the American Revolutionary War in the eighteenth century, the
Napoleonic Wars and the Russian War (otherwise known as the 'Crimean
War') in the nineteenth century, the First and the Second World Wars in
the twentieth century, and the Iraq War in the early twenty-first century.
This *longue durée* approach has made it possible for us to identify three
factors that have emerged as qualifiers in the mobilization of Shakespeare
at times of war: the nature and extent of the conflict (such as 'total war'
versus 'proxy war'), Shakespeare's shifting cultural capital, and the individual aims of the agents and networks involved. Because of the varying
interplay of these three factors, the history of Shakespeare at war does not
progress linearly.

One of the features that makes this collection distinctive is its 'material
history' – its focus on archival objects, such as theatrical props, playbills,
and production photographs, along with newspaper articles, broadsheets,
prints, posters, and pamphlets. This material approach is a vital and illumi-
nating one: each essay in the collection concentrates on a specific, local history of Shakespeare at war and shows that, by slowing down and offering rich
descriptions of a material object and its significance, we can recover untold
and forgotten histories from the archives that shed light on Shakespeare's
wartime appeal and the role of the arts during conflict. Objects and their
history of use and valuation – the position of, for example, a cabinet card
of Shakespeare within the papers of Irish nationalist Michael Davitt (as
Andrew Murphy considers in Chapter 6) – witness an intersection of different agents, aims, and interpretations, which often challenge established
critical priorities. This material history offers fresh insights into the ideologies, affiliations, and agendas of those who 'recruited' Shakespeare at times
of war and shows that even the most belligerent or oppositional acts of
appropriation were qualified by the intersectional identities of those who
produced them or by the divided responses that they elicited.[2] There are
also parallel histories of Shakespeare's use during conflict to critique war,
to contest his relevance, and to reflect on the experiences of non-elite or
marginalized voices (see Monika Smialkowska's discussion in Chapter 9
of the gender hierarchies on display in a 1916 Shakespeare gala at Calais).
Indeed, Shakespeare's appeal for a specific community – for an audience,
readership, government, armed force, or nation – is variable, non-uniform,
and often changes during a conflict. In place of a single, linear history of
Shakespeare's reception during wartime, our aim – through the structure,
content, and material focus of the collection – is to embrace and recover a
plurality of voices and histories.

The most recent conflict to erupt in Europe since this project got underway – Russia's invasion of Ukraine in February 2022 – shows that Shakespeare is still routinely invoked at times of war. On 8 March 2022, Ukrainian President Volodymyr Zelensky addressed the British Parliament and cited *Hamlet* to sum up the existential threat faced by his people: 'The question for us now', he said, 'is to be or not to be'. Then he added, emphatically, that the answer to that question was 'definitely yes, to be'.[3] *Hamlet* was also the play that the resident company of the Ivan Franko Academic Drama Theater in Kiev decided to revive on 15 March 2022 to underline the need to take a stand against invading Russian forces. Making a transhistorical link with an earlier period of conflict, the production was dedicated to 'the people of the UK for ongoing support of Ukraine & in recognition of the Blitz of WW2 in which the UK's civilian population was also bombed'.[4] These uses tap into a history of oppositional readings of this play in Ukraine, as well as resistance to imposed Russian translations of Shakespeare in the years following the First World War, which strove to 'confirm the right to stage Shakespeare in Ukrainian', as Irena R. Makaryk has explored.[5]

In at least one respect, however, the way in which Shakespeare has been mobilized in Ukraine so far confirms that it amplifies, and never simplifies, fundamental questions that deepen our understanding of complex situations, even as they unfold. When Zelensky made his appeal to the British Parliament, both parties knew that British military support was at the time unfeasible, because it would automatically trigger the involvement of all other NATO countries and therefore lead to the escalation of this conflict at a global level. However, his reference to *Hamlet* helped him to challenge what kind of support – humanitarian, diplomatic, financial, and so forth – heads of state, military leaders, and international organizations believe to constitute 'involvement' in a military conflict. Similarly, the dedication of the *Hamlet* production staged by actors of the Ivan Franko Theater to the 'people of the UK' as fellow victims of brutal regimes foregrounded the tension between an ethical imperative and civic duty, since Britain was about to issue a veto that made direct involvement of its citizens as a voluntary militia illegal.[6] In short, the use of Shakespeare's *Hamlet* right at the outset of this conflict aligned the international community with its main character in a renewed effort to establish what course of action constitutes an ethical versus a purely strategic or even pragmatically necessary response to a violent crime, or even what constitutes a (war) crime.

By prioritizing how Shakespeare is used at times of war, rather than how war is represented in Shakespeare, we are able to see how embedded

Shakespeare has become over the centuries, not just in Britain but, as this most recent example suggests, globally, and that this relevance is not exclusively linked to his most warlike plays. Admittedly, *Henry V* has been a firm staple during wartime – sometimes through high-profile productions, such as Laurence Olivier's 1944 film version (see Edward Corse's discussion in Chapter 17) – although it has not been performed as frequently as one might assume. *Hamlet* has, for example, proven to have quite wide appeal during wartime. The play, of course, involves a political usurpation, but many wartime readings have pursued a different emphasis: on Hamlet as a questioning individual painfully dislocated from his society, on the cultural fame that this play has acquired globally, and on the rhetorical template offered by its most famous soliloquy.[7] As discussed, this speech has been invoked most recently in Ukraine, but it has a long history of wartime mobilization: as this collection shows, it was used by Wilhelm II during the First World War when describing the conflict as an existential question for Germany (see Marius S. Ostrowski's discussion in Chapter 11) and in a range of print parodies during the Napoleonic Wars (see Lidster's discussion in Chapter 4). While plays such as *Othello* and *Much Ado About Nothing* do not depict active combat per se, the former is set within a military community and the latter within a surrounding wartime context, and these plays have been adapted to reflect on how the costs, consequences, and conduct of war permeate and implicate all aspects of a society (see discussions by Maria Aberg, Jonathan Shaw, and Iqbal Khan in Chapters 24–26). Plays that are even more removed from the immediacy of conflict, such as *The Taming of the Shrew*, and uses of Shakespeare that focus on the dramatist himself as a cultural combatant (see, for example, Irena R. Makaryk's and Reiko Oya's discussions in Chapters 5 and 20, respectively) have also played important roles during conflict, sometimes presenting the arts as aspects of society, allied with notions of freedom of expression and democracy, that are being defended through the war effort.

Casting a wide net over the past two-and-a-half centuries, this material history of Shakespeare at war uses its distinctive focus to shed light on some of the core political issues dominating a conflict, the wartime role played by the arts, and the shifting cultural capital of Shakespeare for different communities. In this reception history, Shakespeare is both of an age *and* for all time: he is often used to respond directly to the immediacy of a specific conflict and carry topical currency, but he is also part of a long cultural history that is always under negotiation and reveals a shifting set of priorities, values, and even prejudices. This collection of essays, which doubles as a critical companion for the *Shakespeare at War* exhibition (held at the National Army Museum in London, 2023–24), shows what can be gained from a material focus on this history. By exploring the lives of significant objects – their provenance, uses, and resonances – we can work to recover the polyvocality of wartime Shakespeare. But the work of 'Shakespeare at War' is never over, and the archives are full of many more exciting and overlooked histories. We hope that our focus in this collection prompts us all to slow down, look again, and pay attention to the layered responses found within this important critical tradition and the trail of fascinating archival objects that it has left behind.

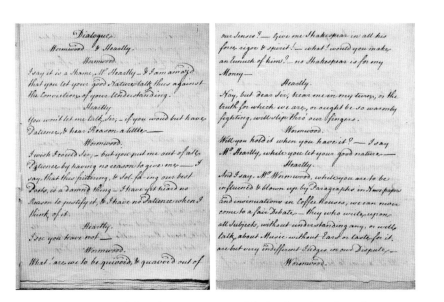

Figure 1   David Garrick, opening pages of the 'Dialogue', performed as prologue to Garrick's *The Tempest* (1756) (LA 123 Larpent Collection, The Huntington Library, San Marino, California).

CHAPTER I

'The Truth for Which We Are Fighting'
David Garrick's The Tempest (1756) and Inclusive Britishness during the Seven Years' War

Sonia Massai

Figure 1 shows the first two pages of a 'Dialogue' between Heartly and Wormwood written by eighteenth-century actor, playwright, and stage manager David Garrick.[1] Heartly is an actor who is about to start performing in Garrick's operatic version of *The Tempest*, which opened at Drury Lane on 11 February 1756. Wormwood is a critic who loves Shakespeare but dislikes opera because he believes that music enervates and emasculates the listener. 'What! are we to be quiver'd & quaver'd out of our Senses?', he exclaims. And then he adds, 'Give me Shakespear in all his force, rigor & spirit! – what! would you make an Eunuch of him? – no[,] Shakespear is for my Money – ' (i^r–i^v). Later in the 'Dialogue', Wormwood reiterates his love for Shakespeare and his hatred for 'capering, & quavering', which he finds 'Unnatural, & abominable' (iii^r). When challenged by Heartly – 'But English music, Mr. Wormwood? … would you chuse that your Country shou'd be excell'd in any thing by your Neighbours?' – he concedes: 'In manufactures? – no – from the casting of Cannon, to the making of Pins, … but your capering & quavering, only spoil us, & make us the Jests, who shou'd be the Terrors of Europe' (iv^r).

The military language deployed by Wormwood and his belligerent stance against Britain's neighbouring nations on the Continent establish a link between Garrick's operatic adaptation of *The Tempest* and the imminent escalation of the French and Indian War (1754–63), which was fought against the British in the North American colonies, into the Seven Years' War (1756–63), the first conflict that had Europe as its epicentre while involving an unprecedented number of global 'theatres of war'. In this essay I argue that Garrick's operatic *Tempest*, generally dismissed as a flop and as an embarrassing misjudgement on Garrick's part, in fact takes on greater topical significance and political resonance when reconsidered in its wartime context and alongside its original prologue.[2] Garrick's opera and 'Dialogue' are representative examples of wartime appropriations of Shakespeare, which, as this collection shows, often served as important platforms for the fashioning of current attitudes towards military conflict. In the second of the two pages of the 'Dialogue' reproduced in Figure 1, Heartly captures this very specific purpose of (re)playing Shakespeare at times of war when he urges Wormwood (and his audience) to 'hear [him], or', he warns, 'the truth for which we are, or ought [to] be so warmly fighting, will slip thro' our fingers' (i^v). What is remarkable about this short dialogue (twelve pages in all) is that this rousing call to arms comes from a dubious, foppish character, whose notion of 'truth' is swayed, as Heartly points out, by 'Paragraphs in Newspapers and insinuations in Coffee houses' (i^v). As this essay goes on to show, the 'Dialogue' sounds a note of caution that invites reflection and possibly reconsideration of the motives for going to war. It also provides an important perspective on the opera, which would otherwise seem consistently aligned with Wormwood's aggressive and exclusive nationalism.[3]

§

Garrick pared down Shakespeare's play quite radically by cutting the number of its original characters and the lines they speak in order to make space for thirty-two songs. It is therefore surprising to find as many as four named sailors in it, since there are none in the original: Trinculo and Stephano, who are described as '*a Iester*' and '*a drunken Butler*' in the list of dramatis personae appended to the earliest printed edition of Shakespeare's play in the First Folio of 1623, are joined by Mustacho and Ventoso in the opera, where they are respectively listed as '*Boatswain*', '*Master of the ship*', '*Mariner*', and '*Mate*'.[4] Also noteworthy is that Garrick did not invent Mustacho and Ventoso. He borrowed them from an earlier adaptation of *The Tempest, or the Enchanted Island* by William Davenant and John Dryden, which had premiered at the Duke of York's House on 7 November 1667. Along with Stephano and 'Trincalo' (*sic*) (A4^v), these two new characters play a significant part not only on the island, as reimagined by Dryden and Davenant, but also in the opening scene.[5]

In Shakespeare, the play opens with '*A tempestuous noise of thunder and lightning*'. '[*A*] shipmaster, *and a* boatswain [*and* mariners]' then enter, as they try and save the ship from splitting or running aground. Instead of keeping below deck, Alonso, the King of Naples, his brother Sebastian, his son Ferdinand, his councillor Gonzalo, and Prospero's brother, Antonio, disrupt the crew as they go about doing their jobs as best as they can. 'You mar our labour … You do assist the storm', complains the boatswain, as he overrules his social superior, Antonio. When Gonzalo urges him to be patient, the boatswain retorts, 'What cares these roarers for the name of king?' (1.1.0.1–16). The dramatic shift from the crew's insubordination, which mirrors the fury of the elements, to the peaceful setting of Prospero's long narrative account of how he has in fact caused the storm to bring his enemies under his control acquires topical significance when read in relation to changing British policy for control over the sea. According to Paul Franssen, its main extra-dramatic purpose was to signal a break away from Elizabeth I's policy of 'open seas' to the establishment of 'sovereignty of the seas' under James I.[6] In the Dryden–Davenant play, the sailors and their officers' drunken brawling and their greater prominence have instead been linked to charges brought against the British Navy following the Dutch invasion of the Medway during the Second Anglo–Dutch War (1665–67).[7]

By the time we get to Garrick's opera, the four sea-faring characters had acquired an established presence on the English stage, where the Dryden–Davenant play had displaced the Shakespearean original for nearly a century. But their significance shifted once again. Relative to the overall brevity of the text, these characters are even more prominent in Garrick's opera than in the Dryden–Davenant play. Compared to their Restoration predecessors, they are also significantly rehabilitated, mostly as a result of Garrick's omission of Shakespeare's opening scene. The beginning of Garrick's opera is significantly different from both its Shakespearean and its Restoration antecedents in being remarkably quieter and orderly. The opening stage direction – 'The Stage darkened – represents a cloudy sky, a very rocky coast, and a ship on a tempestuous sea.' (B1^r) – suggests the use of a painted backdrop. Ariel is the first character to enter, singing a song borrowed from the Dryden–Davenant *Tempest*: 'Arise, arise, ye subterranean winds' (B1^r). Then Prospero enters with Miranda to claim complete control over the elements and all the other characters on the island. When Garrick's Boatswain, Master of the ship, Mariner, and Mate are reunited and meet Caliban at the end of Act 1, they still fall out over who should be in charge of the island, but their exchange is much shorter than in the Dryden–Davenant adaptation, where it would have stirred uncomfortable memories of the English Civil War and Interregnum (1642–60). In Garrick, the four seafaring companions are garrulous rather than seditious. Trincalo (*sic*) ends up leading the others because he had the good fortune of getting to shore 'on a butt of sack' (C3^v) and wine is their most treasured possession on the island. As in William Hogarth's contemporary print *The Invasion, Plate 2: England,* conviviality is not juxtaposed but rather conducive to comradeship and valour. In Hogarth, the English love for 'Beef and Beer' animates the revellers outside a country tavern in the foreground and sustains the well-disciplined soldiers training in the background. In his twin print, *The Invasion, Plate 1: France,* the French, by contrast, look bedraggled and malnourished, huddling anxiously underneath a sign that advertises 'Soup Meagre a la Sabot Royal'.[8] Overall, the prominence and rehabilitation of the four seafaring companions in Garrick register a renewed optimism in the strength of the nation's naval power. It is significant in this context that, despite crushing land battles in the American colonies in the early stages of the French and Indian War, the British Navy had avoided defeat for Britain by taking hundreds of French vessels, thus cutting off reinforcement of enemy troops and ammunition.

In this respect, the 'Dialogue' would seem to bolster this nationalist element in Garrick's opera. When trying to persuade Wormwood about the stirring power of 'English music', Heartly asks him to consider how, if 'sounded in the Ears of five thousand brave Englishmen, with a Protestant Prince at the Head of 'em', it would rouse them into action. Heartly, whose 'good nature' Wormwood often praises (and patronizes), uncharacteristically encourages the music-hating critic to imagine how the roused soldiers would 'drive every Monsieur into the sea, & make 'em food for sprats and Mackrell' (v[r]). It is perhaps the culinary appeal of 'sprats and Mackrell' that contributes to changing Wormwood's appreciation of music so quickly, as suggested by his sudden and cordial admission of defeat: 'I see my Error – but I'll make amends – let us meet after it [the opera] is over, & take a Bottle to Sprats & Mackrell' (vi[r]). Conviviality, fuelled by 'sack' in the 'low' plot of Garrick's opera and by 'Sprats and Mackrell' in the 'Dialogue', produces the necessary optimism and fellow feeling required to repel foreign invaders. However, the next section of this essay shows how both Garrick's opera and his 'Dialogue' register current anxieties about Britain's ability to retain control over the fast-expanding frontiers of the Empire, which in turn qualify this optimistic outlook about the imminent outbreak of a new war in Europe.

§

Caliban is one of Shakespeare's most prominent and vocal outsiders. Both Prospero and Miranda call him 'savage' (1.2.355), 'thing most brutish' (1.2.357), and 'slave' – 'poisonous slave', 'most lying slave', and 'Abhorrèd slave' (1.2.320, 345, 351).[9] Caliban disputes their account of how he came to be enslaved and reclaims ownership over the island: 'This island's mine by Syrcorax my mother, / Which thou tak'st from me' (1.2.332–33). Even more crucially, his language sounds quite the opposite of 'savage' or 'brutish'. This is most memorably the case when he reassures Trinculo and Stephano that 'the isle is full of noises, / Sounds, and sweet airs, that give delight and hurt not' (3.2.127–28). It seems especially strange that Garrick, who champions the power of music to move the heart and rouse the spirit in the 'Dialogue', should cut these lines from his opera, since Caliban goes on to recall how 'Sometimes a thousand twangling instruments / Will hum about mine ears; and sometime voices, / That if I then had waked after long sleep, / Will make me sleep again' (3.2.129–32). Caliban's character is in fact the most drastically abridged role in the opera as a whole: he does not feature in the first act, as he does in Shakespeare; he speaks just a handful of his original lines when he stumbles on Trincalo and his other seafaring companions in the second act; and he does not return in the third and final act. Caliban is not even mentioned in the Argument prefaced to Garrick's opera.

The extent to which Garrick cut Caliban's role is even more remarkable when his opera is compared to the Dryden–Davenant adaptation, where Caliban not only speaks most of his original lines but has also acquired a sister, named Sycorax after their mother. Also worth noting is the increased threat posed by Caliban and Sycorax to the European visitors. As in Shakespeare (but not in Garrick), Caliban admits that, had Prospero not 'prevent[ed]' him, he would have 'peopled else / This isle with Calibans' by sleeping with Miranda (1.2.350). The risk of miscegenation is higher in the Dryden–Davenant play, because Caliban's sister displays a similarly active and unruly sexuality: first she throws herself at a reluctant but ultimately acquiescing Trincalo, who wants to inherit the island by marrying her; and then she offers to 'marry that other King and his two subjects [Stephano, Mustacho and Ventoso] to help [him] anights' (G1ᵛ). Despite these notable expansions of the 'low' plot, Dryden and Davenant also cut Caliban's most poetical lines quoted above ('This isle is full of noises …'). In Garrick, Caliban becomes a minor role: his sensitivity has all but disappeared, along with his subversive resistance and most of his original lines.

The fact that Caliban becomes increasingly unthreatening by the Restoration and increasingly marginal by the mid-eighteenth century is symptomatic of growing (rather than abating) anxieties generated by the expansion of Britain's colonial territories. According to Linda Colley, the territorial gains secured by the end of the Seven Years' War left Britons 'in the grip of collective agoraphobia, captivated by, but also adrift … in a vast empire' that both fascinated and challenged them with its riches and its strangeness.[10] Telling in this respect is a related adjustment to the way in which the island is represented. In Shakespeare, the island is often a projection of the emotions experienced by its inhabitants. The noises that 'give delight' to Caliban and 'hurt [him] not' drive the king and his party frantic with fear. Similarly, the island seems in turn 'barren' or 'fertile', and has 'fresh springs' but also noxious 'brine-pits' (1.2.339) and 'unwholesome fen' (1.2.322–23), whose 'wicked dew' Caliban threatens to use to poison Prospero and Miranda. Similarly, in the Dryden–Davenant adaptation the riches that the island can yield – 'Every dainty you can think of, / Ev'ry Wine which you would drink of' (F3^r) – are offset by hidden and nightmare-like dangers. Alonso tells his party how 'he pull'd a Tree, and Blood pursu'd [his] hand' (C4^r). He then urges them to 'Beware all fruit but what the birds have peid [pecked]' (D1^r) and warns them that even the 'shadows of the Trees are poisonous' because 'A secret venom slides from every branch' (D1^r). In Garrick's opera, all hidden dangers have disappeared. The island is neatly divided into 'Prospero's cell' (B1^v ff.) and 'the wild part' (C2^v ff.), and the characters who inhabit these spaces never get to mix or interact with each other.

The island's 'wild part' would therefore seem to be fully contained in Garrick. However, the 'Dialogue' strikes a very different note from the opera by offering an interesting corrective to the marginalization of Caliban. When Heartly urges the audience to 'protect her [English music]' because it is 'distress'd' by the common view that it is a minor art, he extends his appeal to encompass all other kinds of oppression: ''Tis the known principle of a Brittish [sic] Breast, / Those to befriend the most, Who're most opprest' (vi^v). One could argue that Garrick's Caliban does not evidently fall into the category of the oppressed, since his character is so thoroughly sanitized, and its significance so drastically reduced. In fact, I would argue that the extent to which Caliban's 'distress' is removed from, or rather repressed in, Garrick's opera is symptomatic of the systematic denial that was proving necessary to make the colonial enterprise seem compatible with 'the known principle of a Brittish Breast'.

§

The war-related resonance and colonial anxieties that this essay has identified in Garrick's *Tempest* and in his 'Dialogue' take on additional significance when considering that Garrick's paternal grandfather was a French émigré Huguenot. David de la Garrique left France to resettle in London after the revocation of the edict of Nantes in 1685, which had granted limited rights to French Protestants since the end of the French Wars of Religion in 1598. Garrick's career was punctuated by repeated attacks from critics who targeted both his lack of professional training as an actor and his French descent. As early as 1742, in a tract called 'A Clear Stage, and no favour: Or, Tragedy and Comedy at War', its anonymous writer claimed that advertising '*Puffs*' should Garrick's 'way precede, / [so] England may his foreign Actions read' (10). In a similar vein, in 1755, Theophilus Cibber, the son of classically trained, 'old school' actor and theatre manager Colley Cibber, who was following in his father's footsteps, complained 'that an *Englishman*, the Son of an *Englishman*, who … has been judged one of the greatest Ornaments of the *English* Stage … should be obstructed … by the Son of a *Frenchman*' ('An Epistle from Mr. Theophilus Cibber to David Garrick, Esq.', 1755).

Given Garrick's background, one might assume that the tension this essay has highlighted in his *Tempest* and accompanying 'Dialogue' between supporting the war effort and cautioning against oppressing those that are distressed stemmed from personal circumstances. However, a quick glance at news stories published by the press in early 1756 suggests that public opinion was similarly divided. On 1 January 1756, for example, none other than Colley Cibber, Garrick's rival, had his 'Ode for the New Year' published in *The Whitehall Evening Post*. In it, he compares the fast-expanding British Empire to the imperial power of ancient Rome by referring to the reigning King George II as a Caesar: 'Hail! Hail! Auspicious Day, / Advancing to prolong / The years of CAESAR's Sway.' Cibber's poem shared the front page with a lengthy 'Description of the Azores.'[11] A woodcut showing a ship, anchored just off a rocky coastline, surmounted by a fortified citadel opens this feature, where the islands are described as 'very fertile in Corn, Wine, Variety of Fruits' and 'breed[ing] great Quantities of Cattle'. The syntax attributes active agency to the islands, suggesting that they offer an endless supply of labour-free goods:

> The very Rocks, which elsewhere are generally dry and barren, produce here a good sort of Wine … The Land yields plenty of good Wheat and Fruits; and their Pasture Grounds such Numbers of large Oxen, Sheep, and other Cattle, that here is no want of any Necessaries of Life.

The article goes on to mention a quasi-magical crop unique to these islands, 'an extraordinary Root, … as big as a Man's two Fists, cover'd with long, and small Fibres, of a Gold Colour, not unlike Silk'. Predictably a distinction is then drawn between the naivete of the inhabitants, who 'only use [it] to stuff their Beds', and what an 'Ingenious Hand' could do with it.

The combined effect on the reader of this front page is comparable to a reading of Garrick's opera and 'Dialogue' that singles out its nationalist emphasis on the role of the arts (and of English music more specifically) to rouse the British to repel a potential French invasion on the home front and to continue to pursue colonial ambitions overseas. However, on the same day, the same reader might have read another article about the 'State of Europe' in *The London Evening Post*, which advocated for peace and power-sharing among all European nations: reflecting on the fact that '*France* has no *Quarrel*, no *Shadow* of a *Quarrel* with the *Germanick* Body', its author regards the possibility of hostilities breaking out between these two countries as 'the *greatest* of *Absurdities*'. The same article then goes on to report the unconfirmed news that the devastating earthquake that destroyed Lisbon on 1 November 1755 had also impacted the Azores. After inviting its readers to reflect on 'the prodigious Loss the Portugueze Monarchy has suffered … by these tremendous Convulsions of the Elements', this article reprints the same description of the Azores that the *Whitehall Evening Post* had published on its front page.

Reading these two newspapers on the same day would have had a comparable impact to heeding to the qualified, more inclusive nationalism that emerges from Garrick's 'Dialogue' and opera. Garrick's wartime appropriation of *The Tempest* and news stories published at the time suggest that both the London stage and the London press shared divided views about the ongoing colonial war overseas and the potential outbreak of another war in Europe. In the next essay, building on his earlier study of Garrick's *Harlequin's Invasion* (1759), Jonathan Crimmins shows that Garrick continued to uphold 'a cosmopolitan stance of neighbourly reconciliation' in a farce that, while drawing on nationalist sentiments, abounds in ironic qualifiers that ultimately undermine them.[12] His neglected operatic *Tempest* and even less well known 'Dialogue' represent a similarly complex appropriation of Shakespeare, which, as this essay has shown, initiated a tendency, still popular today, to turn to Shakespeare to process conflicting attitudes to war and to negotiate divided allegiances exacerbated by it.

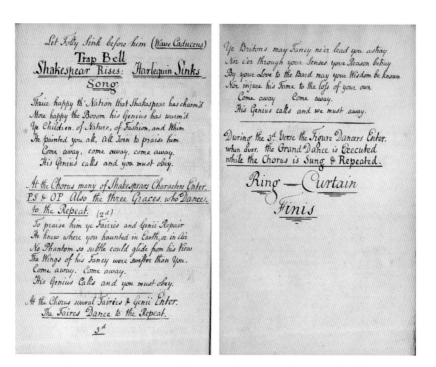

Figure 2   Manuscript of *Harlequin's Invasion: A Christmas Gambol*
(MS G.3936.1, Barton Collection, Boston Public Library).

CHAPTER 2

The Seven Years' War (1756–1763) and Garrick's Shakespearean Nationalism

Jonathan Crimmins

With beautiful flourishes on 'Ring — Curtain / Finis', the last pages of David Garrick's *Harlequin's Invasion* are the manuscript's most ornamented (see Figure 2). It is the prompter's copy, and Drury Lane's prompter, Richard Cross, pays special attention to the stage direction: 'Shakespear Rises: Harlequin Sinks.' He gives us two beautiful Ss: a wispy airy S to lift up 'Shakespear' and a harpooning arrow on top of the S that pantomimes 'Sinks'. The play is structured around an enmity between Shakespeare and Harlequin. The opening scene, for instance, closes with trumpets, fife, drum, and the god Mercury enjoining the assembled crowd: 'Let all hands, and hearts, do their utmost endeavour. / Sound trumpet, beat drum, King Shakespear forever.'[1]

Harlequin's Invasion premiered on 31 December 1759, at the end of a year of important military victories for the British in the Seven Years' War, and, as John O'Brien writes, 'Shakespeare's ascendancy in the play needs to be understood as a sign of British cultural pre-eminence designed to rhyme with a military puissance.'[2] In August, the British Navy defeated the French Mediterranean Fleet in the Battle of Lagos. In late November, the British victory at the Battle of Quiberon Bay put an end to the threat that 'Monsieur Harlequin' would cross the Channel with his legions 'on an ocean of canvas in flat bottom boats' and invade the coast of Britain (see Amy Lidster's discussion in Chapter 4 for a resurgence of this threat during the Napoleonic Wars).[3] *Harlequin's Invasion* ends with the invasion repulsed in the midst of a storm like the one that helped destroy the French fleet. Celebrating this decisive victory, the play would seem to easily merit the claim John O'Brien makes that it is 'the most aggressively and openly nationalist eighteenth-century English pantomime', as if 'Shakespear Rises: Harlequin Sinks' tells us definitively how the play should be read.[4]

During the Seven Years' War, Shakespeare's plays were easily enlisted in support of British nationalist sentiment. In 1759, for instance, when Covent

Garden produced an adaptation of *Cymbeline* by William Hawkins, the opening prologue pitched the play as timely and instructive: 'the poet begs you to see / From an old tale, what Britons ought to be'.[5] Unlike Thomas d'Urfey's adaptation, which focused on *Cymbeline*'s love story, Hawkins boasted that 'in these restless days of war's alarms', his adaptation 'Not melts the soul to love, but fires the blood to arms'.[6] Shakespeare was a potent tool for arousing anti-French bellicosity because he already functioned as a figurehead for the cultural rivalry between the two nations. As Howard D. Weinbrot writes, 'The more the French denigrate Shakespeare and insist on the rules, the more the British elevate Shakespeare, the irregula.'[7] Shakespeare's irregularity – flaunted unities, blended genres, and mixed tones – buttressed self-aggrandizing notions of England as a rugged, untameable nation.

Shakespeare's irregularity, however, also had the effect, according to Frans De Bruyn, of opening new lines of thinking about Shakespeare: 'By personifying Voltaire as a cultural bogeyman, the English created a critical space that permitted them to entertain new ways of understanding and appreciating Shakespeare's achievement.'[8] In other words, in the eighteenth century, Shakespeare helped very good readers like David Garrick develop a more capacious aesthetic. If Shakespeare was to be England's premier playwright – foremost not despite his irregularity but because of it – then a playscript might not have to be scripted quite so simply. Garrick repeatedly tailored the strangeness of Shakespeare into theatrical forms that the eighteenth century found most hospitable to strangeness, time and again proving his commitment to the strange things theatre makes possible.

Harlequin's Invasion is in fact a strange play. It is a mock *Cymbeline* – staged at a moment when Garrick was preparing to present a restored, nearly unaltered *Cymbeline* – that appears to have been cobbled together from older material in collaboration with the comic actor Richard Yates.[9] Understanding precisely what Garrick is saying in this antic absurdist play about war, nationalism, and Shakespeare requires us to recognize that while, as actor, writer, and manager, Garrick routinely championed Shakespeare, it was not necessarily in order to endorse notions of a swaggering British masculinity and its unruly violence. Comparing an earlier partial manuscript of the play held by the Huntington Library's Larpent Collection with the full manuscript held by the Boston Public Library's Barton Collection, I argue that one sees in Garrick's revisions his love of irony, his eclecticism and celebration of intermixture, all elements of the play that run counter to its seeming bellicose nationalism. *Harlequin's Invasion* rather harbours abiding suspicions about violence and nationalism, more consistent with a critique of war-making. The *annus mirabilis* of 1759 finds Garrick looking past wartime nationalism to peace and reconciliation.

The play begins with a crowd assembling in Charing Cross. Forge, a blacksmith, gets the first line, entering with a proclamation and exclaiming, 'Huzza Boys!—Here it is, jolly hearts! This will be the making of us all, huzza!'[10] The implication is that joining the war gives each of them a chance at fortune, rank, or glory, and might thus prove to be their 'making'. It is all a set up for an extended joke. Neither Forge nor anyone in his cohort can read. They have no idea what the paper says. But is the grim insight that patriotism is profiteering couched as a joke in order to blunt a politically unpalatable critique, or is it such a time-worn truism that we chuckle like a shrug? Are the play's nationalist messages the easiest ones to read because the play's comedy offers a cluster of ironies to answer simple questions? Or is it that we tend to accept the premises of nationalism as if they are synonymous with political wisdom? What if, before we consider the relationship between nationalism and war, we ask the simpler question implied by the first line: namely, what does war make?

Of course, Forge's bellicose exuberance cannot mean the making of all of us all at once and certainly not all of us equally. Many will die, be imprisoned, maimed, traumatized, or otherwise ruined. It can only mean *all* in the sense of *potentially any* of us. Even as it implicitly means only some, the *us* nonetheless creates a unit, since all must strive that some might achieve. There are various spoils for the surviving victors; for the dead, romanticized ceremonies that smother grief with honour. Every loss and every gain is garnered in the name of the larger us, that mythical unity gathered together and directed by enmity – which ought to make this moment in the play an exemplar of Carl Schmitt's defining criterion of the political: 'the specific political distinction to which political actions and motives can be reduced is that between the friend and enemy'.[11] Indeed, the contagious huzzas and the repeated flourishes of fife, trumpet, and drum seem to suggest that by the end of the scene the Londoners have united against the common enemy, rallying under a nationalist banner that symbolizes their shared hostility.

The contested passage of the Militia Acts in 1757, which raised a defence force to protect England against a French invasion while the army occupied North America, expanded the *all* and the *us* beyond the more limited sense of the professional military class. The populist nationalism of the scene, therefore, seems to celebrate the widening of wartime beneficiaries to regular citizens, now suddenly subject to lottery recruitment. Yet, rather than unifying the nation in a wartime posture, the Militia Acts, as

J. R. Western explains, proved divisive and difficult to implement: 'To get the law enforced, its partisans set going an agitation in the counties parallel to that in parliament.'[12] In this context, Garrick's opening scene reads like a parody of these campaigns to bolster support for the militia, contrasting the jingoism of the crowd with Taylor Snip's prudent reluctance, in the scene that follows, to trade his shears for a sword.

The opening scene also makes clear that the question of who is included in the widening populist *us* is less than simple. The group includes Taffy, a Welshman, who would have been included in the lottery, but also Bog, an Irishman, who would not. Ireland was under British rule in the period, and many Irishmen had joined the French forces with plans to participate in the invasion of the English coast, hoping to restore Irish sovereignty. It includes Corporal Bounce, who belongs to the professional army, boasting that as a soldier he can swear, fight, drink, and wench (Taffy interjects 'teeve and steal too'), but cannot read.[13] Lastly, it includes Gasconade, a Frenchman. It is not clear whether Gasconade is a French national or an immigrant, but he functions as the boastful French counterpart to the British Bounce. The group is thrown together to emphasize, as E. J. Hobsbawm points out, and as Garrick, whose grandfather was a French Huguenot, surely understood, that England's path to nationalism was 'evidently incompatible with definitions of nations as based on ethnicity, language, or common history' (see also Sonia Massai's account of Garrick and 'inclusive Britishness' in Chapter 1).[14] Nationalism's friend–enemy distinction – then and now – must supersede the many categories of difference that constitute London's polyglot population, and *Harlequin's Invasion* shows that the enmity that unites the group under the banner of patriotism is as dangerous domestically as any external threat.

Examining the revisions Garrick made to the draft scene in the Larpent collection helps make it clear that *Harlequin's Invasion* has a different story to tell about the *us* of nationalism than Schmitt's insistence on the primacy of enmity. If Garrick portrays a nation of bubbling antagonism, it is primarily a comic cauldron, one of workaday hostilities between culturally various people that diffuse into a disjunctive co-dependence that is for the most part peaceful. The play suggests that the friend–enemy distinction (to use Schmitt's terms) that rules wartime nationalism is less effective at nation-building, less effective at the level of the political, than everyday cycles of peevishness and annoyance dissipating into toleration and mundane social intercourse.

The manuscript draft portrays a scene in which Mrs Snip, wife of the tailor, convinces her daughter Dolly to be glad that her father headed out to capture and murder Harlequin. Mrs Snip argues Dolly out of her romantic infatuation with Harlequin by promising that her father will be made a baronet. Dolly is pleased. She hates being 'plain Dolly' and has gotten a taste of 'Quality doings' from a stay with her aunt, housekeeper for 'Lord Bantems'.[15] Mrs Snip also persuades Dolly to snub her current suitor, the tailor Abraham. It all ends badly for Dolly, who loses Abraham to her cousin, becoming the butt of their jokes. Set in a wartime play about nationalism, this conventional satire of class ambition takes on broader implications. Along with other scenes, it suggests that wealth and rank, more than notions of otherness, motivate jealousy and hatred. Noting that Dolly stands to become 'Lady Doll Snip all the World over', the scene observes the historical fact that the class interests of British aristocrats are international and cosmopolitan. Nationalism is a tool to motivate commoners through chauvinism and xenophobia.[16] Schmitt's friend–enemy distinction operates in the play, not as the essential criterion of the political, but rather as a secondary mechanism. It weaponizes internal divisions based on class and rank, activating internal ambitions and resentments, and channels them externally toward a demonized foe.

The draft uses softer language than the revision to describe Snip's quest. In the early version, Dolly says, 'I hope, Mama, that my Papa has not put on a sword to destroy Mr. Harlequin.'[17] In the revised scene, Dolly enters weeping and protests that she is 'ashamed to see my Papa so blood thirsty and look so like a madman as he did'.[18] The revisions heighten Dolly's distaste for her father's decision and give us a stronger verbal image of Snip, formerly peaceable, formerly reluctant, transformed by the call to arms into a madman. Likewise, revisions to the end of the scene add lines that bring about a similar transformation for Dolly. Dolly begins the scene calling Harlequin 'that dear, sweet, charmingest of all creatures'.[19] She admits that she hid him in her bedroom for three exciting days and would do it 'again, and again and again'.[20] But after her mother calls her a 'Jack-bite hussy' and promises that she will be 'qualitified' if Harlequin is killed, Dolly announces that she would 'cut off his head myself if I had him here'.[21] These revisions thus emphasize a dangerous facet of nationalism: the capacious *us* that jingoism creates, as people imagine themselves as citizen soldiers, is unified only by a common willingness to kill and possibly die for individual gain. It turns tailors into murderers, poisons love with ambition, and endorses bloodthirstiness as patriotism.

Other additions to the scene juxtapose the language Dolly uses to describe her aspirational husband, a captain, with her description of her three-day romantic encounter with Harlequin. Once her mother convinces her that she might become 'qualitified', Dolly decides she will 'frump' her current suitor, Abraham, imagining that she would then be in the position in which, were she 'to chuse for myself, I should like a Captain'.[22] Mrs Snip replies, 'I love a soldier, too. Everybody loves 'em. They have done so much and deserve so much that they may do what they will with us.'[23] Unlike the tailors, who Mrs Snip claims to have reformed and improved with her attentions, the officers of the army, and patriotism in general, demand that women submit to whatever they wish. This joke about what might be considered Mrs Snip's sexual generosity is like many offhand jokes about the army in the play, which taken collectively imply that patriotism's blustering violence ramifies domestically as lawlessness and chaos.

The revisions also add language that makes Dolly's interaction with Harlequin mirror her description of what she finds exciting about the prospect of marrying a captain. Of captains, she says, 'They look so bold & are so bold, & are so grand when they March up to one—So—They look as if they wou'd Eat a body—It frightens one a little, but it does one's Heart good to see 'em—.'[24] In the added material, Dolly describes the moment Harlequin transforms into an ostrich, saying, 'he walked about so stately and looked so grand, and when I went up to him he clapped his wings so (mimics the ostrich) that my very heart leaped within me'.[25] In both cases, she describes them as 'so grand'; in both cases, she demonstrates their gait (marked by 'So' in the text); and in both cases, her heart palpitates with excitement. The revised scene thus juxtaposes the two types of eroticism, both predicated on an overwhelming, compelling presence of the exotic and the strange. In the first case, Dolly lusts after one of her countrymen plumed with a uniform and gun, transformed into someone dangerous by a wartime regime. The nationalist fervour sweeping through Dolly pairs the mythical joys of violent hate to the fantasy erotics of fear. In the second, Dolly lusts after a Frenchman, whom she entertained for three days, enjoying his animal exuberance and astonishing physical agility. Dolly's Harlequinade fervour is less mythical than actual, rooted in the joyful erotics of a sexually compelling display of theatricality.

Pitting these two types of transformation against each other – one, ambition united and transformed into war profiteering; and two, natural variety transformed by theatricality and loosely united as a playscript – *Harlequin's Invasion* consistently denigrates the transformations that serve the nationalist fervour. We begin the play in a scene of direct address – Forge's rallying cry to us 'Boys' and 'Jolly Hearts' – as if participating in the larger us of the nation were harmless or indeed jolly. Mercury channels this joy with a parade, music, a nationalist song, all the effects of theatre, toward a single antagonism that he promises is 'the road to renown'.[26] All the participatory and unifying delights of theatre are transformed by hatred. Glorified as spectacle, hate masquerades as grand and stately fun. The remainder of the play, however, uses Harlequin and his marvellous transformations to restore theatrical play and the daily enjoyments of theatre as a force for national unity that can accommodate the many differences that exist in a nation.

Unsurprisingly, for Garrick, Shakespeare is the exemplar of this unifying play of differences. Near the end of *Harlequin's Invasion*, Mercury says of Shakespeare, 'Ye children of Nature, of Fashion, and Whim, / He painted you all, all join to praise him.'[27] The line introduces a procession of Shakespeare's characters, giving the audience a visual representation of his transformative powers. In so far as Garrick is substituting Shakespeare's marvellous variety of characters for the farcical transformations of Harlequin, it is not, as O'Brien would have it, to position 'Harlequin as Shakespeare's demonic other, the rival whose illegitimate usurpation of the stage must be exposed and repulsed'.[28] If Shakespeare is to be equated with nature it is because he is nimble and playful like Harlequin. Just as the play calls attention to the fluidity of citizenship, it calls attention to other fluidities that valorize nature and Harlequin as polymorphous. Garrick celebrates a Harlequin Shakespeare over a nationalist one.

In *Harlequin's Invasion*, Garrick builds a different sort of myth for Shakespeare than the myths of bellicose nationalism. Garrick's myth is predicated on a celebration of difference that is united in the same way that natural fecundity is harmonious. Nationalist myths, however, yearn for unity as a totality that regulates, suppresses, and subsumes difference via antagonism, which is why the best way to read Schmitt is to read his claims about the political not as a penetrating description of some essential truth of the human as a political animal, but rather as the fundamental assumptions of a fantasy that tries to enact the claims it proffers. The claims to universality and essentiality are aspirational, conditions nationalism hopes to enact through the political. The 'great myth' for Schmitt is a unifying narrative that eradicates internal divisions through xenophobic enmity and creates a homogeneity rooted in the enthusiastic rejection of some forms of difference: 'Out of the depths of a genuine life instinct, not out of reason or pragmatism, springs the great enthusiasm, the great moral decision and the great myth.'[29]

That Schmitt calls this fascist myth a 'life instinct' flags an important point about the difference between how he and Garrick view nature. Schmitt subordinates the procreative abundance of natural forms to a single unifying drive: the struggle for survival as predation. Garrick's myth attributes to Shakespeare the values that 'the eighteenth-century culture was attributing to the natural – beauty, spontaneity, sublimity'.[30] While the call to arms in the first scene of *Harlequin's Invasion* associates nature with nationalism – 'The name of King Shakespear has charms, / To rouse you to actions of glory', and that ''Tis nature calls on you to save her' – the remainder of the play works to undermine nationalist unity with nature's dexterity and variety.[31]

On the night *Harlequin's Invasion* premiered, Richard Cross recorded strong receipts at Drury Lane of £200, noting that the play 'went off with applause'.[32] Although *The Weekly Magazine; or, Gentleman and Lady's Polite Companion*, called the play 'absurd' and complained about the 'stupid Taylor and his more stupid wife', it continued to be a successful afterpiece for several seasons.[33] Despite these charges of absurdity, the play, and its success, suggests that comedic variety is more crucial to Shakespeare, to his ability to draw a plethora of characters who all seem true to life, than any nationalist zeal rooted in some unruly masculinity. The play valorizes nature's spontaneity, its transformations, and improvisations, more so than glory or sublimity, which gestures beyond itself to an unspeakable unity so serviceable to nationalism's call for annihilation as self-sacrifice. That Schmitt's grand narrative about nature is so much less imaginative than nature itself is not the worst indictment one can make of nationalist ideology. But it is crucial to recognize this component of nationalistic logic because of the way it authorizes the shallow worship of violence. Perhaps the most absurd, farcical, and saddest trick of all is how often we allow this sadistic fantasy to pass as pragmatism, realism, or realpolitik.

Figure 3   Paul Revere, 'The Bloody Massacre perpetrated in King Street, Boston on March 5th 1770 by a part of the 29th Reg[iment]' (Boston, 1770) (Collection of the Massachusetts Historical Society).

CHAPTER 3

Revolutionary Shakespeare
Julius Caesar *and the Rhetorical*
Fashioning of Ideologies of Freedom

Esther B. Schupak

Paul Revere's engraving of the Boston Massacre is a masterful piece of visual rhetoric somewhat at odds with the reality of the event it depicts. Its title, 'The Bloody Massacre perpetrated in King Street, Boston on March 5th 1770 by a party of the 29th Reg[iment]' (Figure 3) implies malice aforethought and an organized attack against which the colonists were innocent victims, when the historical record makes it clear that the event was a street riot that got out of control – with violence erupting on both sides. On the right side of the engraving, the soldiers are lined up in a neat diagonal that allows the viewer to see the brutal joy on the soldiers' faces, earning the sobriquet in the verse caption 'fierce Barbarians grinning o'er their Prey', particularly the one at the end of the line who occupies the central position in the picture. Perfectly aligned in an almost balletic neatness, the stance of the British regulars further implies a level of premeditation and organization that was absent from the actual event. In contrast, the Patriot group lacks any kind of organization, the dominant shapes on their side rounded and seemingly randomly distributed. Colour-wise, the strident red of the British contrasts with the softer blues and browns of the rebellious citizens, and these gentler hues highlight the redness of their bleeding wounds. The scarlet blood, refracting the scarlet of the redcoats, implicitly reifies the guilt and violence of the British and concretizes the interpretive label of 'massacre'. Abject in the face of violence, those Patriots not collapsed by their injuries raise their hands in protest and surrender. Similarly, the presence of a woman, clasping her hands together in fear, emphasizes the victimhood of the colonists. Employing verbal as well as visual rhetoric, the verses at the bottom further sentimentalize the scene and radicalize the rhetoric implicit in the image, a rhetoric that would later be reflected in the advertisement of a republican-inflected *Julius Caesar* performed by the American Company. The rhetoric embodied and magnified in this engraving would be associated with the cultural capital of Shakespeare's *Julius Caesar*, a drama whose republican conflicts were closely linked to the heart of the revolutionary project.

The importance of colour to the rhetorical impact of the image seems to have been appreciated by Revere, who employed an artist who had emigrated from Spain to Boston, Charles Remick, to colourize the engraving.[1] The emotional impact of the reds particularly enhanced the sentimentalization of this incident, in which five people were killed, and turned it into a 'massacre' with the propagandistic weighting of that word. In fact, defended by John Adams, most of the soldiers were exonerated – they had been attacked by a large mob and used their guns out of panic, self-defence, and desperation. But the mere facts were subsumed in the cultural memory of the enraged colonists. While no one incident could be said to have ignited the revolution, this one had an impact that was felt throughout the colonies. In the wake of this event, even Governor Thomas Hutchinson, a strident opponent of the Patriots, felt the need to withdraw the British military presence from Boston.[2]

The wave of patriotic feeling evoked by the Boston Massacre was capitalized upon by the American Company, the pre-eminent theatre company in the British North American colonies, who chose that kairotic moment to perform a *Julius Caesar* that was inflected with the same anti-British sentiment apparent in the engraving. Performed in Philadelphia only three months after the unfortunate occurrence in Boston, the advertisement for the play entailed the same militantly republican overtones as Revere's engraving. Still entitled 'Julius Caesar', the advertisement nonetheless emphasized the republican aspects of the drama by highlighting the 'Deaths of Brutus and Cassius' with a font nearly as large as the title of the play, with 'Battle of Philippi' printed in capital letters underneath. The rest of the advertisement echoes the same kind of sentimental language as that found on the bottom of the Revere engraving:

> Containing the noble struggles for liberty by that renowned patriot Marcus Brutus: the death of Caesar in the Capitol, the remarkable orations of Brutus and Antony, upon that occasion. The first shewing [sic] the necessity of his death, to give Freedom to the Roman People; the latter to enflame their minds, and excite them to a commotion, in which the orator succeeds, and is the cause of the civil wars between Brutus and Cassius; of the one part, and the triumvirate, Octavius, Antony, and Lepidus, of the other; which last was finally establish'd by the decisive Battle of Philippi.[3]

Clearly, the author of this advertisement considers republican Brutus to be the real hero of *Julius Caesar*, and the Rome of the drama has been transposed to New England and to the colonists' revolutionary politics, using the lexicon that was particularly resonant in this period: 'liberty' functioning as a key term in the philosophy of the revolution, with Brutus described as a 'patriot'. To the authors of this advertisement, the assassination is not a controversial, debatable action as it was during the Renaissance, when students were, as a matter of course, asked to debate whether the assassination was a justified tyrannicide, a debate with origins in the works of Cicero and Cassius Dio, but still at issue in the Renaissance: instead, Brutus's speech 'shew[s]' the 'necessity of [Caesar's] death'. Conversely, Antony is portrayed as a demagogue whose rhetoric has the capacity to 'enflame their minds and excite them to a commotion', and is himself therefore the cause of the Civil Wars. Even Caesar is not assassinated or killed, let alone murdered. Instead, his ending is nominalized as a 'death' without perpetrator. Although the drama itself has a tradition of being interpreted both ways, as either republican or monarchical in its ideology, this advertisement skews heavily towards the republican, thus recruiting the play to serve in the revolutionary project.

Drawing connections between Shakespeare's political-historical theatre and current events was a typical mode of theatrical engagement for the eighteenth century, where 'colonists quoted Addison, Thomson, Pope, Milton, and Shakespeare as political authorities hardly less often than they quoted Locke or Montesquieu'.[4] Indeed in his *Ideological Origins of the American Revolution*, Bernard Bailyn asserts that 'the heritage of classical antiquity' was central to the written discourse of the Revolution.[5] Taking an omnivorous approach to political theory, the colonists would not have been surprised to see Shakespeare's ancient Rome invoked in their struggle with the British, as it often was in other forms of discourse.[6] One would therefore assume that performances of Shakespeare's *Julius Caesar* would have been widespread in the colonies and the early republic. In fact, I have found records of only two performances of *Caesar* taking place in the years preceding the Revolutionary War and only four in the years immediately after the war, until 1800.

But if this was the case, then we need to ask, why did the American Company – or any of the other six companies performing in British America – fail to continue the strategy of attracting audiences by engaging with revolutionary rhetoric? Why didn't performances of *Julius Caesar* sweep the colonies?

Douglass's Legitimation of the Theatre

In order to answer these questions, we have first to consider how theatre gained a foothold in the colonies despite considerable resistance. Anti-theatrical feeling coalesced around three issues: first of all, religious feeling. It was most famously the Puritans, Quakers, and other dissenters who inveighed against the corruptive influence of the theatre – and the theatre faced the most strident opposition in the North, with Boston, for example, enacting penalties not only for performance, but even for mere attendance.[7] Religious opposition was not exclusive to the Congregationalist North and existed throughout the thirteen colonies. However, religious anti-theatricalism was less vehement in the South, which throughout the early American period was more friendly to the theatre. The second locus of opposition to the theatre was financial, as it was felt that the theatre fiscally drained the cash-strapped colonies and wasted funds on extravagance. In a similar vein, the theatre was seen as potentially distracting apprentices and subordinates from their employment.

Despite the considerable opposition to theatre in the colonies, in the 1760s theatre started coming into its own as part and parcel of gentrification as British America transitioned from a 'survival culture' to a genteel culture predicated upon consumption of consumer goods and British cultural artifacts.[8] Nevertheless, theatrical companies continued to face resistance, and the only successful way to establish such an enterprise was always to seek permission from those who held power, that is, representatives of the British government. David Douglass, the manager of the American Company, discovered the importance of this deference upon the first occasion he neglected to do so: opening a theatre in New York in 1758. William Dunlap, himself a pioneering theatre manager and historian of early American theatre (writing in 1832), explained Douglass's plight as follows:

> [Douglass] appears to have been by descent and education a gentleman … He had failed to bow the knee to power even before he had approached within its bounds, and he was thus made to lick the dust before a gracious permission was granted, to enlighten his judges, their satellites, and the people entrusted to their care, by the recitation of the pride of English poetry and wit.[9]

The incident referred to here by Dunlap seems to have been caused both by Douglass's failure to seek official permission before building a theatre and by his political naivete, neither of which errors he repeated. Because the theatre in colonial America was seen as a dubious enterprise, Douglass had to perform a substantial amount of obsequious 'kissing up' to provincial governors in order to obtain permission and support for playing. In fact, the theatre was perceived so negatively that such obvious manoeuvring was only the most readily apparent rhetorical strategy in a long list of other strategies, which included: giving charity performances, being sensitive to religious holidays and religious issues in general, writing letters to the editor minimizing theatrical profits, and, before leaving a city, always advertising that anyone to whom Douglass was in debt should 'come forth and be satisfied'.[10] A crucial part of this rhetorical strategy was to cultivate relationships with the powerful, by joining the Masons and hobnobbing with the elite who could afford to attend and whose conspicuous presence was part of the cultural capital of the theatrical enterprise.[11] Of course, in colonial America the quickest and most effective avenue to political power was through association with the British power structure, chiefly through strong relationships with the reigning governors. The American Company thus became quite quickly linked to the British elite, upon whom they depended for legitimation.

This linkage naturally did them no favours with the Sons of Liberty and other Patriot groups, who nurtured republican ideals. However, the American Company had also developed strong connections to the Patriot elite, the American gentry whose political interests lay in revolution: George Washington and Thomas Jefferson, for example, regularly attended performances, with Washington even purchasing a subscription to contribute to the building of the theatre at Williamsburg.[12] This attendance and support for the theatre did not necessarily entail a predilection for the drama as *entertainment*. The theatre was, first and foremost, an important site for networking and for establishing one's place within the social elite, an elite that included Patriots – hence, the performance of *Julius Caesar*, and the more numerous performances of *Cato*. As Johnson has remarked, 'From seven stages in six colonies, Douglass spoke on American soil the words that would become the mantra of the revolution, the words that would prepare them to be Americans.'[13] But those words were spoken from stages that were, in a sense, theatres royal, associated with British hegemony. This association rendered republican performances – such as the production of *Julius Caesar* linked to the Boston Massacre – a vexed enterprise.

The American Company thus inhabited a fundamentally contradictory and tenuous position in the midst of what British Americans of the time often – and correctly – dubbed a 'civil war', a war that was to be particularly harsh for civilians of both sides, with loyalists persecuted by Patriots and vice versa.[14] Associated with British hegemony but also implicated in republican rhetoric, the American Company wisely decamped to Jamaica in 1774.

The Theatre as a Site of Conflict

What had allowed the theatre to grow and even flourish during the period before the revolution was the process of gentrification and the culture of consumerism that developed as a result.[15] However, revolutionary ideals directly contradicted the dominant cultural values of gentility and refinement, which had originated in the courts of Europe and spread outward to the colonies. According to Richard Bushman, when republican values were adopted, 'the glories of court life became shameful and subversive, a seductive and debilitating influence ... Refinement, the court, and European oppression were opposed to republican simplicity, virtue, and freedom.'[16] This austerity was influenced by the religious culture of New England, the earliest flashpoint of the revolt, but also had a firm basis in republican ideology heavily inflected by stoicism, symbolized by the predominance of references to the (in)famously Stoic Cato. Indeed, *Cato*, a drama written by Addison about the staunchly republican Cato the Younger and his attempt to defeat Julius Caesar, 'quoted, paraphrased, parodied, inspired, and emplotted the resistance ... it was one of the last performed during Douglass's final season as a civic benefit, and the theatre was so crowded the audience was sitting on the stage'.[17] The 'Catonic image' was 'central to the political theory of the time', and this image and its associated principles stood in opposition to the very idea of theatre.[18] Therefore, as an element in the cultural complex of Britishness, urbanity, and gentility, theatre was on the whole implicated as decadent. As John Adams admonished his wife,

> But let us take Warning and give it to our Children. Whenever Vanity, and Gaiety, a Love of Pomp and Dress, Furniture, Equipage, Buildings, great Company, expensive Diversions, and elegant Entertainments get the better of the Principles and Judgments of Men or Women there is no knowing where they will stop, nor into what Evils, natural, moral, or political, they will lead us.[19]

Spending money on luxuries such as elaborate clothing and housing – and theatre tickets – was not simply profligate; it was also a first step on the road to 'evil', not merely moral evil, but also political evil, which in Adams's thinking was linked to the aristocratic and monarchical. Like the religious Congregationalists who viewed the theatre as a devilish seduction, to fervent republicans, theatre participated in a degenerate axis of corruption that was fundamentally antithetical to their interests. Republicanism, in its American – especially northern – incarnation, went hand in hand with a simple, austere lifestyle.

Taxation without Representation

The association of American colonial republicanism with austerity has its roots – at least partially – in the politics of the time, where taxes on imported goods were the primary locus of contention in the colonists' struggle with Britain. After having invested heavily in military expenditures to protect the colonists in the French and Indian War, Britain felt justified in imposing taxes in order to defray the considerable costs of the conflict. The passing of the Sugar Act more than tripled the duties on imported sugar, and the Currency Act, which prevented the colonies from printing their own money, was followed by the infamous Stamp Act, which imposed a spectrum of paper, publishing, and documentary taxes on the colonies. The colonists, who viewed their own legislatures as autonomous and coequal with Parliament, saw these acts as tyrannical domination, as 'taxation without representation' – the first step on the road to further tyrannies, with Boston's Town Meeting asserting that 'a deep-laid and desperate plan of imperial despotism has been laid, and partly executed, for the extinction of all civil liberty'.[20] To resist these trespasses on liberty, the colonists boycotted imported goods. These boycotts were imposed not only by the twinges of individual conscience, but also by the public shaming of those who failed to adhere to the policy. Wearing simpler clothing, drinking coffee instead of tea, and generally making do without luxury goods became potent political symbols during this period, as asceticism became an intrinsic element of republican activism in the United States. As John Adams wrote to his wife,

> Frugality, OEconomy, Parcimony [sic] must be our Refuge. I hope the Ladies are every day diminishing their ornaments, and the Gentlemen too. Let us Eat Potatoes and drink Water. Let us wear Canvass, and undressed Sheepskins, rather than submit to the unrighteous, and ignominious Domination that is prepared for Us.[21]

Women were central to the fulfilment of this economic agenda since they often were the primary customers for British goods, and therefore 'the first political act of American women was to say "No"'.[22] Wearing homespun (at least in theory), avoiding tea, abstaining from imports of all kinds, were political statements at the heart of the revolutionary ethos. In the context of this ideological framework, the frivolity of attending the theatre was perceived as being morally and politically antithetical to the republican ethos, even when the performance was of a republican drama such as *Julius Caesar*.

It may have been this perception that motivated a mob's destruction of the New York theatre on 5 May 1766, just a month after the Stamp Act was repealed. According to the *Maryland Gazette*, the explanation for this event lies in the same constellation of issues that Adams brought out in his letter to his wife:

> The play advertised to be acted on last Monday evening, [gave] offence to many of the inhabitants of this city, who thought it highly improper that such entertainments should be exhibited at this time of public distress, when great numbers of poor people can scarce find means of subsistence, whereby many persons might be tempted to neglect their business, and squander that money, which is necessary to the payment of their debts, and support of their families ... The audience escaped in the best manner they could; many lost their hats and other parts of dress. A boy had his skull fractured, and was yesterday trepanned, his recovery is doubtful; several others were dangerously hurt; but we have heard of no lives lost. The multitude immediately demolished the house, and carried the pieces to the common, where they consumed them in a bonfire.[23]

Again, the primary objection here seems to be the frivolity and waste of money entailed in theatrical entertainments. At the same time, this event also highlights a much darker aspect of the revolution: the mob violence that was often enacted by the Patriot Sons of Liberty (and sometimes in later years by their opposite numbers among the loyalists). Like the patriotically inflected performance of *Julius Caesar* after the Boston Massacre, this was a kind of performance. This 'street performance', on occasion later executed by the Committees of Safety and/or Correspondence, could entail anything from a violent riot of the kind described above to a relatively innocuous raising of a Liberty Pole (in lieu of a Maypole), to parading effigies of royal governors, to a tarring and feathering that involved grievous bodily injury. In this sense then, the Sons of Liberty were in their creation of spectacle competing with the more conventional theatre, which, oriented as it was toward the financial elite and the culture of London, was destined to lose. As Bruce McConachie observes, 'For the next twenty years, the primary form of theatre in America would be amateur republican performance in the streets, not professional playing on conventional stages.'[24] Indeed, the Continental Congress would eventually interdict all theatrical performances during the period of hostilities.

Rhetorical Potentialities of *Julius Caesar*

Despite the mixed fortunes and conflicting allegiances of formal theatrical performance in the colonies, the Philadelphia staging mentioned above makes it apparent that the rhetorical potentialities of performing

Julius Caesar during the early republican period were at times recognized and acted upon. In addition to the Philadelphia performance linked to the Boston Massacre, another important performance occurred after the war. When the theatres were closed in New York during the winter of 1790, Washington had *Julius Caesar* staged in the presidential residence.[25] The actor William A. Duer described this event as follows:

> I was not only frequently admitted to the presence of this most august of men, in propria persona, but once had the honor of appearing before him as one of the dramatis personae in the tragedy of Julius Caesar, enacted by a young 'American Company' (the theatrical corps then performing in New York being called the 'Old American Company'), in the garret of the Presidential mansion, where before the magnates of the land and the elite of the city, I performed the part of Brutus to the Cassius of my old school-fellow, Washington Custis.[26]

This event, occurring only seven years after the Revolutionary War and in the presence of the privileged elite of New York, would have been more than merely light entertainment for a president who enjoyed the stage. Rather, like Obama's kitchen garden or Clinton's jogging jaunts, the leisure activity of this well-loved president perhaps would have served as an inspiration to the people, in this case strengthening the ethos of republicanism and fostering political cohesion by invoking the recent conflict.

Another famous theatrical performance – also ordered by George Washington, who well knew the power of theatre – took place at Valley Forge. Anyone who has grown up in the United States is familiar with the legendary suffering of the colonial forces at Valley Forge: the lack of proper uniforms, the lack of food and medical care, the many soldiers who died in that terrible winter. In the absence of sufficient funding from the Patriot Congress, there was little Washington could do to physically ameliorate the soldiers' conditions, but he could and did use theatre to remind them of the ideology for which they fought. Staged at least twice, *Cato* was performed as part of a larger festive occasion, involving an orchestra and public dinner with all the officers. The republican fervour in which this performance participated can be glimpsed in a diary account, written five days before the staging:

> The entertainment was concluded with a number of patriotic toasts, attended with huzzas. When the General took his leave, there was a universal clap, with loud huzzas, which continued till he had proceeded a quarter of a mile, during which time there were a thousand hats tossed in the air. His Excellency turned round with his retinue and huzzaed several times.[27]

The enthusiastic reception is clear, but of course, Addison's *Cato* was only one element of this production, with George Washington also performing his role of inspirational general. Indeed, to the audience, Washington himself would have been simultaneously identified with and supplemental to the historical Cato depicted in the play, the fervent republican who had died for the cause of liberty.[28]

After this production, the Continental Congress strengthened their opposition to the theatre on 16 October 1778, proclaiming that 'who shall act, promote, encourage or attend … plays, shall be deemed unworthy to hold such office, and shall be accordingly dismissed', a threat that George Washington seems to have taken to heart as there were no more American military theatrics.[29] While this decision was in keeping with the stoic and anti-British ethos promoted by the Patriots, it reduced the opportunities available to recruit Shakespeare's *Julius Caesar* to the republican project. However, as the war receded into the past, the play was performed more frequently in the early days of the United States, from the presidential residence to the theatre, demonstrating the emotive power of Roman history in a fictive-historical theatrical enactment.

BUONAPARTE's SOLILOQUY

At Calais.

Written and designed by G. M. WOODWARD.

TO go, or not to go? that is the question;—
Whether 'tis better for my views to suffer
The ease and quiet of yon hated rival,
Or to take arms against the haughty people,
And by invading end them? T' invade,—to fight,—
No more; and by a fight, to say, we end
The envy and the thousand jealous pangs
We now must bear with; 'tis a consummation
Devoutly to be wish'd. T' invade,—to fight;—
To fight?—perchance be beat: aye, there's the rub;
For in our passage hence what ills may come,
When we have parted from our native ports,
Must give us pause;—there's the respect
That makes th' alternative so hard a choice.
For who would bear their just and equal laws,
Their sacred faith, and general happiness,
That shew in contrast black our tyrant sway,

Our frequent breach of treaty, and the harms
Devouring armies on the people bring,
When he himself could the dark shame remove,
By mere invasion? Who would tamely view
That happy nation's great and thriving power,
But that the dread of falling on their coast,
(That firm and loyal country, from whose shores
No enemy returns,) puzzles the will,
And makes us rather bear those ills we have,
Than fly to others that we know not of?
Thus conscience* does make cowards of us all:
And thus the native hue of resolution
Is sicklied o'er with the pale cast of thought;
And enterprizes of great pith and moment,
With this regard, their currents turn awry,
And lose the name of action.

      * Alluding probably to Egypt.

Folio Caricatures let out for the Evening, at R. ACKERMANN's, 101, Strand, London, where New Caricatures are published daily.

PRINTED BY D. N. SHURY, NO. 7, BERWICK STREET.

Figure 4   George M. Woodward, 'Buonaparte's Soliloquy At Calais' (1803).

CHAPTER 4

Hamlet *Mobilized*
Political Parody during the Napoleonic Wars

Amy Lidster

In September 1803, from his well-known shop on the Strand in London, Rudolph Ackermann published a broadside with the title 'Buonaparte's Soliloquy At Calais' (Figure 4) that mobilized *Hamlet* in the service of anti-French propaganda following the breakdown of the short-lived Treaty of Amiens – in effect from 27 March 1802 to 18 May 1803 – that had temporarily halted war with France. It testifies to the appeal of Shakespeare during wartime – not, in this case, through a performed or read play, but through an extracted textual fragment that is appropriated to respond directly to the ongoing conflict. 'Buonaparte's Soliloquy' is attributed to George M. Woodward, a prolific caricaturist during the 1790s and 1800s whose drawings were typically etched by others, including, in this instance, Isaac Cruikshank. This graphic satire offers a parody of Hamlet's much-quoted 'To be or not to be' soliloquy, adapted for Napoleon who is debating whether or not to invade Britain: 'To go or not to go' replaces the famous opening question, while the rub for Napoleon is the risk of defeat. Above the printed soliloquy, a hand-coloured caricature of a concerned and disgruntled Napoleon is shown in an oversize French bicorne that seems to play into contemporary satires, particularly in Britain, of his supposedly small stature.[1] With his arms and legs crossed, he leans against a signpost with the direction 'Road to England' pointing across the Channel. Woodward's prints typically advance pro-government and anti-French sympathies, and here, Napoleon's representations in image and text are designed to work together to ridicule Britain's adversary amidst growing concern over the threat of a French invasion, which reached a peak in 1803–05, when Napoleon placed his 'Armée d'Angleterre' along the Channel.[2] Created and published within the first few months of the Napoleonic Wars, this graphic satire seems designed to unite British readers in derision of Napoleon. But it stops short of offering a rousing call to arms, a strategy witnessed in other print propaganda from the same time.[3]

A closer look at Woodward's parody reveals how Hamlet's deeply religious and philosophical questioning about 'self-slaughter', prompted in the play by the political usurpation orchestrated by his uncle Claudius, has been repositioned to offer a secular soliloquy about Britain's contemporary wartime context that sets up clear polarities of good and evil. The parody follows Hamlet's speech line by line, retaining some words, phrases, and complete lines (including the final eight of the soliloquy), but has a very different tone and effect: where Hamlet's soliloquy is searching, interior-focused, and lacking in resolution, Napoleon's is fixated on the external world and earthly gains. Napoleon himself concedes that his desire for territorial conquest is unjustified and describes Britain as a superior rival: a 'happy nation' with 'just and equal laws ... sacred faith, and general happiness', which serve to highlight 'in contrast black our tyrant sway, / Our frequent breach of treaty'. The parody relies on readers' familiarity with the original to achieve its full effect: for Hamlet's 'heart-ache' and 'thousand natural shocks / That flesh is heir to' (3.1.62–63), a spiritual reflection on unbidden suffering and bodily decay, Napoleon describes his 'envy' and 'the thousand jealous pangs' that the French must bear if Britain remains unconquered. This local rewriting concentrates on external wants and unjust wartime aggression that underline the parody's potential as anti-French propaganda. Together, the image and text condemn Napoleon and his chances of success and present Britain's wartime involvement as defensive. Napoleon is not simply 'opposing' British forces and aiming to 'end them', as the fifth line could read if it were to follow the original; he is, instead, 'invading' in order to 'end them'. The broadside's confidence should not, however, be accepted unquestioningly as an accurate reflection of the views of British readers. As this essay argues, Shakespearean quotation and parody could be used to construct, rather than reflect, united public opinion on the necessity of war and confidence in British defences.

What the broadside does reveal is confidence in Shakespeare's appeal for readers and their desire to participate in political commentary and reflection. This parody of Hamlet's soliloquy was circulated widely, the text appearing in other publications both in Britain and abroad, including the September 1803 issue of *The Monthly Visitor and New Family Magazine*, one of a number of new 'moralizing' magazines in London that invited a female readership.[4] Ackermann, publisher of the broadside, was a key figure in networks of export and exchange, and his shop at 101 Strand, known from 1798 as 'The Repository of Arts', was a fashionable location for the sale of old master paintings, watercolours,

and hand-coloured prints and caricatures, such as this one, and it became
a hub for polite urban culture. Ackermann, who was originally from
Saxony, also maintained strong links with Germany and was close friends
with Johann Christian Hüttner, London correspondent for the Weimar-
based journal *London und Paris* in which 'Buonaparte's Soliloquy At
Calais' also appeared, without the image, in 1803.[5] Published by Weimar
editor Friedrich Justin Bertuch, *London und Paris* brought reports about
politics and cultural life from these two major cities to satisfy a readership within German states that lacked a similar metropolis.[6] Hüttner
sent caricatures, including many by James Gillray, from London, which
were printed alongside French caricatures, with commentary supplied by
Carl August Böttiger. 'Buonaparte's Soliloquy', which, Böttiger claims,
is 'not without sharp wit and innuendo, but still treated with some subtlety', is described as one of many similar parodies that were circulating
in Britain: 'Die Engländer haben hundert Parodien auf diesen berüh-
mten Monolog' ('The English have a hundred parodies of this famous
monologue').[7] The journal prints this textual parody both in English
and in a German translation, and is closely followed by Gillray's graphic
satire, 'The Flying Sword run mad', which depicts Napoleon as a winged
sword raging about his desire for conquest and the liberty of the British
press. This caricature is itself an adaptation of Gillray's 'Maniac-raving's,
or Little Boney in a strong Fit' (London, 1803), which shows Napoleon,
rather than the visual synecdoche of the sword, and was seen as too dangerous to print in the Weimar journal.[8] The edited version was prepared
specially for *London und Paris*, and one of the scattered papers on the
floor beneath the sword of Napoleon reads 'Soliloquy' – a new visual
addition that possibly alludes to the parody of Hamlet contained within
the pages of the journal, a text that acquires, in this print context, another
companion image. The politics of *London und Paris* shifted in response
to events and censorship during the Revolutionary–Napoleonic Wars;
but the journal tended to offer, as this example suggests, broad support for Britain's position and notably refrained from printing French
political caricatures.[9]

The appearance of Woodward's parodic soliloquy in a range of
publications therefore draws attention to the appeal of Shakespeare as a
vehicle for political and cultural participation that was also allied to the
consumption of fashionable goods by a growing readership not limited
by national or state boundaries. Rather than testifying to fixed position-
takings or political views, it also reveals a heteroglossia of shifting opinions
and tensions during this period of renewed war with France, a conflict

that would lead to, in German states, the establishment of Napoleon's Confederation of the Rhine in 1806 and French control over the press.

§

The practice of parodying Shakespearean speeches during wartime and appropriating quotations for use in graphic satire was an eighteenth-century development. Jonathan Bate identifies George Bickham's 'The Stature of a Great Man or the English Colossus' from March 1740 as one of the earliest examples of a political caricature that clearly uses a Shakespearean quotation – in this case, from *Julius Caesar* – to set up an 'ironic comparison' between Robert Walpole and the play's title character in order to criticize the de facto first prime minister's reluctance to engage in war with Spain.[10] These practices gathered momentum as the century progressed, not only within Britain, but also abroad, and Hamlet's 'To be or not to be' soliloquy offered a malleable rhetorical template. In 1769, prior to the outbreak of the American Revolutionary War, the slogan 'Be taxt or not be taxt, that is the question' was used by American Patriots to promote the campaign for independence, while in 1776, a Loyalist adapted the same speech to question whether to sign a boycott of British goods: 'To sign or not to sign? That is the question.'[11] Unlike parodies that expose or ridicule the source text, these examples testify to the high valuation of Shakespeare: as Samuel Taylor Coleridge puts it, 'Parodies on new poems are read as satires; on old ones (the soliloquy of Hamlet for instance) as compliments.'[12] They also testify to Shakespeare's growing global reach within British colonies that did not yet have a long-established history of Shakespearean performance and publication. Shakespeare's lines, extracted from their original context are, as Bate describes, 'used as a weapon, turned against the follies of a later age'.[13] These practices reached their height during the Revolutionary–Napoleonic Wars, and, as David Francis Taylor discusses, Shakespeare's plays were 'by far the most common source of material for political caricature' at a time of prolonged conflict that was marked by an obsessive interest in position-takings and the participation of a growing public in political debate.[14] The early years of the French Revolution and Revolutionary Wars had divided both parliamentary and public opinion in Britain, and satires often represented political debate in ambivalent or ambiguous ways. William Dent's 'Revolution Anniversary: or Patriotic Incantations' (1791) casts opposition Whigs, including Richard Brinsley Sheridan and Charles James Fox, as the witches in *Macbeth*, presenting them as revolutionary sympathizers who gleefully consign George III's crown into a cauldron of 'French Spirits'. It seems to announce the dangers of revolutionary fervour within parliament; but through its comic presentation, it also seems to downplay or dismiss this threat and even appeal to the witches' anarchic potential.[15]

At certain pivotal points during the French wars, however, political parodies and caricatures prompted blunter, didactic interpretations that could mobilize Shakespearean quotation for the purposes of political propaganda. The renewal of war in 1803 and Napoleon's growing power as First Consul and then Emperor of France in 1804 was one of those moments that led to an outpouring of loyal publications and fundraising. Even Sheridan, who had spoken out against war with France, now took steps to support 'Our King! our Country! And our God!' through the circulation of a speech from his popular play *Pizarro* as 'Sheridan's Address to the People' (1803). Woodward's parody of Hamlet's 'To be or not to be' was not an isolated example, although it potentially had the greatest reach, given its use in other journals and connection to networks of European trade and export. From 1803 to 1805, a spate of parodies adapted Hamlet's famous soliloquy to reflect on the threat of a French invasion, and were printed in, for example, *The Times* (London), *The Anti-Gallican*, *The Gentleman's Magazine*, and *The Quebec Mercury*. Most adapted the soliloquy for Napoleon, who debates the strategic merits of an invasion: 'To invade or not to invade' is the most common opening question posited in this spate of parodies. They are documents of wartime propaganda that are unambiguously patriotic, expressing support for Britain's war effort and condemning Napoleon as, by turns, cowardly and tyrannical. And, indeed, they are quite unusual in their representation of Napoleon in the position of Shakespearean protagonist. As Taylor has shown, Napoleon was often castigated as Harlequin, and a number of graphic satires about 'Harlequin's Invasion' also appeared at this time.[16] These wartime Hamlet parodies therefore represent an exchange between past and present that involves the celebration of a British writer: they announce Shakespeare's influence as an established cultural symbol, as well as his topical wartime currency, which at this point increases in 'legibility' as the parodies become less tied to the minutiae of Westminster political life and concentrate on broader lines of conflict.[17]

The invasion parodies differ in the vehemence of their attack on the French leader and, conversely, the nature of the praise directed towards Britain. In the anonymous 'Parody of the Soliloquy in Hamlet', printed in *The Times* on 31 August 1803, Napoleon describes Britain as the 'yet unconquer'd Country, from whose bourne / No enemy returns', conceding that, with their 'hearts of oak', Britons 'do make cowards of us all'.[18]

His reluctance is owing to a fear of defeat – 'T''invade, to fight – / To fight, perchance to fall' – and his desire for invasion is linked to the silencing of Britain's scorn and confident mockery of Napoleon's France: he wishes to end the 'thousand British taunts', 'the jests and laughs of the Isle, / The People's scorn, the Press's contumely'. Napoleon's grievances are most directly aimed at press agents and public opinion. This parody was printed with some important variants in *The Quebec Mercury* on 23 December 1805, another example that testifies to the export and circulation of these topical Shakespearean parodies beyond the British Isles. Introduced by a prefatory remark supplied by a subscriber, the lightly revised parody was intended to appeal to readers within the British colony of Lower Canada who were loyal to Britain: 'Mr Cary, – Sir. The following Parody on Hamlet's soliloquy, in Shakespeare, may perhaps suit your loyal readers; and by inserting it, you will favour a Subscriber.'[19] *The Quebec Mercury*, founded by Thomas Cary in 1805, was a staunchly loyalist political newspaper that advocated for the Anglicization of the colony. The parody has been altered in two significant ways: first, Napoleon's motivation – Britain's contemptuous mockery of France through the public and the press – is shifted to emphasize, instead, the dangers of Britain's military and naval strength. It is the soldiers and the sailors who rebuff France with 'whips and scorns', a revision that draws attention to the conflict's immediacy and aggrandizes Britain's wartime power. Second, this version channels most of its satirical attack at Napoleon himself by changing the parody's use of the first-person plural to first-person singular. It emphasizes Napoleon's own dread of defeat and his desire for conquest, and not, by extension, France's, a more amenable interpretation for a newspaper that was published in a French- and English-speaking colony: Britain's strength 'makes *me* rather keep the pow'rs *I* have, / Than fight for others which *I* know not of!' (emphasis mine). A different parody in *The Times* on 11 September 1805 – still based on this same soliloquy and reproduced in *The Spirit of the Public Journals for 1805* – similarly places culpability most squarely on Napoleon, whose views dominate through the first-person singular and express a fear of 'the oppressive thought of English liberty', again serving to flatter Britons and their political systems.[20]

Perhaps the most critical portrait of Napoleon is presented in a parody by 'R. P. C.' that appeared in *The Anti-Gallican* (1804), a publication of tracts, speeches, poems, and songs about the invasion threat that were dedicated 'To the Volunteers of the United Kingdom, who with an impulse of genuine patriotism, have offered their services to defend the rights of their country from the violation threatened by an implacable foe', and

supported by an epigraph from *King John*: 'Nought shall make us rue, /
If England to herself do rest but true' (cf. 5.7.117–18).[21] The main target
of the parody is Napoleon, and his fear of defeat is directly linked to a
fear of his own mortality: 'How soon a ball or bullet may decide / The
premier CONSUL's fate, – must give me pause.'[22] Where Hamlet in the
play debates the merits and justification of 'self-slaughter', Napoleon is
at pains to preserve his earthly life. The legibility of the parody does not
rely on a nuanced understanding of wartime debate nor on a line-by-line
comparison with Hamlet's original soliloquy to achieve its main design as
anti-Napoleonic propaganda that offers a call to arms for Britons. But a
contrastive analysis nevertheless packs an additional satirical punch that
underscores Napoleon's secular and aggressive concerns in contrast to
Hamlet's philosophical questioning in response to an act of political usurpation and murder. This parody presents Napoleon as a tyrannous leader
with an insatiable desire 'To conquer ENGLAND; desolate her towns; /
Her bulwarks burn; and drench her plains with blood'. Indeed, of all the
invasion parodies, it departs the most from Hamlet's original soliloquy,
offering instead a vivid description of the desolation that Napoleon would
bring if the fear of his own loss of life did not hold him back.

While these parodies respond to the urgency of the invasion threat and
are unambiguous in their political sympathies, they do not circumscribe
meaning absolutely and could prompt different acts of reading, particularly because of the original soliloquy's Horatian interest in rational disputation over opposing positions. From October 1792 until December 1805,
a series of about one hundred and fifty Shakespearean 'Parodies' appeared
in *The Gentleman's Magazine*, written by Reverend Thomas Ford, vicar of
Melton Mowbray, and for the most part printed under the pseudonym
'Master Shallow'.[23] One of Ford's parodies in August 1803 adapts Hamlet's
soliloquy to concentrate on the question of British armament in anticipation of an invasion – the question is 'To arm, or not to arm?'[24] Unlike the
others, Napoleon is not the speaker of the parody, which is instead presented from the perspective of an unspecified British voice. Ford's politics
were loyal and conservative, as were those of *The Gentleman's Magazine*,
and the parody offers explicit support for readying British defences and
attacking Napoleon's 'fleet of large flat-bottom'd boats, / And by opposing sink them'.[25] However, Ford departs from the weighing of alternative positions that is one of the key structural features of the soliloquy:
Hamlet begins by contemplating the desirability of death and then re-
evaluates this position because of the unknowability of what happens after
death. Similarly, in all the parodies already considered, Napoleon begins

by imagining the benefits of invasion, only to be dissuaded from this path by his fear of defeat. In Ford's parody, there is no such turning point and the 'rub' becomes a 'horror' that simply reinforces the need for armament and defence:

> ... to fight, defend,
> Perchance to fail – aye, there's the horror;
> For in defeat what miseries may come
> If we once kneel to this usurping monster,
> Must rouse us all.

The second half of the parody goes on to relate the horrors that would accompany Napoleon's unresisted invasion and, as opposed to ending with Hamlet's inaction and lack of resolution, the parody offers a call to arms that aims to 'Stir up all ranks to rush into the field, / And pant for action'. But because of the original's well-known structure and the disputation of one course of action followed by another, Ford's parody could unintentionally prompt readers to question the desirability of renewed war with France: the question 'To arm or not to arm' initially sets up an expectation that both sides of the argument will be considered. Ford's vivid description of the horrors of French conquest in Britain is also an account that evokes the 'miseries' of war and the risks of engagement and defeat. The parody argues that it is more honourable to 'die with harness on our backs', alluding, somewhat forebodingly, to Macbeth's decision to die in battle (cf. 5.5.51), rather than be 'pinion'd down with manacles and screws'. It does not shore up optimism of a British victory, but draws attention to the costs and consequences of war.

Indeed, Ford's parody is instructive because it helps to qualify assumptions about the function and impact of Shakespearean quotation during wartime. While Shakespeare was most conspicuously and consistently used at the renewal of war with France to support British defences and to ridicule Napoleon, it does not follow that these parodies testify to united public opinion about the necessity of war, to untrammelled optimism about its outcome, or to the rigidity of political opinion that could be divided neatly into pro- or anti-war, loyalist or Jacobin sympathies. Instead, the political situation was more volatile and malleable than a cursory survey of patriotic propaganda might suggest. Joseph Cozens draws attention to high desertion rates in the army and militia between 1803 and 1805, and challenges the view that this was a period of popular loyalism.[26] Political parodies and propaganda that seem confidently to announce support and high morale for the war effort often testify to fractures and limitations.

After almost a decade of ongoing conflict and a short-lived peace treaty, war weariness and division were evident throughout many cross-sections of the British public. The period of the Revolutionary Wars (1792–1802) was marked by heated position-takings, pamphlet exchanges, and the prominence of debating societies that took different views on the conflict and applied foreign disputes to domestic issues in Britain. For some, the pursuit of French liberty was a spur for parliamentary reform in Britain and widening participation in politics. Opposition to the Revolutionary Wars led to outbreaks of unrest, including a protest on 29 October 1795 that involved an attack on George III's carriage as individuals threw stones and cried out 'Peace! Peace! No War!'[27] Of course, the events of the 'Terror' in France and Napoleon's later consolidation of power as he declared himself First Consul in 1799 shifted the balance and nature of political debate in Britain. In retrospect, Napoleon's later actions and invasions of, for example, Portugal and Russia could be seen to justify war and the preparation of British defences. However, in 1803, it was Britain that failed to uphold the terms of the Treaty of Amiens by refusing to evacuate troops from Malta. Contemporaries drew attention to the British government's self-serving interests in the French wars: Gillray's 'The Plumb-pudding in danger' (1805) shows Prime Minister William Pitt and Napoleon greedily cutting into a pudding that represents a globe of the world. The caption accompanying the image adapts a line from Shakespeare's *The Tempest*: '"the great Globe itself and all which it inherit", is too small to satisfy such insatiable appetites.' Considered alongside high desertion rates, a growing war weariness, and the difficulty of expressing oppositional views, the practice of Shakespearean quotation can be seen, by turns, to reveal and conceal these tensions, rather than witnessing undisputed public support for renewed conflict.

What is particularly revealing about Shakespeare's use during this period is the malleability, adaptability, and currency of both the plays and the figure of Shakespeare himself to reflect on the renewed wartime context, sometimes offering clear-cut propaganda and other times facilitating political discourse that could draw attention to the divisive debates underlining this period of conflict. Hamlet's famous soliloquy becomes a rhetorical template for carrying out topical wartime debate, whilst also capitalizing on a connection to the past – to an established cultural figure and text that carry with them a set of assumptions, priorities, and values. To return to the material text with which I began, Woodward's graphic satire, published by Ackermann and circulated without the image in publications such as *London und Paris*, also draws attention to transnational exchanges – not only in terms of a growing global interest in Shakespeare, but also in terms of shared political and cultural debates that permeate state boundaries. It is also an exchange that crosses different media and readerships, as a hand-coloured graphic satire and as a text-only parody that circulated more widely in journals and magazines. In its different material forms, this parody could be a focus for cultural discussion and wartime propaganda, offering a reminder of the different ways in which Shakespeare could signify. *London und Paris* concentrated on the cultural and fashionable life of its two capital cities, but also on the political conflict between them that embroiled German states when Napoleon oversaw their organization into the Confederation of the Rhine in 1806, which brought the press under French control. While the journal continued to publish, from this date no political caricatures similar to 'Buonaparte's Soliloquy' appeared within its pages. The reproduction, in 1803, of a British parody that offers anti-French propaganda sheds light on the Weimar-based journal's own political sympathies and freedom to engage in debate and print politically charged content. At a material level, the exchange and provisionality of these parodies draw attention to broader issues about the multiple roles Shakespeare is called to perform during wartime, as networks of global users extract and adapt his plays for topical wartime debate, propaganda, and cultural discussion.

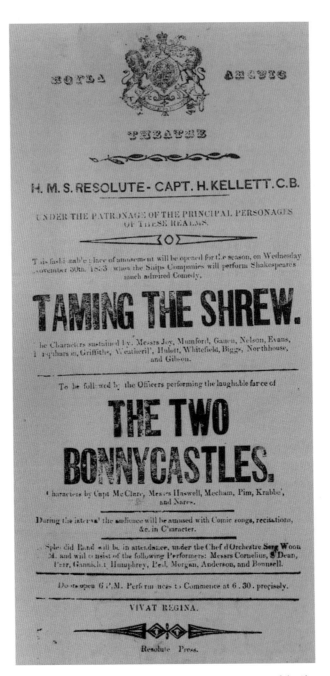

Figure 5   *Royal Arctic Theatre on board the Resolute presents: Taming of the Shrew* and *Two Bonnycastles* (Library and Archives Canada, W. T. Mumford fonds, C-096563).

CHAPTER 5

Shakespeare, the North-West Passage, and the Russian War

Irena R. Makaryk

The much-anticipated new theatre season of 1853–54 was launched on Wednesday 30 November with 'Shakespeare's much admired Comedy, *Taming the Shrew*'. The playbill invited audiences to 'This fashionable place of amusement': not an elegant London playhouse, as its conventional phrasing suggested, but a snow stage specially created for the Royal Arctic Theatre on board the *HMS Resolute* commanded by Captain Henry Kellett (see Figure 5). Here, the spectators would find all the usual elements of a Victorian theatre event: a prologue composed for the occasion, a mainpiece (*Shrew*), an afterpiece (J. M. Morton's farce *Two Bonnycastles*), and, during the interval, 'Comic songs, recitations, etc., in Character'. A 'Splendid Band' under 'the Chef d'Orchestre Serg[eant] Woon' augmented the audience's pleasure. The delighted spectators were drawn from the crews of four ships – the *HMS Assistance, Intrepid, Pioneer*, and the *Resolute* – all overwintering in the same area in the High Arctic under the general command of Sir Edward Belcher.

From the Royal Arctic Theatre's name encircling the British Coat of Arms and suggesting monarchical patronage, to its rousing finish – 'VIVAT REGINA' – the playbill produced by the 'Resolute Press' employed (and parodied) well-known rhetorical and typographical conventions. Set in type by William T. Mumford (Carpenter's Mate) on a portable printing press supplied by the Admiralty, the playbill offered a small indication of the great importance of these wildly popular shipboard theatricals. Encouraging social cohesion and boosting morale, Shakespeare in particular served both to remind the crews of Britain's great theatrical and literary legacy, and to unite their hearts and minds in affirming their loyalty to Navy, Queen, and Country. Such expressions of unity and resolve were accented as rumblings of imminent war with Russia increased. Mumford, an enthusiastic thespian, was involved in almost every aspect of the production. His unpublished private diary, found in Library and Archives

Canada, constitutes an important source of information for understanding the process of creating shipboard theatricals under some of the most difficult conditions imaginable: many months of sunless days, extremely cold temperatures, and anxieties about basic survival. An invaluable resource for understanding the dangerous conditions that men endured in the Arctic, Mumford's diary provides copious details about shipboard life from the rarely extant point of view of the men rather than the officers.[1]

The Rivalry with Russia

Shortly after the Napoleonic Wars, the British Admiralty returned to a project that had been attempted in Shakespeare's day: the search for the North-West Passage. Second Secretary to the Admiralty Sir John Barrow urged a renewal of that endeavour and 'of not allowing others, especially Russia, "a naval power of but yesterday", to snatch from Britain the honour of solving this great problem'.[2] It was hoped that the discovery of the Passage would accelerate Britain's trade advantage by reducing the number of months it took to travel to the west coast of America and, further on, to China and India. Moreover, it would signal to the world Britain's undisputed leadership in scientific and geographical exploration; and, most importantly, it would incontrovertibly assert its naval power while thwarting Russian expansionist ambitions. Among the many tasked with searching for the fabled Passage was Sir John Franklin and his crew of the *Erebus* and the *Terror*. Mysteriously, they disappeared sometime after 1845.

Like the concurrent search for the North-West Passage, the events leading up to the Russian War took place in the context of this period of British national and imperial self-assertion. Although later misnamed the 'Crimean' War, the Great War with Russia, or simply the Russian War (as its contemporaries called it), was not confined to a small area of the Black Sea, but was waged on a much broader stage, including the Baltic, the White Sea, the Arctic, the Pacific coastline of Siberia, the Sea of Azov, and the Black Sea.[3] At this time, Britain's primary striking force in European warfare was the Navy, not the army, and it was in part because of its maritime might that the struggle was extended into many theatres of war. The aim was to destroy Russian naval power, to harass commerce, block ports, and attack all 'Russian establishments around the world'.[4] In contrast, the role of the British Army, although important, was conceived as support for what was expected to be primarily a French and Turkish land campaign.[5]

As search vessels were combing the Arctic for any scrap of information about the fate of the Franklin expedition, Anglo–Russian rivalry was reaching its height.[6] War was finally declared on 28 March 1854. One of the most important reasons for this declaration was Britain's attitude to Russia. Stereotyped as 'a savage power, aggressive and expansionist by nature, yet also sufficiently cunning and deceptive to plot with "unseen forces" against the West and infiltrate societies',[7] Russia gained this reputation through numerous aggressive acts. Its expansion southward (the annexation of Crimea, 1783); its brutal response to the struggles for freedom of the Poles (1831) and of the Hungarians (1849); its invasion of Moldavia and Wallachia (July 1853); and, shortly after, its destruction of the Turkish fleet at Sinope – all these offered reasons for deep concern.[8] A crusading war fever swept Britain, which was played out in newspapers, pamphlets, and broadsheets, as well as in public venues including taverns and churches.[9] Hostility to Russia became 'a central reference point in a political discourse about liberty, civilization, and progress that helped shape the national identity'.[10] For the first time, a war was initiated not just by government leaders but also by the pressure of the press and the force of public opinion.[11]

Expecting to employ its naval superiority to roundly thrash Russia's fleet, Britain carefully timed its declaration of war to coincide with the break-up of winter ice in the Baltic – the anticipated location for the major theatre of war.[12] Joining forces with its historic foe, France, and allegedly in defence of Turkey after Russia had encroached on its territory, Britain was eager to maintain the status quo in terms of global power dynamics. Keen to torpedo Russia's ambitions in the worldwide imperial struggle for power, Britain hoped to destroy its navy and halt its ever-expanding territorial reach. A dispute about the rights of Catholic monks in Jerusalem ignited the final spark, though the protection of British trade routes remained the central, though occluded, British agenda, and one in concert with efforts to discover the North-West Passage.[13] Both aimed to outmanoeuvre Russia.

Allied naval squadrons attacked Russian towns and ports, destroyed military installations, and disrupted shipping, fishing, and trade routes even in that most inaccessible of regions, the Far North.[14] The British presence there indicated how important this territory was to its concerns with the future of its trade.[15] The smallest of the theatres of war were in the Arctic: in the White Sea and the Barents Sea.[16] Any extended campaign there was impossible because the waters were ice-free only for a very short period. Officers experienced with the Arctic waters like Erasmus Ommanney, Samuel Cresswell, Edward Inglefield, Bedford Pim, W. J. S. Pullen, and Sherard Osborn, who had served on the Franklin search vessels, were soon diverted from one task in order to engage in another with the same aim: besting the Russians at war.

Shipboard Shakespeare

For those serving on Arctic ships, the twin maladies of monotony and nostalgia for home were acutely experienced. Crews endured many months of sunless days locked in the seemingly endless landscape of ice and snow. As Commander of the *Pioneer*, Sherard Osborn noted, 'Nothing struck one more than the strong tendency to talk of home, of England: it became quite a disease … We gladly sought refuge in amusements.'[17] Deprived of the familiar markers of space and time, the crew created their own equivalents of the comforting rituals and routines that recalled home. They engaged in an astonishing range of shipboard activities, which included theatricals, masked balls, magic shows, Guy Fawkes Day ceremonies, comic recitations, pageants, shipboard periodicals, glees, and 'orchestras'.

The most popular and the most anticipated of all were theatricals. Since Sir Edward Parry's expeditions earlier in the century, these had proven to best help raise spirits, create a sense of community, and instil a patriotic spirit. Nearly all of the forty Franklin search vessels staged plays. Both a distraction from homesickness and yet a replication of home, theatricals intentionally mirrored all the conventions of the London stage tradition while also emphasizing the Navy's valuable contribution in maintaining the power and prestige of the Empire. They took on resonant imperial names such as the Queen's Arctic Theatre, the Royal Victoria Theatre, or – as in the *Shrew* playbill – the Royal Arctic Theatre. Each theatre event celebrated the crew's loyalty and service to the Navy, the Crown, and the British Empire.[18] Shipboard periodicals, poems, songs, recitations, and theatrical events constantly referenced the Empire and the crews' own gallant part in the mission to make it ever greater.

The Arctic theatrical repertoire was understandably dominated by light fare. Of all the Shakespeare productions that took place in the Arctic, *Taming the Shrew* is the best documented by its contemporaries. Once the choice of play had been decided, three weeks of intense activity began. Throughout the daily rehearsals, Mumford referred to the play as *Catherine and Petruchio*, David Garrick's eighteenth-century adaptation of Shakespeare's comedy. The playbill, however, prominently advertised the play as Shakespeare's; only the journal of Émile Frédéric de Bray provides firm evidence that the 30 November event began with a play by Shakespeare 'arrangée par Garrick'.[19]

The deliberate substitution of 'Shakespeare' for 'Garrick' points to the potency and usefulness of the Bard's name as a resonant signifying and unifying force. As shorthand, Shakespeare's name invoked a 'shared symbolic universe'.[20] A common denominator of British identity, 'Shakespeare' was embraced both by officers and men, thus flattening naval, social, and professional hierarchies. The tacit understanding of a shared British cultural tradition was reflected more generally in the whole theatrical event, which employed the full panoply of London theatrical rituals and practices, beginning with the playbill and ending with theatre reviews 'published' in the shipboard periodicals.

Since the men, not the officers, were performing 'Shakespeare', their skill and capacity to embody the National Bard's work endowed them with considerable prestige, certainly more than if they were 'simply' performing a farce by Garrick. No strangers to the Bard's works, many of the sailors, both men and officers, privately read and enthusiastically discussed the plays. A Frenchman who had volunteered to join the British search for Franklin, Joseph René Bellot, recorded with evident surprise that 'Mathison, one of our men, reads *Othello*, and I am astonished to hear all the sailors talk to me of Shakespeare; one prefers *Macbeth*, another *Hamlet*; I doubt if Molière is so popular among French sailors.'[21]

George McDougall, Mate on the *Intrepid*, and a member of the Theatrical Committee of Management whose duty was to oversee all the theatrical productions, was at pains to explain how difficult and time-consuming a business it was to put up a theatre in the extreme circumstances of the Arctic, and yet how much pleasure was derived from it: 'The very fifes had to be manufactured out of brass curtain rods, whilst a tin fiddle occupied the tinker for several days.'[22] While the props were being constructed, the Royal Arms were raised on the gable front of the Royal Arctic Theatre. On 21 November, with the temperature hovering at minus thirty-one degrees, beer was brewed in anticipation of the post-theatrical celebration, while the carpenters began to paint the scenery, a task completed five days later. Meanwhile, the band practiced on board the *Intrepid*. On 23 November, the men spread sails over the heavy canvas housing to roof the theatre. Despite the plunging temperature that reached minus thirty-five on 24 November, it was decided that the play was to go ahead on the upper deck of the *Resolute*. The ship was a busy hive of activity, particularly for the carpenters. After cleaning the lower deck, new-hinging the captain's cabin door, and completing other smaller tasks on 26 November, Mumford recorded that the dresses had been 'issued to the actors and actresses'.[23] Most officers brought with them one or more costumes for masquerade balls, a tradition in various ports of call around the world. The men, however, had to have their costumes made on shipboard using whatever materials were at hand. McDougall, who also served as the chief scene painter and general dressmaker, ruefully observed that proper materials were significantly lacking. Dress and bonnet-making ('extremely puzzling') posed a special problem, while stage makeup had to be created from soot, blacking, chalk, and anything else that could serve.

The raked snow stage was arranged near the foremast with the audience seated in front of the mainmast. Underscoring the ship's hierarchy, the few chairs available were set aside for the 'royal box' of the captain and his guests, while the men sat on trunks. Deck banking was dug out for the orchestra and sledge flags were hung up along the sides of the *Resolute* – a visual sign both of naval pride and of welcome to the crews of other ships as they made their icy way in the dark to attend the performance.

The space of the *Resolute* was everywhere transformed into a paeon to the Navy, Britain, and the Empire. An elegant chandelier, made out of swords' bayonets, beads, lamps, and candles, was fitted and hung by Mumford. The upper deck was well festooned with banners and numerous colourful naval and British flags. A canopy of flags and Captain Kellett's coat of arms were placed over the 'president's [captain's] seat' (an armchair) at the foot of the mainmast. Once seated, Kellett was presented with a copy of the playbill printed on silk as a memento of the event.[24]

The 'talented brass' kept the impatient audience occupied before the curtain finally rose to a successful performance that began with a Prologue recited by Mr C. Anderson. Recording his evident 'surprise', McDougall observed that 'the characters were admirably supported', the language 'well delivered, and all appeared to enter into the spirit of the immortal bard'.[25] Notably, the 'immortal' Shakespeare, not Garrick, was invoked as the 'spirit' unifying the performance. It was a spirit – as de Bray noted – that imbued the ensemble with 'un brio extraordinaire'.[26] Richard Roche (Mate on the *Resolute*) similarly assessed the performance as having been carried out with 'great éclat', especially its knockabout farce. He noted that the shrew 'was excessively well tamed' and that Petruchio, despite a 'very broad North Country accent', had 'acquitted himself to the intense satisfaction of a numerous & delighted audience'.[27]

Shakespeare, hilarity, sent-up theatrical conventions: these were binding agents, reminding sailors of their common heritage and reinscribing the 'blank' space of the Arctic into a 'British' space, one that was united through camaraderie, patriotism, laughter, and reminders of home. As public events and iterative rituals staging familiar English practices, Arctic theatricals created a bond in the hearts and the minds of the sailors. 'Shakespeare' generated an enthusiasm and unity in which the individual, absorbed by the naval community and incorporated into the larger British nation, experienced the pleasure of the renewal of national identity and purpose.

Penned especially for the occasion, the Prologue echoed these sentiments. Written in halting rhyming couplets by Mumford (Baptista) and Able Seamen T. Northhouse (Kate), both of the *Resolute*, together with James Nelson (Grumio) of the *Investigator*, the Prologue gloried in Britain's naval power, which reached even into their 'wastes remote'. Employing some elements of the Bard's metatheatrical toolbox, the Prologue linked the snow-packed stage of the *Shrew* to the 'stage' of 'sweet' home that dwelt in the deepest recesses of their hearts. While gently hinting at their anxiety about a safe return from such a treacherous and unforgiving landscape, the men expressed their hope that, in the following year, they would return home to the land of their 'Gracious Queen':

> Our sign, the well-known British Coat of Arms
> Whose banners name o'er these wastes remote
> As proudly as e'er they waved o'er decks …
> 'Gentlemen' we thought this year to play a part
> On homes sweet stage which claims our inmost heart
> But still we hope, our Gracious Queen, God bless her
> Will see her loyal subjects this time next year.[28]

Fixing the performance in the place and time of their Arctic adventures and linking 'Shakespeare' to royal symbols and authority, the Prologue concluded with a brief introduction to the play:

> These three short acts will show in modern life
> How well was 'tamed' a young shrew wife
> For Nature indeed has often gone astray
> But if Husbands will command, Wives <u>must</u> obey.[29]

The men's creditable performance of 'Shakespeare' and their evident knowledge of popular Victorian theatre culture elevated them to a certain level of authority. Yet, like the women's experiences they impersonated, the carnivalesque suspension from 'Nature' was temporary, ending with the evening, when 'command' led back to 'obey'.

A ritual element of theatricals, the Prologue was recited by Charles Anderson, Able Seaman, and gunroom cook on the *Investigator*.[30] A fine actor, singer, and musician, his name appears on various playbills in these different capacities, including on that of the *Shrew* in which he also served as one of the musicians. Evidently, his many talents were much respected. Only from de Bray do we learn that he was Black:

> In the interval several men sang comic songs and we discovered some excellent actors among *Investigator*'s men, among others a Black who recited a prologue composed for the occasion. Nothing more amusing than this Black arriving in black evening dress and white waistcoat to recite in his patois a bit of verse and trying hard to imitate the manners of a man of the world.[31]

The text of the Prologue, with its earnest expressions of British loyalty and pride on the one hand, and anxiety about a safe return home on the other, seems to have been at significant odds with the manner of delivery, perhaps intentionally mirroring Quince's hilariously inept performance of the Prologue to 'Pyramus and Thisbe' before *his* 'betters'. Anderson's parody of the speech patterns, dress, and mannerisms of an upper-class toff may have cut two ways: while serving as an obliging object of laughter, he was likely also mocking those 'gentlemen' who displayed some of these same uppity mannerisms. The laughter evoked was thus simultaneously ridiculing *and* unifying. Indeed, in the special circumstances of the small, contained environments of ice-locked ships, the usual cultural and hierarchical distinctions that pertained on land were not only hard to maintain[32] but were also met with significant displeasure and pushback when captains attempted to do so.[33] The fluidity of hierarchical distinctions in the Arctic is clearly reflected by the fact that the Prologue was penned not by someone in power or authority but, rather, by a carpenter's mate and two able seamen, and, moreover, delivered by a Black cook. The affirmation of unity and resolve was of paramount importance in these isolated circumstances and with war brewing in the wings.

   Anderson's performance requires a few more words of comment. Only a few months earlier, Captain Robert McClure, Anderson, and his mates from the *Investigator* were forced to abandon their ship. Trekking across the Arctic, they were eventually saved from starvation and certain death by the *Resolute*'s officers to whom McClure announced the joyful news: he had beaten the Russians and discovered the North-West Passage – though he had done so by walking rather than sailing through it. Celebrating Queen, Country, Navy, and Bard, the *Investigator*'s participation in the *Resolute*'s theatricals attests to Shakespeare's power as a vehicle of social cohesion, morale-boosting, and patriotic pride. Bringing the November evening's entertainments to a close, the 'Splendid Band's' performance was followed by a rousing chorus of 'God Save the Queen' and three cheers for the performers', uniting all in a ritual celebration of British values.[34]

Home

News of the war with Russia eventually reached Mumford and his companions on 26 August 1854, putting 'the whole ship' into a state of 'extreme excitement'.[35] Finally reaching the shores of England in early September, Mumford concluded his journal with a reference to the first victorious British engagement in the Russian War, the battle of the River Alma (20 September 1854): 'Saluting in honour of the Battle of Alma – off Gravesend … made fast at 7 pm when leave was at once granted to the "Resolutes" and at 7.30 we once more set foot in Old England to the great joy of all concerned.'[36]

While there is no record of Mumford taking part in any other naval adventure, many officers turned from searching for the Franklin to their new commission: attacking the Russians on the Arctic coast and on other fronts. Fittingly bringing together British objectives designed to thwart Russia, Sherard Osborn completed editing the Arctic journal of Robert McClure's *Narrative of the Discovery of the North-West Passage* while in the Sea of Azov. It was a book that captured the imagination of many readers, including Queen Victoria,[37] for whom McClure's discovery helped remove some of the stain of the British disasters in the Crimea.[38] Mumford's play-bill brings to light this rich, complex, and forgotten moment in British wartime history in which 'Shakespeare' played a unique part as catalyst for affirming national identity, British naval pride, and loyalty to the Crown. 'Shakespeare' brought 'England' to the Arctic.

Figure 6   Cabinet card of James Sant's portrait of 'Shakespeare "as youth"' (Michael Davitt Papers, The Library of Trinity College Dublin (IE TCD MS 9649/183)).

CHAPTER 6

'Now for Our Irish Wars'
Shakespeare, Colonialism, and Nationalism in Ireland

Andrew Murphy

The object chosen as the point of focus for this essay is an image titled 'Shakespeare "as youth"' included in the Michael Davitt papers at Trinity College Dublin (Figure 6). The Davitt material was deposited at Trinity between 1978 and 1982 by the Davitt family and by Davitt's biographer, T. W. Moody, Professor of Modern History at Trinity. The piece is a photographic souvenir cabinet card, reproducing a portrait of a young Shakespeare by James Sant (1820–1916). Sant was a highly successful portraitist who 'gained popular acclaim for his idealized depictions of childhood … which were widely disseminated through engravings'.[1] The image of Shakespeare certainly is 'idealized' in Sant's portrait: the poet is presented as a soft-featured, long-haired boy, set in a pastoral landscape.

Cabinet cards, consisting of a photograph mounted on a card backing, were popular in the later nineteenth century. Oftentimes they were used for family portraiture, so the present item is a little unusual in what it depicts. The image under consideration here is part of a substantial body of photographs collected by the noted Irish nationalist Michael Davitt (1846–1906). Davitt is best known for his work as a land-rights activist, but he was also a member of the radical Irish Republican Brotherhood, which aimed to break the connection between Britain and Ireland by force of arms. In 1867, Davitt took part in a raid on a military installation in England with the aim of securing arms to be transported to Ireland as part of what was envisaged as a general uprising against British rule. Though the insurrectionary project failed, it helped to maintain the momentum of separatist militancy, which culminated in the 1916 uprising.

Davitt was himself an avid photographer and his papers include a substantial collection of images, mostly souvenir portraits of one sort or another. The great bulk of the photographs are of noted persons connected in some way with Irish history and politics. The Sant image stands out as rather anomalous within the collection and, in this sense, we might see its inclusion as rather surprising. However, consideration of the ways in which Shakespeare was appropriated and deployed within the context of a conflict in Ireland that extended over several centuries makes the presence of the image seem less strange (an issue also discussed by Katherine Hennessey in Chapter 12 in connection to the Easter Rising). While Shakespeare served as a kind of cultural 'anchor' for the colonial community in Ireland in the period from 1690 onwards, the playwright was increasingly adopted by nationalists almost as a kind of 'honorary Irishman' from the 1790s. Davitt's interest in Shakespeare is thus all of a piece with the investment in the English playwright that we find in other noted nationalist leaders from Theobald Wolfe Tone to Patrick Pearse. Over the long duration of Shakespeare appropriations in Ireland, we discover that the playwright is adopted as an emblematic figure by those on *both* sides of the political divide: nationalists as well as unionists. And, indeed, as noted in the closing section of this piece, there are times when – strangely and unexpectedly – Shakespeare even has the capacity to bring those on both sides of the divide together.

§

In *Richard II*, having just learned of the death of John of Gaunt, Richard declares,

> … Now, for our Irish wars,
> We must supplant those rough rug-headed kern,
> Which live like venom where no venom else
> But only they have privilege to live.   (2.1.155–58)

The play does not, in fact, follow Richard to Ireland, which remains an off-stage territory, a land of venom and conflict. But while England's military experience at the hands of Ireland's 'rough rug-headed kern' was often fraught, from Shakespeare's time onwards the island witnessed a progressive chronology of English/British military success on the island. At the time when Shakespeare was writing *Henry V*, in 1599, English control over Ireland stood in the balance in the face of a separatist campaign led by Hugh O'Neill. Just three years later, however, the Irish and their Spanish allies would be decisively defeated at the Battle of Kinsale and, over the course of the seventeenth century, further conflicts would lead to a thorough weakening of native Irish power. As the century drew to a close, the conflict between James II and William of Orange played out its final stages in Ireland, culminating in the defeat of James's forces at the battle of the Boyne in 1690. All of these conflicts had the effect of increasingly strengthening the colonialist position in Ireland, so that the 'supplanting' imagined by Richard II increasingly became a reality. By the later stretch of the seventeenth century, less than 10 per cent of Irish land remained in the hands of the native Catholic community.

The eighteenth century in Ireland was substantially a period of colonial hegemony, as the settler community tightened its grip on political and economic control. Shakespeare served a central function in the *cultural* formation of that community. There was a flourishing publishing trade in Dublin in this period and Irish editions of Shakespeare began to appear from 1721, when George Grierson issued texts of *Othello*, *Hamlet*, and *Julius Caesar*. Grierson published his Shakespeare texts in parallel with a strong line of anti-Catholic publications, some of them – such as *God's Goodness visible in our deliverance from Popery with some fit methods to prevent the further growth of it in Ireland* (1735) – celebrating the colonial community's ascendancy over the native population. In 1725, Grierson published the first Irish complete edition of the plays and six more collected editions would appear with a Dublin imprint before the end of the century.

Grierson's premises were located close by Smock Alley, where Dublin's most enduring theatre of the period was located. The theatre had first opened in 1662, and remained in business until 1788, serving during this time as Dublin's pre-eminent theatrical venue. For most of its existence it was designated a 'Theatre Royal' and it was much frequented by the upper reaches of Irish society. Shakespeare was an absolutely central staple of the Smock Alley repertoire, but in fact, the most extravagant Shakespearean production of the period was staged not at Smock Alley but in Dublin's Phoenix Park, at a property owned by Luke Gardiner, Viscount Mountjoy. In January of 1778, Gardiner commissioned a production of *Macbeth*, with Gardiner's wife, Elizabeth, playing the part of Lady Macbeth. The Irish *Freeman's Journal* hailed the production as 'a sure mark of the advances which this country had made of late years in civilization and literature', and the *Hibernian Magazine* noted that the Gardiners had 'built a temple to Shakespeare' at the Phoenix Park property.[2] The *Journal* praised Elizabeth Gardiner for a performance that was 'animated, impassioned, and even extravagant'.[3] The *Hibernian* registered that the performances were given in front of a 'brilliant assemblage of the first people in Ireland, with the presence of the Viceroy on the second, and his lady on the first night ... all vying with each other in magnificence'. None in the assembled audience, however, outshone Elizabeth Gardiner herself. Her costume was made of 'a gold-ground silk, ornamented with artificial and silver flowers, and with diamonds to the amount of one hundred thousand pounds'.[4] The opulence of the evening served as a clear indication of the extent to which the colonial exploitation of Ireland had succeeded over the course of the eighteenth century – and of how the colonial community had grounded itself culturally, using Shakespeare as a touchstone.

Not much more than a decade after the Phoenix Park *Macbeth*, French aristocrats found themselves being beheaded for far less than wearing gold-ground silk dresses with a hundred thousand pounds' worth of diamonds attached to them. Soon enough, the French revolutionary ideas that set the guillotines in motion in Paris found their way to Ireland and they provided intellectual inspiration for an emerging coalition of radical Protestants and a disaffected Catholic peasantry, who came together as the 'United Irishmen' with the intention of breaking the link with Britain and establishing a republican form of government in Ireland. The leader of the movement was Theobald Wolfe Tone (1763–98) and in 1791 he published a tract entitled *An Argument on Behalf of the Catholics of Ireland*. In one section of his tract, Tone draws on Shakespeare to help advance his argument, adapting Shylock's famous speech in *The Merchant of Venice* to Irish ends. As a Protestant himself, Tone specifically addresses his own community, arguing in favour of equal rights for Catholics in the following terms:

> Shall they not say to us, 'Are we not men, as ye are, stamped with the image of our Maker, walking erect, beholding the same light, breathing the same air as Protestants: Hath not a Catholic hands; hath not a Catholic eyes, dimensions, organs, passions? Fed with the same food, hurt by the same weapons, healed by the same means, warmed and cooled by the same summer and winter, as a Protestant is. If ye prick us, do we not bleed? If ye tickle us, do we not laugh? If ye poison us, do we not die? And if ye injure us, *shall we not revenge?*'[5]

In addition to arguing in favour of Catholic equality, Tone is also pressing for essentially seeing Catholic natives and Protestant incomers as a single community who would benefit from working together to break the colonial connection.

That joint effort to overthrow the colonial administration was launched in 1798, when Tone led the United Irish coalition in a militant uprising. The campaign was a failure, but the uprising signalled the resumption of regular armed conflict in Ireland, with further militant campaigns breaking out repeatedly over the course of the ensuing century and beyond. Tone's repurposing of Shylock's speech in *The*

Merchant of Venice can be said to have signalled something else as well. Where previously Shakespeare had largely been the possession of the settler community, serving, as we have seen, as an important element in their cultural formation, now he was being deployed on behalf of the *colonized* Irish and, in this new era, the playwright would regularly be adopted by Irish nationalists.

A notable instance of this process is the case of the militant nationalist Michael Davitt. Davitt was born in 1846, as Ireland was in the grip of an intense famine. Though Davitt's own family survived, they fell behind with their rent and were evicted by their landlord. The family moved to England, settling in Haslingden in Lancashire. At the age of 9, Davitt began work at the local cotton mill, but in 1857 an accident with a piece of machinery led to his losing his right arm. In the wake of this accident Davitt was – though a Catholic – sent to the local Wesleyan school, where he studied for four years.[6] His life story from this point closely mirrors that of many of the nineteenth-century working-class autodidacts.[7] He was 'a voracious reader, his love of books follow[ing] his footsteps all his days from the Mechanics' Institute in Haslingden to the National Library in Ireland'.[8] Davitt ended up serving time in prison for his political convictions, and he carried on his studies while in custody, where, in one stint, 'He was allowed any books he requested, apart from those on current affairs or newspapers.'[9]

The Irish poet W. B. Yeats described an encounter with an elderly Davitt and observed of him that 'I watched him with sympathy. One knows by the way a man sits in his chair if he have emotional intensity, and Davitt's suggested to me a writer, a painter, an artist of some kind, rather than a man of action.'[10] But Davitt had indeed, in his younger days, been a man of action. In 1865, he joined the Irish Republican Brotherhood (IRB), a clandestine organization that aimed to forward the republican, separatist programme originally mapped out by the United Irishmen. Two years later he played a significant part in an ambitious plot aimed at securing Irish independence. Members of the IRB in Britain were to mount raids on a set of military installations, plundering the stores for arms and ammunition. As a later account indicates, 'The telegraph wires were to be cut, and the railroads not required for operations to be torn up.' The arms and supplies acquired in the raids were to be transported by commandeered trains to Holyhead, 'where possession was to be taken of one or more steamers, in which Ireland was to be reached and the standard of insurrection raised'.[11] By now a local commander in the IRB, Davitt was charged with leading the attack on Chester Castle, but his group of militants realized at the last moment that their plan had been betrayed and the attack was aborted, with Davitt's group making its escape. The entire plan to secure weapons in Britain failed, but the uprising in Ireland went ahead nevertheless, though it was quickly put down by the British forces.

While Davitt escaped capture following the abortive raid on Chester Castle, he was not so lucky three years later, when he arranged to meet a contact at Paddington railway station in London. Davitt had 'in his possession ... 150l. in bank notes, some two or three pounds in gold and silver', and his contact was carrying a bag filled with packages that 'were found to contain 50 well-finished six-chamber revolvers' – these weapons were destined to be deployed in service of the conflict in Ireland.[12] The authorities put 2 and 2 (or perhaps we might say 150 and 50) together and Davitt was charged with felony-treason and sentenced to penal servitude. It is in his recollections of prison life that Davitt demonstrates his clear knowledge of Shakespeare. In his *Leaves from a Prison Diary*, he recalls a stint spent at Newgate prison and remembers that the first book he was given to read there had previously been in the hands of another prisoner who 'had written – "Good-bye, Lucy dear," throughout the book, upwards of as many times as the love-smitten hero of *As You Like It* had carved the name of Rosalind on the trees of Arden Forest'.[13] That Davitt was acquainted with a broader range of Shakespeare's writings beyond just this single play is attested by another story from his prison writings. One of his fellow inmates, he relates, 'did me the honour of requesting me to become the critic of a piece of blank verse, which, he declared, had elicited from the schoolmaster an opinion that Shakespeare had nothing equal to it in any of his works'. Davitt notes that he was 'deeply interested in the individual who could beat Shakespeare hollow', but, when the piece of writing was produced for him to examine, his own knowledge of Shakespeare's work – and his broader reading – made it possible for him very easily to discern that it consisted of nothing more than 'a string of unconnected lines stolen from Milton, Shakespeare, and Young's *Night Thoughts*'. So much, Davitt concluded, for 'Shakespeare's rival'.[14]

Davitt's interest in Shakespeare is also signalled, as we have seen, in the cabinet card of Sant's Shakespeare portrait. In the greater collection, we find many pictures – either photographs or photographic reproductions of engravings or paintings – of Irish nationalist leaders, including Robert Emmet, who led an abortive uprising in 1803, Daniel O'Connell, who successfully campaigned for Catholic emancipation early in the nineteenth century, and of Charles Stewart Parnell, who fought a parliamentary battle for Irish Home Rule in the closing decades of the century. There are photographic images too of scenes of nineteenth-century evictions in Ireland – scenes with which Davitt would doubtless have felt a particular connection. Sant's Shakespeare portrait is thus a curious inclusion in this broader company.

In addition to Sant's rather romanticized Shakespeare, Davitt also possessed two further related images: pictures of William Charles Macready and of Henry Irving. Both were, of course, among the fore-most Shakespearean actors of the nineteenth century. Macready had a strong Irish connection. His father had been born in Dublin and had acted at Smock Alley before relocating to London, where his son followed him into the acting profession. Macready *fils* ventured to Dublin a number of times in the period 1820 to 1850, playing various Shakespearean roles over the years. Irving also played in Dublin regu-larly in the later decades of the century. In November 1876, for instance, Edward Dowden, Professor of English at Trinity College, went to see him as Hamlet at the Theatre Royal, and noted in a letter to a friend that he 'was certainly a wonderful success here … the students were a flood of enthusiasm'.[15] It is unclear whether Davitt might have attended any of Irving's Dublin performances (he had been only a child during the period of Macready's Irish appearances). Certainly, at the point when Dowden saw Irving play Hamlet, Davitt was still in prison in England. Though based in Ireland in his later years, Davitt was often out of the country, so it is possible that he might not have coincided with any of Irving's performances at the turn of the century. But the presence of the images of two such prominent Shakespearean actors in Davitt's photo collection, together with the Sant portrait, certainly indicates an interest in performed Shakespeare and in the biographical Shakespeare as well as in the text of the plays.

The trio of images that we find in Davitt's photo collection reflect a nationalist investment in Shakespeare that persisted into the high period of Irish militancy in the opening decades of the twentieth century. One militant nationalist activist at this time – Darrell Figgis (like Davitt, a gun-runner) – went so far as to write a substantial book about Shakespeare, an extended study taking into consideration Shakespeare's life, craft, thought, and personality, among other topics.[16] Interest in the playwright extended to the very highest levels of the militant separatist movement, with Patrick Pearse, the leader of the 1916 uprising, being virtually a Shakespeare obses-sive. Fellow insurrectionist Desmond Ryan noted, for instance, the almost neurotic impulses that Pearse experienced in relation to acquiring editions

of the playwright's works: Pearse loved, he tells us, his 'many editions of
Shakespeare, all of which he watched in the booksellers' windows, nobly
renounced, entered, fingered, steeled himself, fled whole streets away, lin-
gered, wavered, turned back and purchased, radiant and ashamed until he
saw the next'.[17]

Where Davitt suffered incarceration for his militancy, Pearse paid
for his with his life. His execution by firing squad in 1916 occasioned
a striking Shakespearean coda to his career – and to the general history
of political appropriations of Shakespeare in an Irish context – as indicated in a contemporary account of a lecture on *Julius Caesar* delivered by
Wilbraham Fitzjohn Trench. Trench had succeeded Edward Dowden as
Professor of English at Trinity, with his qualification for the job resting
largely on a book he had written, entitled *Shakespeare's Hamlet: A New
Commentary*.[18] As a moderate unionist, the Trinity professor had little
sympathy with the aims of the 1916 separatists. Some months after the
rising, Trench found himself giving a talk to the National Literary Society
in Dublin and his lecture had the rather intriguing title 'Shakespeare's
Brutus in Ireland'.[19] Early in his talk, Trench offered an unambiguous
portrait of Shakespeare's politics: 'The basic principle was conservation;
it was that settled order was society's chief interest. Order appeared
to Shakespeare as it must have done to any of his contemporaries, to
be best secured under a monarchical system.' Trench noted, however,
that in *Julius Caesar* Shakespeare presents his audience, in the case of
Brutus, with a republican idealist. Trench is damning in his assessment of
Brutus's programme and actions: 'Brutus never did a bit of constructive
work. He murdered an intimate friend, he plunged his country into civil
war.' 'Such men', he notes, 'were to be found in the French Revolution.
They were also to be found in Irish history.'

With the uprising very much in recent Irish memory at the time, it
does not take a great deal in the way of close reading to see what Trench
is getting at here: the image of Pearse begins, we might say, to emerge
from behind that of Brutus. But the figure of Brutus can be a pecu-
liarly malleable one in wartime contexts and, having established him as
a fundamentally negative figure, Trench's text takes rather an unexpected
turn. Brutus, Trench observes, 'was not only a self-opinionated theorist,
misled, and misleading others. Still less was he only a murderer and a
traitor; he was also a pure-souled patriot, acting without a thought of
self-advancement for what he mistakenly supposed to be the cause of his
country.' The word 'patriot' here has, of course, strong resonances in a talk
that is being delivered not just in the wake of the uprising but, indeed,

while the greater war was still raging. Trench concludes his talk with an even more remarkable observation:

> Brutus represented a type that recurred in critical times – the ardent theorist, the man of ideas endeavouring to lead the men of action, the criminal who was a hero, the man whose deeds were to be condemned and his motives admired, the idealist, the visionary, taking his place among the traitors, one to be mourned over and to be loved.

Given the barely disguised melding of Brutus with Pearse here, the conclusion reached is quite astonishing: that Pearse, the militant nationalist idealist, might actually be seen as a patriot and is, despite his actions, worthy not just of being mourned following his execution, but also of being loved – as much by the community of unionists as by nationalists.

The 1916 uprising was followed in time by an Anglo–Irish war that culminated in the greater part of Ireland gaining independence in 1922, finally bringing to an end larger-scale conflicts between Britain and Ireland (the question of Northern Ireland is, of course, a separate matter). Trench's comments on Pearse essentially effect the closing of a cultural loop in relation to Shakespeare and the Irish wars. Where the playwright served as a kind of cultural talisman for the colonial community in the eighteenth century, before subsequently being adopted by nationalist native intellectuals in the nineteenth and early twentieth centuries, Trench's comments offer a moment in which a settler-descendent, conservative unionist is willing to register the honour and nobility symbolized by Pearse's nationalist, separatist sacrifice. What links Trench and Pearse is their common enthusiasm for Shakespeare and it is through Shakespeare that Trench is able to celebrate Pearse, while nonetheless opposing his political views. Irish wars and Shakespeare, we might say, finally have the effect of drawing the strangest of bedfellows together.

Figure 7   Double-page spread from *The Sphere*, 7 December 1914 (pp. 22–23)
(reproduced by kind permission of the Syndics of Cambridge University Library).

CHAPTER 7

Shakespeare and the Survival of Middle England
Weekly Journals, 1914–1918

Stuart Sillars

On 7 December 1914, *The Sphere*, one of the leading illustrated weekly journals of the day, published a double-page spread which, in its use of word and image, drew together ideas of contemporary patriotism and the love of the nation, expressed through an understanding and love of Shakespeare (Figure 7).[1] When drawn together, each part of the spread makes clear the place of Shakespeare in the imagination and beliefs of the very specific readership that the journal addresses. That a major part of it was printed in colour, then a rare and costly process, shows its importance. Together with its main competitors, *The Graphic* and *The Illustrated London News*, *The Sphere* was read regularly in what might be termed Middle England, by the well-educated classes who, largely of commercial and professional interests, had conservative yet firm tastes in poetry, theatre, and the visual arts. Throughout the war, all three made extensive use of references to Shakespeare, harnessing his works as the embodiment of an ideal kind of Englishness, silently subsuming within it the more complex and often vexed lived experience of Britishness.

One feature of *The Sphere*'s pages is immediately remarkable: the use of the spelling 'Shakspere' in the feature 'This Dear, Dear Land', when the more familiar version had already been adopted by editors and critics. This anachronism suggests the magazine's conservative nature, following as it does the form used by John Bell in the eighteenth century, but later adopted as more historically authentic and made widely known by Edward Dowden in *Shakspere: A Critical Study of his Mind and Art*, which was first published in 1875 and reprinted several times, including in 1906, close to the date of this feature. Widely read in the first decades of the new century, the spelling's adoption by *The Sphere* suggests something of the antiquarian in the interest of its readers. The journal's use of the older form, as if something innately more accurate, is a social distinction of no small significance at that time and perhaps since.

71

Aside from the spelling, the most arresting quality of these pages is the sheer size of the text and images. Each page measures 38 by 26.5 cm (15 × 10.5 inches), roughly the same as an A3 page in present-day terms. Full page illustrations were not unusual in the magazine, but most pages had only two or three smaller images, generally surrounded by accompanying or at times quite unrelated text. The use of colour is also rare within the magazine, and was used only for the Christmas number or occasions of state. The size of both images and text would therefore have made a powerful statement to the reader.

Moving from left to right across the spread, in the direction followed by Western readers' eyes, makes clear the multiple ways in which it operates to convey its message and mood. First, at top left comes a twilight photograph of a British naval ship. Its immediate caption, 'Guarding the Shores of Britain', suggests the sense of security often associated with the Royal Navy, developing by implication the view of British history as established and maintained by seafaring. Its caption describes the image as 'From a direct camera study', again playing to its readers who, at that time, would have found 'direct photography' of this size and kind an impressive novelty. This suggestion that the image was made out of doors with a large, glass-plate camera – no easy feat in a winter coastline – adds a different kind of authority, raising it to the highest state of the photographic art at the time.

All these elements are drawn together by the large caption beneath, 'This Dear, Dear Land', printed in large italic capitals. The words, here and on the opposite page, are from lines spoken by John of Gaunt, close to death, in Act 2 Scene 1 of *Richard II*; but they are carefully edited to seem intensely patriotic. They would have been well known to readers of the time. For many, John of Gaunt's speech would have been learned while at school, and perhaps recited on Empire Day, then celebrated on 24 May in every school and many places elsewhere. Building on the Education Act of 1870, which made elementary education compulsory for all, the 1882 'Standards' were introduced to test and certify skills of reading. Standards VI and VII stated that each pupil should 'Read a passage from one of Shakespeare's historical plays, or from a history of England'. The overlapping is important, suggesting as it does that the nation's history and the works of Shakespeare – united around an emphasis on 'Englishness', which, once again, elides the complexity of being 'British' – are essentially one and the same. On the basis of much popular writing and discussion, it is clear not only that the history plays were regarded as accurate records, but that Shakespeare's work in general was seen by some as an embodiment of national identity and purpose. The most popular texts for the Standards' tests were Portia's 'quality of mercy' speech from *The Merchant of Venice* and the 'seven ages of man' from *As You Like It*, yet also popular was Gaunt's speech. Many who read *The Sphere* might well have remembered the lines in that context. When read here, they would not only have seemed familiar, but also became freshly linked with an accompanying image of the nation's naval and imperial power.

The speech is not, however, presented in its entirety, being shortened as it so often was when quoted as an embodiment of national fealty. The first nine lines are omitted – those where, seeing himself as 'a prophet new inspired' (2.1.31), Gaunt speaks of the intemperance of Richard's behaviour, concluding that it will soon destroy itself in its profligacy: 'Light vanity, insatiate cormorant, / Consuming means, soon preys upon itself' (2.1.38–39).[2] It is perhaps ironic that the part of the speech most directly related to the play's action, and the most forceful in utterance, has in general become the least known, the lines quoted in *The Sphere* and elsewhere having become detached from their surrounding context. Yet the opening lines are not the only part to be omitted. At the close of the famous paean of praise to the nation comes the bitter statement that the land 'is now leased out ... / Like to a tenement and pelting farm'. Specifically, Richard's 'England' is compared to a tenancy, land rented but not owned – a reference to the king's need to make large borrowings to fund his way of living – and a 'pelting' or paltry farm. Clearly these lines have no place in the text when it is to be repurposed as an account of an ideal 'England'.

This abbreviation also has a further uplifting effect on the reader, since the whole speech as quoted has no main verb, becoming, therefore, a simple catalogue of the nation's glories. This absence of verb brings with it an absence of tense, and hence of time: all of the qualities praised in the speech in consequence become eternal, so that England's glory will never end. Read at the coming of war, this quality would surely have had a powerful resonance. The grammatical operations might not have been realized by many of *The Sphere*'s readers, but their effect would remain forcefully present. In the play, Gaunt's angry final lines are almost spat out in contempt. In *The Sphere*, the passage instead ends with lines relating to England's militant glory, now presented as its permanent state: 'England, bound in with the triumphant sea / Whose rocky shore beats back the envious siege / Of watery Neptune' (2.1.61–63). Seen in their contemporary context, the lines offer yet another allusion. Only a few years before, Britain had been involved in a race with Germany to build more Dreadnoughts – heavily armoured fighting vessels whose primary purpose was to retain its traditional sea power. Popular demands had coined the slogan, 'We want eight, and we won't wait.'[3] The 'envious siege' was therefore bound to acquire even more immediate resonance in linking this historical context to the pressures of the current conflict.

Within the frame of popular feeling in winter 1914, all these allusions seem quite reasonable to hear as contemporary echoes within Gaunt's speech. One other aspect of the lower half of the first page is important: the 'camera study by Frank E. Huson', which visually presents the line 'set in a silver sea'. The image is one of daylight calm, balancing the twilit scene shown above, echoing in miniature the endlessness of the passage's grammar. In practical terms, it suggests that Britain's naval power over the seas is similarly without end, physically and metaphorically surviving the darkness of present days.

If these references to naval power were not enough, further force is added to the speech by the quotation, at the head of the second page, of a single line: 'This fortress built by Nature for herself' (2.1.43). The image beneath gives the words a special kind of literalism, showing the 'fortress' as the clifftops guarded by a single sentry, almost suggesting that no more is needed since Nature has provided the country with this unbreachable barrier. And the fortress, of course, is the Shakespeare Cliff in Dover, known as such since at least the middle of the nineteenth century after a scene from *King Lear*. Again, the text is considerably modified, the whole compressed into an imagined stage setting: there is no mention of the highly complex passage where Gloucester is persuaded by Edgar that he was standing on the top of a cliff and jumped from it, being given to understand that he has miraculously survived the fall (4.5). Doubtless few then knew of the cliff's name as coming from this passage in the play: the mere allusion to Shakespeare is enough. Beneath, the caption makes its function more explicit, with the line 'Guarding the White cliffs of old Albion' – Albion, the whole, ancient kingdom, as named in Shakespeare's text (*King Lear*, 3.2), not simply 'a Cliff near Dover'. There is even a half-ironic further caption – 'Drawn by Philip Dadd at a certain place' – following military prohibition of naming the place for fear of aiding the enemy. The final line makes all this a little more explicit in its half-quotation of Shakespeare's text, calling it 'this island realm'.

One more circumstance gives added weight to the cluster of allusions that surround these two pages. In addition to the magazine's yearly subscribers, the Christmas number of *The Sphere* would have been bought and read by others who, unable or unwilling to receive it regularly, bought it as a special part of the Christmas celebrations. It would therefore have been seen and read by a wider constituency, perhaps also becoming part of family celebrations and the subject of discussions among different generations. Seen thus, the spread developed a carefully edited but well-known passage from Shakespeare to bring the work's patriotic potential to a wide range of people. Yet despite this wider readership, the number's cost – at one shilling rather than the fivepence of the usual issues – was only within the reach of the relatively well-off. This was at a time when the wages of a clerk were generally one pound ten shillings – the 'thirty bob a week' that was bemoaned in the title and text of John Davidson's celebrated poem of 1905. Industrial workers, with little security of employment, often earned less than a pound to cover a week's expenses. The readership of *The Sphere* was certainly part of a privileged, well-educated elite. For these readers, the spread would have confirmed a social, intellectual, and political understanding of the inevitable rightness of the War's cause, protected by the Royal Navy and supported by the strength of the British Empire.

These qualities are shared in some measure by subsequent articles published in *The Sphere* and its two close rivals. Shakespeare features once again in short quotations introducing articles that often have no relevance to the plays, but reveal a world in which some knowledge of Shakespeare's plays was an established part of their readership's everyday life. Reviews of Shakespeare's plays in performance and newly published books peppered the three magazines, repeatedly linked to the rightness not only of the British cause but of notions of Britishness – and indeed 'Englishness' itself – as landscape, tradition, and a particular order of thought and way of life. Even photographs of new cars were posed in or near Stratford-upon-Avon, reminding those wealthy enough to consider purchasing them as a link between their status and Shakespeare's heritage.

As the war moved on, allusions to Shakespeare changed in tone, becoming more serious and in many cases subtler and more ingenious. Attitudes towards the war's management changed as the fighting became more intense and more costly in material and suffering. Shakespeare's works became firmly a part of the war effort because of the way they epitomized important values for the readers of these weekly journals, especially in comparison to those of the enemy. Indeed, allusions to Shakespeare as the essence of Englishness – revealing that telling elision between English and British identities – occur in several discussions of German approaches to his works. Some address the opinions of Heinrich Heine and other poets as readers of the plays or as advocates for the inclusion of Shakespeare into the German canon. On 22 April 1916, within *The Graphic*'s regular series 'The Way of the War', an anonymous article celebrating the Tercentenary of Shakespeare's death hails the dramatist as 'one of the few links remaining between this country and Germany, which speaks of him as "Unser Wilhelm", very much as it does of its own Kaiser' (see also Marius S. Ostrowski's account in Chapter 11 about the 'Germanizing' of Shakespeare in both high-brow and low-brow German culture). The next paragraph, though, proceeds to challenge this claim: 'it is difficult to find anything in Shakespeare that is not English – and aggressively English', putting him 'quite beyond the pale of the whole spirit of portentous Prussia'. Next come words from a speech by Lord Bryce describing the current state of England: 'The old spirit of devotion is alive again in Great Britain … never has England shown herself worthier of the greatest tradition of her greatest days … An England that does this is an England worth fighting for.' The article introduces this passage by describing it as 'A thing that would have gladdened the great and essentially English heart of William Shakespeare', its statement before the quotation placing Shakespeare, by extension, at the centre of English life and the nation's heroism in the war.

The article closes with a direct statement of Shakespeare's essential Englishness for which the war is now being fought. The idea is reinforced by the page's illustrations. At its top are three small photographs. The first shows 'Stratford-on-Avon College boys in the procession to lay wreaths on Shakespeare's tomb', marching past the grammar school that Shakespeare himself may have attended. In the centre is a view of the Memorial Theatre in Stratford; at the right is Shakespeare's tomb in Holy Trinity Church, 'covered with memorial flowers'.[4] The three images show Shakespeare as thoroughly embedded, in war as in peace, in education, performance, and civic life. Were this not enough, another image at the foot of the page shows the importance of Shakespeare in the midst of the fighting. An open-air performance of a Shakespeare play is captioned, 'A play produced in the open for the amusement of French soldiers in the War Zone', and elsewhere in the article it is praised as 'proof positive of the high spirit of our great ally'. This feature underlines the presence of Shakespeare's plays in the war zone, and specifically in France, thereby rejecting the German assimilation of 'Unser Wilhelm'. The coming together of all these elements, in an article celebrating the Tercentenary, stresses forcefully and repeatedly the presence of Shakespeare as a national force at this time of war.

Shakespeare remained central in illustrated magazines throughout the conflict – and we should remember that what we would now read as nearing the end of the war was then one of its darkest periods. A discussion of the uses of propaganda in *The Graphic* on 23 February 1918 has the following exhortation: 'We must follow the bent of our own national genius.

Shakespeare said that a long time ago – "to thine own self be true"; and our subsequent experience, not least the experience of the present war, shows that he was profoundly right.'[5] In the same vein, 'Political Portraits' by Charles Whibley in the *Illustrated London News* offers a direct statement of pride in Shakespeare's place in the national imagination at that time. The histories are referred to as 'the epic of our race'; Portia's account of the German suitor, of whom she thought 'very vilely', is quoted in full; and 'Germany's preposterous claim to the racial ownership of our national poet' is countered by the belief that the works 'must not be touched by hostile undiscerning hands'.[6]

Perhaps the most explicit statement uniting Shakespeare to the actuality of war came in an article from *The Graphic* on 22 April 1916, which asked directly, 'Did Shakespeare Enlist?' In this article, John O'London developed an argument voiced in 1859 by William J. Thoms, founder of *Notes and Queries*, an early critical journal devoted to literary studies, that Shakespeare had fought for his country. The article itself develops the idea of Shakespeare as soldier, first by citing aspects of his life, then by succinct quotations from the plays resting on detailed knowledge of military events that supposedly reveal his service in the field. It proposes that Shakespeare's early patron, Robert Dudley, first Earl of Leicester, visited Warwickshire in 1585 and that the boy Shakespeare might have been taken by his father to see Queen Elizabeth's visit to Kenilworth, one of Leicester's seats. That year, soldiers marched through Warwickshire urging young men to join the fight against the Low Countries. O'London imagines that Shakespeare might have witnessed the parades and become entranced. The article also quotes from a letter by Leicester's secretary that mentions 'Will, my Lord of Lester's jesting player'.[7] All this evidence is conjectural, but biographical speculation was popular in Edwardian England and is mobilized here to suggest that Shakespeare himself fought for his country.

The article continues by citing passages from the plays to point out knowledge obtainable only from military service. Quotations include 'you must put in the pikes with a vice' (*Much Ado about Nothing*, 5.2.14–15) and 'As level as the cannon to his blank' (*Hamlet*, 4.1.42). More sustained argument is revealed in *Troilus and Cressida*, where Ulysses rants against a soldier who neglects his duty: such a man will 'like a gallant horse fall'n in first rank, / Lie there for pavement to the abject rear / O'er-run and trampled on' (3.3.161–63). *Romeo and Juliet* includes the powerfully direct 'deadly level of a gun' (3.3.103), and a more complex military metaphor, when Friar Laurence describes Romeo's suicidal thoughts as 'Like powder in a skill-less soldier's flask' (3.3.132). Thoms reads this line as a reference

to 'match locks', lighted matches of the present day that closely resemble
the earlier gunpowder pouches. The argument is clinched in a final, single-
sentence paragraph, linking the practice to current fighting: 'It may be
remarked, in passing, that our soldiers in Flanders are now subject to a
similar sort of accident in their use of trench bombs and grenades.'

The article is inventive, if fanciful, both in Thoms's original and in
O'London's conclusion, but it reveals the importance of Shakespeare study
and discussion – for educated readers as well as specialists – as a part of
life during the war. It also links Shakespeare to current debates about the
need to introduce conscription. The Somme offensive, beginning in early
April, had failed to achieve its promised success and already fallen into
static and costly trench warfare. For those who knew even a little about
the carnage of the opening offensive, the lines from *Troilus* would have
a terribly literal relevance. Already in January 1916, the Military Service
Act had called on men to 'attest' their willingness to serve if called for.
But this appeal did not suffice and, on 24 May, conscription was finally
introduced. While the campaign for conscription was still very strong, the
appearance of O'London's article, suggesting that even Shakespeare might
have joined the forces, can easily be seen as a powerful contribution to the
debate. A month after writing the article, the author left to take up a post
at the *Daily Mirror*, a paper campaigning vigorously for conscription and
the more forceful prosecution of the war. Seen within the conservative and
staunchly nationalist context of the weekly journals examined in this essay,
the underlying message of this article seems to be that if Shakespeare –
celebrated national poet and epitome of the nation's cultural identity and
spirit – had fought for his country, surely it was the duty of all thinking
readers of these illustrated journals to do the same.

𝔖𝔥𝔞𝔨𝔢𝔰𝔭𝔢𝔞𝔯𝔢 𝔥𝔲𝔱

(GOWER and KEPPEL STREETS, W.C., 1)

𝔖𝔥𝔞𝔨𝔢𝔰𝔭𝔢𝔞𝔯𝔢

Celebration Performance

APRIL 20th, 7.30 p.m.

To the Memory of William Shakespeare (April 23, 1564—1616)

Under the direction of Miss EDITH CRAIG.

MEN OF H.M. & ALLIED FORCES ONLY.   ADMISSION FREE.

Figure 8   Programme for a Shakespeare anniversary gala at the Shakespeare Hut, London,
April 1917 (Ellen Terry and Edith Craig Archive, © National Trust, image supplied by
the British Library, BL/125/25/2/Ellen Terry Archive/ET/D438).

CHAPTER 8

Ellen Terry Stars at the Shakespeare Hut

Ailsa Grant Ferguson

In a letter to a friend written in 1917, the greatest actress of her age, Ellen Terry, writes that she 'must return to town to collect Falstaff and sich-like [*sic*] trash for my tour which begins 29th this month first showing at Shakespeare hut'.[1] In this letter, Terry is referring to the event related to the archival object I have chosen to discuss in this essay, a single-sheet gala programme owned by Terry (Figure 8), which opens the door to a unique culture of performance, a century after its brief existence. Indeed, a material history of Shakespeare in wartime could not be complete without including an object connected to the inimitable Shakespeare Hut, an unjustly forgotten building and the only built memorial in London for Shakespeare's tercentenary of 1916. This 'Hut' had an extraordinary space hidden within: a 400-capacity purpose-built performance space, where the biggest stars of the early twentieth-century stage performed their wartime duties to entertain the troops – and that stage was run by women. Terry's programme bears witness to the unique and crucial contribution of women's theatre practice to how Shakespeare was presented, utilized, and exploited in the sociopolitical backdrop of the First World War.

Shakespearean commemoration and production were both gendered and politicized in the context not only of wartime necessity but of early twentieth-century feminist activity and philosophy – an issue also considered in this collection by Monika Smialkowska (Chapter 9) and Maggie Smales (Chapter 13). This essay will reconstruct the Shakespearean gala mentioned by Terry from this rare surviving programme, an object that is in essence paradigmatic of the literal and figurative fragility and fragmentation of women's wartime Shakespeare production in the canon of Shakespearean performance history.

§

A vast, mock-Tudor structure incongruously erected among Bloomsbury's leafy squares, the Shakespeare Hut provided entertainments, a safe place to stay, and all manner of conveniences for servicemen on leave. This may seem to a reader today to be an unlikely place to find London's biggest theatre stars treading the boards; yet, as the key object of this essay shows, the Shakespeare Hut in fact offered a significant performance space in the extraordinary entertainments of wartime London. Arguably the greatest theatre star of the turn of the century – and certainly the most renowned actress – the great Ellen Terry herself trod the Hut's tiny stage on many occasions, not only the one evidenced in this programme.[2] While, unfortunately, 'she has been particularly known for her own supporting role in relation to powerful and famous men', here we find her in a female-led theatre at last, directed by her daughter, Edith Craig, and produced by fellow suffragist and actress Gertrude Elliott (aka Lady Forbes Robertson).[3] The Shakespeare Hut's theatre spanned an eventful three years from 1916's compulsory conscription and Entertainment Tax to 1919's slow demobilization and exodus home of newly created young, male diasporas of 'Dominion' troops. Craig and Elliott spent these three years presenting a frantic cornucopia of Shakespearean and other theatrical delights to the tens of thousands of servicemen who visited the Hut.

Terry kept the programme discussed here for the rest of her life, almost perfectly preserved in her own personal papers.[4] The programme's fragile, frugal material form – a small, folded piece of cheap, thin paper – reveals a wartime austerity. The cover pays homage to Sir Johnston Forbes-Robertson, leading actor-manager and prominent member of the SMNT as chair, with two honorary secretaries credited equally below: Lady Forbes-Robertson (his wife) and Israel Gollancz, founder of the Shakespeare Hut. Lady Forbes-Robertson was Gertrude Elliott, stage star and president of the Actresses' Franchise League, leading this substantial suffragist organization with a committee that included Edith Craig, whom we find (as on all the few surviving Shakespeare Hut gala programmes) credited as director further down the cover page in pride of place. Elliott's active management of the Hut is somewhat diffused by her husband's name above and equal placement with Gollancz. Craig, however, avowed as sole director, is granted autonomous female creative direction. Craig's directorial activities since before the war had in some large part focused on her leadership of the Pioneer Players, a suffragist agitprop touring company that continued to flourish in war-time, and her work with the Women's Theatre project of the Actresses' Franchise League.[5] Her direction, therefore, brought with it bold asser-tions of women's right to leadership, agency, and artistic autonomy in the theatre. Wartime, however, had necessarily diluted the political sig-nificance of Elliott and Craig's leadership, at a time when women were taking on traditionally male occupations.

Shakespeare galas at the Hut, therefore, provided an opportunity for women's theatrical leadership to flourish while sidestepping political criti-cism. The audience too is significant here: 'MEN OF H.M. & ALLIED FORCES ONLY'. This phrasing encompassed all servicemen, but we know that the Hut was designed for, and used in particular by, New Zealanders, for whom suffragism was scarcely radical, given that all women in New Zealand had gained the vote back in 1893 (when many of these servicemen were small children or were yet to be born). Craig's directing career was possibly comparatively unknown to the Hut audiences, and she was not particularly associated with Shakespearean production prior to her work at the Hut. However, Ellen Terry added star value to the event, while her vocal support for women's rights added two layers of contemporary sig-nificance to the gala: morale for the troops and a leap forward in the rise of Women's Theatre.

Turning the page of the programme, one finds a wealth of Shakespearean fragments and a large cast of performers crammed onto its small pages. There are curated extracts from Shakespeare's English history plays: *King John*, *Henry VIII*, *Richard III*, and wartime favourite *Henry V*. These are followed by *Coriolanus,* and the evening is uplifted at its conclusion by a comic finale: Ellen Terry as Mistress Page in scenes from *The Merry Wives of Windsor*. Unlike the Hut's other two Shakespeare anniversary galas in 1918 and 1919, which included musi-cal interludes and mini-lectures, this programme consists *entirely* of Shakespearean extracts, aside from an opening organ recital. Here is a programme of pure Shakespearean drama. In this way, this gala is prob-ably the closest to a full evening of Shakespearean production that the Hut ever hosted. However, the fragmentary nature of the programme allows Craig, as director, curatorial control over the content and the power of selection, to establish a cohesive presentation for the troops. Some of these extracts are undefined but we can infer which scenes were chosen via the dramatis personae and in some cases play-world loca-tions. However, the programme is specific in the cases of *King John* and *Henry VIII*, in that it provides its readers with a brief narrative context to situate the scene(s). Collectively, these clues can help us reconstruct how the original audience experienced the gala. By moving through the show, piecing together the whole from its parts, we can learn about Shakespearean production in wartime, more specifically its function as entertainment for troops, its place in the development of women's theatrical influence, and its role in establishing a very specific performance of Englishness for 'Dominion' troops.

So, let us imagine a New Zealand soldier in the audience, with his own copy of this programme, and to try and see this artefact, and this occasion, through his eyes. Perhaps he arrived earlier that day:

> Teatime on Saturday, the busiest day in the week. Once inside the swing doors, an insistent hum of voices, tramp of booted feet and cheerful rattle of crockery and cutlery. On the left, inside the main door, row upon row of tables, each laid temptingly and bearing a jar of bronze chrysanthemums. On the right, many comfortable chairs scattered about, but chiefly assembled in a triple ring round the huge open fire, in its old-fashioned red-brick grate, that roars and crackles joyfully.[6]

He may have spent a while in the Reading Room writing postcards home to reassure loved ones that he 'managed to secure a cubicle and it was very comfortable indeed. It contained only one bed (a very good one) and a little table cupboard, 1/6 per night'.[7] Now, though, evening falls and, rather than brave the dangers, expense, and unfamiliarity of the London streets, he is safe inside the Hut. It must be his lucky day: the star-studded annual gala is to be held that evening. Entering the concert hall, he meets a young woman in a smart, rose-pink uniform, who hands him a small, folded page to guide him through the evening, and he squeezes through rows of his fellows in stiff khaki to find an empty folding chair, and looks towards a raised stage, with painted cloths draped at the back by way of minimalist, modern set design, while the ubiquitous, monochrome mock-Tudor beams obstinately peak out behind.[8] Surely that tiny stage cannot hold all of the promise of the programme in his hands, *King John*, *Henry V* – *The Merry Wives of Windsor*? Why, 'anyone who could act on that could act on a tea-tray!'[9]

The Hall's four hundred seats are quickly filling up with soldiers, sailors, and airmen clutching their small programmes and squeezing into the rows of seats, while a Mr Amies plays his organ with relish. Then, a hush falls. Our soldier glances down to his programme and finds a helpful explanation for the coming scene, one that alerts him of its relevance to the conflict that is ruling every aspect of his life: 'King John seized the English throne in spite of the undoubted right of Prince Arthur.' This must be a play about the immorality of usurpation and expansion. There is a villain who has tried, wrongfully, to take control. Our soldier also remembers seeing this play mentioned many times recently. Had he not just seen a line or two from it somewhere? 'England never did, nor never shall, / Lie at the proud foot of a conqueror' (*King John*, 5.7.112–13). That was it: he had seen the same words on the proscenium arch of the Old Vic.[10] When he crossed the road to explore that inviting theatre, having arrived at Waterloo Station, he had seen – and paid his fearful respects to – the growing list of actors lost in the war, memorialized on its wall.[11]

He may, too, have been a reader of Shakespeare during his active service, an act of self-education, national (and colonial) identity, nostalgia, or cultural capital that was evident across a wide range of Allied troops, as Edmund King's extensive research on Allied servicemen's accounts of reading has explored.[12] The choice to read Shakespeare in particular, King argues, was a self-conscious one: 'the knowing distinctiveness of this act unifies wartime readers of Shakespeare across the borders of rank and class'.[13] Yet, the memory of a Shakespeare of the classroom or a fragmentary awareness of Shakespeare sewn together from a patchwork of snippets, speeches, and phrases needed no such conscious act of cultural engagement. Not only in wartime London, but across Europe and the Allied 'Dominions', Shakespeare was everywhere. In a rare account of a stay at the Shakespeare Hut and its accompanying sightseeing party trip to Stratford-upon-Avon, New Zealand soldier Francis Bennett sees this as a 'pilgrimage' and writes lovingly of his boyhood discovery of a love of poetry, specifically Shakespeare, through his English teacher, Mr Rockel. Of his teacher, he writes that he 'loved English poetry and ... easily taught me to love it too ... Out in a back paddock I would stand on a hillside and with dramatic gestures deliver Mark Anthony's oration to the mildly surprised sheep.'[14] In his wartime recollections of that Stratford trip, Bennett notes that many of his fellows could also answer Shakespearean quizzing by their scholarly guide, demonstrating the presence of Shakespeare within New Zealander school curricula at the time.[15] We can therefore assume that our soldier, in the Hut that night watching Terry and her fellow actors, may have also been familiar with at least some Shakespearean texts, though not as enthusiastic a fan as Francis Bennett seems to have been. More generally, we can assume with some certainty that our soldier and the audience of New Zealanders around him were likely to have been aware of Shakespeare's presentation both as a paragon of an English 'motherland' and as a stalwart of their schoolboy days.

Back in the Hut theatre, the actors enter the scene and a murmur sweeps across the audience: these are not princes and their manly attendants; these are four teenaged girls, cross-dressed, discussing politics, life, and death.[16] No male voice is heard. The scene that unfolds is heart-rending: a young boy begs for mercy from a trusted adult, ordered to blind him (*King John*, 4.1). Yet after a dark start, the mood lifts, as mercy prevails. Right has won over wrong. Applause and cheers – of perhaps relief for the child or appreciation for the drama and its actors – ring through the hall and the stage is cleared. Our soldier looks down to his flimsy folded page, already beginning to crease and wear, for the next item. He finds another contextual comment to help him: 'Cardinal Wolsey, thinking that Buckingham was growing too powerful, persuaded King Henry that he was conspiring against him in order to seize the throne for himself.' What is this – another usurper, threatening the English seat of power, or a danger within? England, this evening, is beset and must be protected. Here is one more usurper: Richard III, who needs no introduction, it would seem, as the programme gives our soldier no hints or clues. Next, the stage itself fills with soldiers, mirroring its audience. They are fighting an invisible foe and they too, like the 'war-weary soldiers' in the audience, are flagging.[17] Perhaps they have been questioning their reason for war and just want to go home. But one small figure with faux chain mail tights bagging on their small legs steps forward and calls out with the confidence of a King, 'Once more unto the breach, dear friends, once more' (*Henry V*, 3.1.1). They lift their helmet and show the face of a 13-year-old girl. Is this Henry V or Joan of Arc? The soldiers turn and all are young girls – silence falls as players and audience elide. As Fabia Drake, who played the title character reflected,

> We would be playing to soldiers [and] it was decided that the scene we would enact should be from *Henry V* … We had no extras, we had no army, but we had an audience of four hundred soldiers and Edy Craig had the inspiration that I should come out in front of the curtain and speak … to my Army on the floor … Four hundred war-weary men rallied to the cry of 'God for Harry, England and Saint George', springing to their feet and cheering to the rafters.[18]

As the applause dies away, a distinctive voice suddenly carries from the back of the Hall: 'Some are born great …' and our soldier turns to see Ellen Terry, the real Ellen Terry, speaking 'extravagantly' to a middle-aged couple.[19] What, could *the* Ellen Terry be here? Our soldier checks his flimsy programme, which is now beginning to tear. Yes, this star, whose face he has only seen in his cigarette card collection and whose name he has read emblazoned on posters back home, is about to close the show with one of her most famous comic parts.

Terry had toured the Antipodes with her Shakespeare Lectures as recently as 1914, so it is reasonable to expect that many of the soldiers in her audience were at the very least aware of her presence in the country, given the frequent advertisements in the New Zealand press. An example follows below:

> TWO NIGHTS ONLY 19th JUNE. MISS ELLEN TERRY! OUR GREAT-EST LIVING ACTRESS, in her Wonderfully Illuminating Discourses on Shakespeare's Heroines, with ILLUSTRATIVE ACTING … MISS ELLEN TERRY! THE WORLD'S GREATEST ACTRESS, In her Entrancing DISCOURSES ON SHAKESPEARE'S HEROINES, WITH ILLUSTRATIVE ACTING, In which this great artist will portray, in 'her own inimitable' way, the most effective scenes associated with the immortal characters of Shakespeare's drama. No actress of modern times can compare with Miss Terry in her unrivalled power of illustrating to her audience the varying emotions of the great master's heroines.[20]

Terry was, without a doubt, a superstar both in the United Kingdom and in New Zealand. The advertisement's reference to 'our master's heroines' assumes that Shakespeare belongs in New Zealand by virtue of the nation's colonial identity at that time. While, pragmatically, the link with the United Kingdom was essential to the need for voluntary conscription, this was a time of much wider ideological flux in terms of the establishment of New Zealander and Australian identities free of the notion of an English 'motherland'.[21] By piecing together the likely elements of the Hut show, we can find a narrative, or at least some sort of agenda, moving into focus, in which troops are presented with mercy in action (*King John*), the dangers of power hunger (*Henry VIII*), the perils of persuasion above morality (*Richard III*), the galvanizing power of military action, alongside excellent rhetoric (*Henry V*), the fickle politics of war (*Coriolanus*), and, finally, the relief of some morale-boosting comedy to lift the spirits of the men (*The Merry Wives of Windsor*), delivered by that very special guest star.

Here in this Hut performance, Terry showed her comedy skills, but in other galas here she gave her Portia, presenting her audience of servicemen with an accessible Shakespeare, but also, potentially, a radical one. As Katherine E. Kerry explains, 'Terry's special care to present the voices of Shakespeare's women … allies her with the radical tradition of plebeian Shakespeare … She used her voice and her history in the theatre to create a bridge to the future for herself and her daughter's generation of women.'[22] Over a decade after our soldier watched in awe as Terry lit up that tiny stage, the Shakespeare Hut's founder, Israel Gollancz, recalled her time there:

> During the war when she worked in the Shakespeare Hut she won the hearts of hundreds and thousands of soldiers who were filled with wonder at her charm. Many of them came from far parts of the Empire, and had never seen her act, but she had transcended the stage and become part of the national life. She enhanced the dignity of the drama by the public feeling for her. She remained until the end the 'Queen of the stage'.[23]

Ellen Terry's many turns at the Shakespeare Hut might have remained forgotten in the narratives of her life and work, and that of her daughter and feminist collaborators, had it not been for the unlikely survival of some precious ephemeral traces: her programmes and a few mentions in letters and, as in the tribute above, the gratitude of her Hut colleagues. Yet the fragility of the material traces is in direct contrast to the significance of her presence in this unique space, lending it theatrical and cultural credibility, and drawing attention to its female-led project, as well as valuable, mainstream war work.

Leaving the Hall at last on a wave of starstruck excitement, perhaps our soldier meant to keep the small piece of folded paper he has had in his hands throughout the evening. Maybe he pops it in his pocket but then he needs it to write down directions to the station or the address of a fellow soldier. Perhaps another man throws his copy in the waste bin, unimpressed. Another might drop his from his pocket into the mud of terrifying trenches. Another tucks his in his pocket book and makes it home to New Zealand, where it still remains, in someone's attic perhaps, or pasted into an album of wartime mementos. *His* may, one day, be found. However, it is only thanks to one of the star performers, Ellen Terry, and her habit of collecting mementos of her own career, that we even know this show took place. We cannot know how many other such fascinating wartime programmes are lost.

The only known extant copies of programmes linked to events at the Hut are those in the Terry and Craig archive examined here, and in the papers of Israel Gollancz at Princeton. There is every reason to believe that over time more copies of these programmes may emerge from their sleeping places in suitcases under beds, boxes in attics, or from long-discarded books. But, for now, like much of women's contribution to the performance culture of the First World War in Britain, the Hut galas – as well as its weekly and even nightly performances – exist only as flickers in our peripheral historical vision.

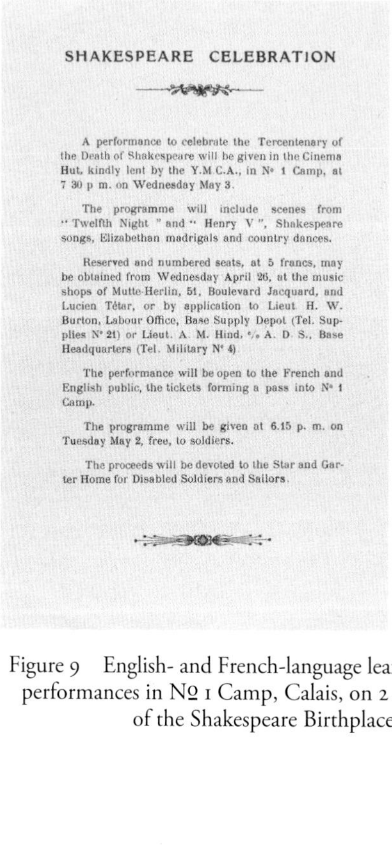

SHAKESPEARE CELEBRATION

A performance to celebrate the Tercentenary of the Death of Shakespeare will be given in the Cinema Hut, kindly lent by the Y.M.C.A., in Nº 1 Camp, at 7 30 p m. on Wednesday May 3.

The programme will include scenes from " Twelfth Night " and " Henry V ", Shakespeare songs, Elizabethan madrigals and country dances.

Reserved and numbered seats, at 5 francs, may be obtained from Wednesday April 26, at the music shops of Mutte-Herlin, 51, Boulevard Jacquard, and Lucien Têtar, or by application to Lieut H. W. Burton, Labour Office, Base Supply Depot (Tel. Supplies Nº 21) or Lieut. A. M. Hind, ℅ A. D. S., Base Headquarters (Tel. Military Nº 4)

The performance will be open to the French and English public, the tickets forming a pass into Nº 1 Camp.

The programme will be given at 6.15 p. m. on Tuesday May 2, free, to soldiers.

The proceeds will be devoted to the Star and Garter Home for Disabled Soldiers and Sailors.

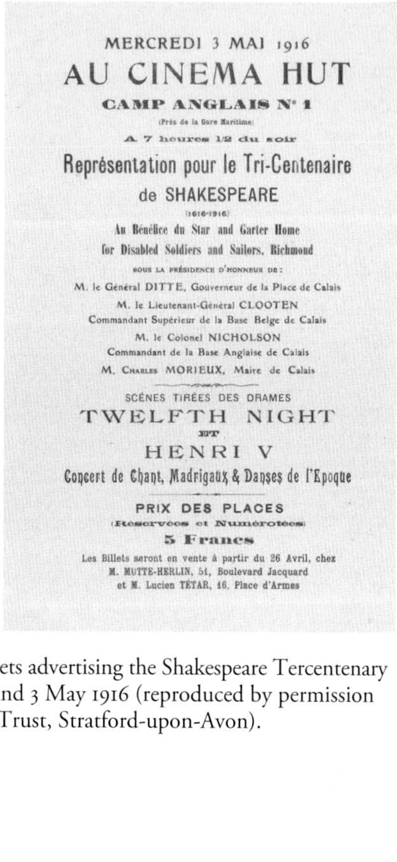

MERCREDI 3 MAI 1916

AU CINEMA HUT

CAMP ANGLAIS Nº 1

(Près de la Gare Maritime)

A 7 heures 1⁄2 du soir

Représentation pour le Tri-Centenaire
de SHAKESPEARE

(1616-1916)

Au Bénéfice du Star and Garter Home
for Disabled Soldiers and Sailors, Richmond

SOUS LA PRÉSIDENCE D'HONNEUR DE :

M. le Général DITTE, Gouverneur de la Place de Calais

M. le Lieutenant-Général CLOOTEN
Commandant Supérieur de la Base Belge de Calais

M. le Colonel NICHOLSON
Commandant de la Base Anglaise de Calais

M. CHARLES MORIEUX, Maire de Calais

SCÈNES TIRÉES DES DRAMES

TWELFTH NIGHT
ET
HENRI V

Concert de Chant, Madrigaux, & Danses de l'Epoque

PRIX DES PLACES

(Réservées et Numérotées)

5 Francs

Les Billets seront en vente à partir du 26 Avril, chez
M. MUTTE-HERLIN, 51, Boulevard Jacquard
et M. Lucien TÊTAR, 16, Place d'Armes

Figure 9   English- and French-language leaflets advertising the Shakespeare Tercentenary performances in Nº 1 Camp, Calais, on 2 and 3 May 1916 (reproduced by permission of the Shakespeare Birthplace Trust, Stratford-upon-Avon).

CHAPTER 9

The 1916 Shakespeare Tercentenary at № 1 Camp in Calais

Monika Smialkowska

On 2 and 3 May 1916, the Cinema Hut at the British Expeditionary Force's № 1 Camp in Calais became the setting for two runs of a gala organized to commemorate the three-hundredth anniversary of Shakespeare's death. The event was advertised through the English- and French-language leaflets reproduced in Figure 9, copies of which are held at the Shakespeare Birthplace Trust's archive in Stratford-upon-Avon, together with other items documenting the occasion: a letter from one of the organizers, Lieut. A. M. Hind, to the librarian of the Shakespeare Memorial Theatre; a playbill in English; some cuttings from local newspapers; and an article from *The Cambridge Magazine*.[1] The leaflets explain that the first Tercentenary performance was to be given free of charge to soldiers, while the second one, the primary subject of the advertisements, was open to the French and British public, with tickets available from two shops in town. Apart from announcing the production's time, venue, ticket price (5 francs), and the charity that would benefit from the proceeds (the Star and Garter Home for Disabled Soldiers and Sailors), the leaflets announce that the programme would consist of select scenes from *Twelfth Night* and *Henry V*, along with songs, madrigals, and dances from Shakespeare's time. The French-language version also lists the event's honorary patrons: the Governor and the Mayor of Calais, along with the British and Belgian Base Commandants.

The leaflets represent significant and intriguing archival objects because they situate the Calais Shakespearean festival at the intersection of several social groups and areas of life: the military and the civilian; the British, the French, and the Belgian; culture, entertainment, and politics. This essay examines the tensions and negotiations between these disparate groups and discourses. The organizers' selection of *Henry V* is of particular interest, considering the event's location and the participants' heterogenous composition: British officers and soldiers, non-combatant local inhabitants, and members of a women's voluntary corps serving in the area. Commemorating Shakespeare under these conditions threw into sharp relief the ideological fault lines that lay at the heart of early twentieth-century national and gendered identities.

Henry V, the *Entente Cordiale*, and Wartime Gendered Identities

It is well documented that Shakespeare was used during the First World War to bolster British patriotism and to create a common ground between Britain and its allies.[2] However, *Henry V*, with its representation of a violent Anglo–French conflict, seems an unlikely play to perform in 1916 Calais to a mixed French and British audience. Yet, as Ton Hoenselaars demonstrates, the play occupied a prominent place in the wartime transactions between the two nations, whose Shakespeare enthusiasts transformed *Henry V*'s representation of the past struggle, culminating in the battle of Agincourt, from 'a potential source of embarrassment' into 'an event that led up to the *entente cordiale* itself'.[3] In the Calais Shakespearean gala, this transformation was accomplished by a careful choice of scenes: Henry's 'Once more unto the breach' speech (3.1), Princess Katherine's English lesson (3.4), and the negotiations surrounding Henry and Katherine's marriage that sealed the 1420 Treaty of Troyes (5.2). This selection shifted the emphasis away from hostility towards the emerging Anglo–French rapprochement, changing *Henry V* 'from a play about war into a play about peace, from a history of hate into a history of love'.[4]

While the *entente cordiale* is a key subtext informing the Calais Shakespearean commemorations, the event also sheds light on the ways in which wartime politics intersected with the problems of gender and sexuality. *Henry V* itself is preoccupied with these issues, foregrounding the overlaps between national identity, political and dynastic (il)legitimacy, masculinity, femininity, purity, and miscegenation. Alan Sinfield argues that the play stages patriarchal anxiety about the 'dependence upon female influence over inheritance, legitimacy and the state', accompanied with 'the fear [of] female sexuality'.[5] Claire McEachern links this feature of *Henry V* to early modern 'associations of political corruption with female corporeality', since, in sixteenth-century parlance, 'female desire is both source and metaphor of civil disorder'.[6] Consequently, the play's male characters strive to suppress female agency, while war, a means of asserting political supremacy, becomes inextricably linked to the subjugation of femininity. *Henry V* expresses this drive towards masculine control in the language of sexual violence. Jordi Coral identifies rape as one of the play's 'central obsessions', arguing that its belligerent rhetoric 'systematically invites us to identify military defeat with violated virginity, or victory with the right to seize the desired lady'.[7] The personal and the political, the military and the civilian become intertwined. In effect, *Henry V* foregrounds human corporeality, questioning what defines male and female bodies and how these gendered bodies' interactions contribute to the construction of national, as well as masculine and feminine, identities.

The intersections of gendered corporeality and the developing sense of English nationhood, central to late Elizabethan political debates, acquired new urgency during the First World War.[8] The global conflict pitted old empires against emerging nation states, bringing to the fore the issue of national identity. Simultaneously, it highlighted and questioned traditional gender roles, as a renewed focus on heroic masculine virtue at the front line was juxtaposed with women's encroachment into previously male-dominated professional and public spheres – an issue that is tackled in Maggie Smales's all-female production of *Henry V*, set during the First World War at a munitions factory operated by women (see Chapter 13).[9] It also foregrounded the significance of the human body, as thousands of wounded, maimed, and dead soldiers, as well as shocking civilian casualties, became impossible to ignore.

In this context, the Calais gala's selection of *Henry V* excerpts is revealing. All three chosen scenes deal with issues of gendered and national identities, and all explore these issues through bodily, often sexually charged imagery. First, Henry's address to his troops during the siege of Harfleur draws a picture of an English masculine body. The king exhorts his soldiers to '[s]tiffen the sinews, conjure up the blood' (3.1.7), making their bodies and emotions hard and unyielding. As Katherine Eggert observes, the speech is 'thick with images of stiffening and arousal', which associate the English troops with their warlike fathers and free them from a reliance on their mothers.[10] Henry urges his men to confirm their legitimacy by their military prowess: 'Dishonour not your mothers. Now attest / That those whom you called fathers did beget you' (3.1.22–23). What matters is their descent from 'fathers of war-proof' (3.1.18), while the maternal connection is evoked 'only as a caution to the negative: if a soldier is not hardened, he proves his mother unchaste', invalidating his familial and national affiliation.[11]

Thus, the first *Henry V* speech that the 1916 Calais audience heard defines an ideal English masculinity: martial, aggressive, obsessed with proving its patrilineal legitimacy. The other two selected scenes complement this depiction of masculinity by staging women's bodies and the confrontation of the masculine and the feminine in an anticipated sexual encounter. As several critics note, the play represents Princess Katherine, the key character in both scenes, as 'the chief prize of war'.[12] The Calais audience first encountered her in the scene in which she is learning English. Although at that point in the play her marriage to Henry is far from certain, her statement '*Il faut que j'apprenne à parler*' (3.5.4; 'I must learn to speak [English]')[13] anticipates her surrender to him in the wake of the French defeat. All the terms that Katherine learns, apart from 'robe', denote body parts (3.4.4–37). Moreover, she mispronounces the English words in such a way that they acquire sexual connotations. As a result, the scene turns into 'an anatomical inventory the items of which become … indecent and extremely vulgar puns', and Katherine is converted into a collection of sexualized parts.[14]

The first two scenes' exploration of wartime gendered identities acquires deeper significance when considered in conjunction with the play's sections left out from the Calais performance. There are two scenes between the 'Once more unto the breach' speech and Katherine's English lesson. The first one – Henry's troops' attempt to storm Harfleur – reveals that the king's depiction of martial English masculinity is wishful thinking. His soldiers, Bardolph, Pistol, and Nym, are exposed as cowards, braggarts, and thieves who 'could not be [men]' even to the boy who serves them (3.2.26). The other omitted section highlights the violence that permeates wartime attitudes to women, as Henry threatens Harfleur's citizens with the 'hot and forcing violation' of their 'pure maidens' if they do not surrender the town (3.4.20–21). Modern critics draw a parallel between the women of Harfleur and Princess Katherine, as their bodies become 'sexual counters in a struggle between the English and French forces'.[15] One can understand why it was not advisable to stage the scenes representing English soldiers as cowards and potential rapists in a British army camp in war-torn France. Nevertheless, it is telling that the selected scenes, with their focus on heroic masculinity and comically sexualized femininity, bookend much more problematic takes on gendered identities in the play, which were elided in the Calais gala.

The final extract from *Henry V* performed in Calais portrays the negotiations leading to Henry and Katherine's betrothal. This scene too is saturated with bodily and sexual imagery. Henry demands that Katherine 'must … needs prove a good soldier-breeder' (5.2.187–8), before engaging in a bout of crude joking with Burgundy about how to make her 'endure handling' (5.2.277). Finally, the French king compares his virginal daughter to cities 'girdled with maiden walls that war hath never entered' (5.2.287–8) and agrees to give her to Henry. The scene thus continues to objectify and sexualize Katherine, as Henry's acquisition of her body in marriage confirms his conquest of France.

Jean E. Howard and Phyllis Rackin explain this conjunction between sexual and military triumph in the context of the early modern evolution of patriarchal attitudes, characterized by 'the cultural transition from a residual status system in which a man's identity was defined on the basis of patrilineal inheritance' to one in which it 'had to be secured by personal achievement'.[16] This 'new version of patriarchy' represented women as 'the objects of sexual conquest and matrimonial possession that provide the final proof of the hero's manhood'.[17] Howard and Rackin argue that this model of patriarchal relations, which has persisted into modernity, relies on separating masculine and feminine spheres of action, defining the battlefield as 'an exclusively male terrain', and reducing women to 'the objects of male protection and the occasions for masculine competition'.[18] They also posit that '*Henry V* is the only Shakespearean history play where male authority is demonstrated in modern terms, by the hero's sexual conquest of a desirable woman'.[19] This feature of *Henry V* may have been one reason why the Calais organizers chose to prioritize the 'women' scenes of this male-dominated play, instead of its more martial, patriotic moments. Apart from emphasizing Anglo–French reconciliation, these scenes presented an idealized vision of a post-war patriarchal order. They promised a return to clearly demarcated gender roles, with men as victorious agents and women as sexualized rewards for masculine wartime heroism.

Enter the FANYs

However, the Calais event's depiction of traditional gendered identities was rendered problematic through the involvement of one group of participants: the members of the First Aid Nursing Yeomanry (FANY). Britain's first women's voluntary corps, the FANY, was established in 1907 to provide first aid and to transport wounded soldiers from the battlefield to medical stations. The members wore uniforms and observed military discipline. When the British authorities rejected their offer of assistance at the outbreak of the war, the FANYs approached the Belgian Army and, in October 1914, were accepted to help organize the Lamarck Hospital for the Belgian wounded in Calais. Their work there, chiefly as nurses and ambulance drivers, was so successful that they soon branched out to run a convalescent home, a canteen, and a mobile bath unit. Finally, in January 1916, they were allowed to work as an ambulance convoy with the British Army.[20]

In many respects, the FANYs were 'New Women embodying modernity': independent, resourceful, encroaching on traditionally masculine
domains with their army-style camp life and uniforms, their presence near
the battle lines, and their performance of tasks such as carrying stretchers,
and driving and servicing motor vehicles.[21] These behaviours exemplified
the wartime destabilization of established gendered identities, which was
accompanied by the fear that the global conflict 'might … have emascu-
lated men by feminizing the wounded, and defeminized women through
the masculinization of those who took on roles previously regarded as
male'.[22] Some reactions to the corps illustrate the unease surrounding their
'defeminized' demeanour. Pat Beauchamp, one of the members involved
in the Calais Shakespeare commemoration, records reading out to her fellow FANYs an article from a British newspaper entitled 'Women Motor
Drivers. – Is it a suitable occupation?' Its author warns that 'Women's
outlook on life will be distorted by the adoption of such a profession, her
finer instincts crushed' and that the job will 'rob her of much feminine
charm'.[23] Beauchamp's colleagues' uproarious mockery of these claims
demonstrates that the FANYs could and did operate successfully despite
such prejudices.[24]

However, doing so required tenacity, diplomacy, and compromise.
Janet Lee argues that the FANYs had to 'renegotiate gender in the context
of wartime service' by simultaneously drawing 'upon, and/or subvert[ing]
cultural mythologies'.[25] One of their strategies was to evoke 'traditional
notions of genteel femininity and its accompanying nurturance, cheerfulness
and devotion'.[26] While for many women the organization's attraction was
its promise of adventure and outdoor physical activities, their wartime service consisted largely of caring duties, especially assisting wounded soldiers.
Nevertheless, the FANYs pushed beyond the limits of stereotypical nurturing
womanhood by acquiring skills previously reserved for men; by demonstrating 'personal heroism, … autonomy, independence and assertiveness'; and
by developing 'comradeship that encouraged a collective female solidarity'.[27]
This level of personal and collective agency was facilitated by their social
background. They were generally well-to-do women who had received a
good education, possessed advanced social skills, and could fall back on the
financial and emotional support of affluent families and friends.[28] Their privileged status, 'respectability', and 'good breeding' also shielded them to some
extent from the suspicion of 'sexual deviance' that accompanied women's
encroachment into the male-dominated arena of war.[29]

The FANYs thus forged a position that was acceptable both to them and
to those among whom they lived and worked, namely the Belgian and,

eventually, the British Army, as well as the French civilians. Nevertheless, this position did not conform to the wartime roles that *Henry V* and subsequent patriarchal discourses ascribe to women: those of potential victims of sexual violence, requiring men's protection; rewards for men's heroism; and carriers of legitimate or illegitimate offspring. Most Great War FANYs were young, unmarried women who served, unchaperoned, near the front line, instead of fulfilling what was seen as the woman's key duty: motherhood.[30] How, then, did their participation in the Calais Shakespeare commemoration affect the event's gender dynamics?

The playbill lists four FANYs who contributed to the Calais gala: Betty (Beryl) Hutchinson, Christobel Nicholson, Norma Lowson, and P. B. Waddell (Pat Beauchamp). In the *Henry V* scenes, Hutchinson appeared as Queen Isabel and Lowson as Alice, the lady attending on Princess Katherine, who was played by 'an Anglo-French Calaisienne, Miss Marthe West'.[31] The most extensive account of the event is an anonymous article in *The Cambridge Magazine*. It might have been written by one of the British officers who organized the performance, as it gives some information about their backgrounds – all former Oxbridge students – and refers to those involved as 'us'.[32] By contrast, the article provides no personal details about the FANYs, though it mentions their service in the British ambulance convoy. It reflects on the difficulties of mounting the show under wartime conditions, emphasizing the constant threat of key players being 'ordered away'.[33] It also describes the programme's components, commenting on individual contributors' performances.

The paragraph discussing the *Henry V* section sheds little light on the participants' interpretation of gendered roles. It describes Marthe West's acting as 'charming', which suggests a conservative portrayal of the French princess as a willing partner in the wooing sequence, an impression reinforced by calling the exchanges between Henry and Katherine 'the royal love-scene'.[34] The most intriguing comment is that West was 'well supported by an Alice (Miss Lowson), whose long silences were as eloquently acted as her few words' in that scene.[35] Lowson's silences, combined with significant gaps and silences in the reports of the event, highlight the ideological tensions that the combination of the *Henry V* scenes and the people involved in their delivery must have produced.

First, the organizers do not explain why they chose a local civilian to play Katherine, the only character not portrayed by an army officer or a FANY. This casting decision could have been intended to strengthen the bond between the French and the British, counteracting any negative associations that *Henry V* might evoke, associations the organizers were aware of, even as they dismissed them: 'The memories of Agincourt are not green enough to have caused a pang to our French visitors, and the note of amity between the two nations, with which the play concludes, made a fitting end to the performance.'[36] The Anglo-French West embodied this amity, crucial for maintaining the *entente cordiale*. Simultaneously, though, she personified the play's problematic gender politics. As a civilian, female representative of an invaded nation, she fitted the roles of a potential victim in need of male protection and a reward for male valour better than a FANY, who dressed in uniform, took care of herself and others, and encroached on traditionally masculine terrains.

This casting choice leads us to the event's final intriguing silence: the paucity of the FANYs' commentary on the Calais Shakespeare commemoration. As we have seen, the male organizers were keen to ensure that there remained a public record of it in *The Cambridge Magazine* and in the cache of documents deposited at the Shakespeare Memorial Theatre. By contrast, Betty Hutchinson talks about it briefly and informally in her unpublished recollections. Only two sentences of the single paragraph describing the Tercentenary gala concern the *Henry V* scenes: 'Henry V speech before Agincourt came into the programme too with Raby playing the King. He had trouble with his armour which was unreliable in dramatic moments, but the French girl who played his Queen was so winsome nothing else was noticed in that part of the evening.'[37] Hutchinson seems remarkably unconcerned with Shakespeare or patriotism: not only does she focus on the performance's quirks rather than the scenes' content, but she also mistakenly places the 'Once more unto the breach' speech before Agincourt instead of Harfleur. In the other two paragraphs related to the Tercentenary celebration, she discusses her costume and a VIP meal after the production, not the programme itself, and she does not mention Shakespeare. She thus appears more interested in the practical and social aspects of the occasion than with its literary or patriotic dimensions.

Surprisingly, considering the Tercentenary event's high profile, Pat Beauchamp does not refer to it at all in her extensive published memoir, despite describing several other instances of the FANYs providing entertainment for the troops. That entertainment, however, was very different from the Shakespeare gala. Organized by the FANYs themselves, it combined comic and serious recitations, vocal and instrumental music, contemporary and topical songs, live drawing of charcoal sketches, kangaroo hop, and a ventriloquist dummy act.[38] Impromptu and leaning towards popular culture, the FANYs' performances were a far cry from the Shakespeare event, with its high-brow content, prominent patrons, and official publicity.

Moreover, they enabled the corps members to choose their own roles, as opposed to acting out gendered identities contrary to the independent, competent selves that they developed through their wartime service. It is therefore no surprise that Beauchamp proudly discussed the FANYs' own programmes and remained silent about the Shakespeare commemoration. Her writing out of Shakespeare from the corps' history indicates that the FANYs might have found popular cultural forms more conducive to expressing their emerging autonomy than canonical literature. The latter, as the Calais use of *Henry V* demonstrates, could be too easily mobilized to perpetuate patriarchal gender roles that Beauchamp and her colleagues strove to challenge.

The Calais gala fits the general pattern of the FANYs' negotiation of their position in contemporaneous gender hierarchies. By participating in it, they nodded towards the established version of wartime femininity: passive, vulnerable, and defined in relation to heroic masculinity. Simultaneously, by performing their daily duties, producing their own entertainments, and telling their own stories, they pushed the boundaries of the accepted feminine identity and redefined it. For us, examining this fascinating event through the lens of the FANYs' involvement leads to some unexpected conclusions. We discover a wartime production of *Henry V* that does not simply or exclusively promote patriotism, martial valour, and the Franco–British military alliance. It also creates a space to debate national identity in relation to gendered subjectivity, juxtaposing the established ideals of masculinity and femininity with the reality of women's increased agency during the global conflict. Crucially, women such as the FANYs contributed to this debate not only by what they said, but also by their actions and their silences. Even when they occasionally performed patriarchal gender roles, they could and did choose how to comment on these performances and, in some instances, to omit them entirely from their histories.

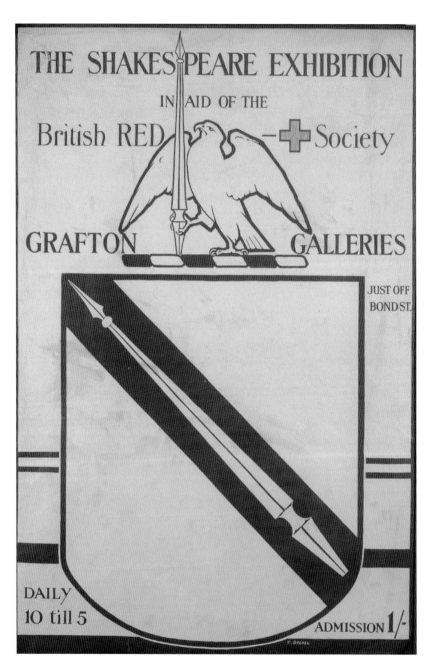

Figure 10   Poster for the Shakespeare Exhibition (1917) (reproduced by permission of the Imperial War Museum (Art. IWM PST 10868)).

CHAPTER 10

Shakespeare Does His Bit for the War Effort
Authorship and Material Culture in the 1917 British Red Cross Shakespeare Exhibition

Clara Calvo

The British Red Cross Shakespeare Exhibition, which opened at the Grafton Galleries just off London's Bond Street on 19 January 1917, was advertised with at least two different posters.[1] One features the symbol of the Red Cross displayed on a white background, the result resembling the English national flag. Another poster – reproduced as Figure 10 and held at the Imperial War Museum – displays, instead of the Red Cross, Shakespeare's coat of arms. This Shakespeare Exhibition poster is a lithograph on paper painted by Charles Buchel (née Karl August Büchel), a British artist born in Germany but educated at the Royal Academy Schools who had a long-standing relation with the London theatre.[2] It is not surprising that the artist chosen for this charity venture was connected with the London Edwardian theatrical scene, given that the promoter of the exhibition was Martin Harvey, an actor-manager who was particularly active for the war effort in collaboration with the British Red Cross.

Unlike other war posters, the Shakespeare Exhibition poster did not have a recruiting purpose. The Imperial War Museum collections hold two other First World War posters that engage with Shakespeare and his works. In a poster deploying a quotation from *Macbeth*, Shakespeare's cultural clout was used to encourage young Britons to enlist in Kitchener's New Army: 'STAND NOT UPON THE ORDER OF YOUR GOING, BUT GO AT ONCE' preceded the order 'ENLIST NOW' (IWM PST 5154). In another poster, which invites British people to recycle metal objects in wartime by taking them to the 'salvage dump' (IWM PST 13407), Shakespeare does his bit for the war effort with a quotation from *The Two Gentlemen of Verona*: 'USE DOTH BREED GOOD HABIT IN MAN'. By 1917, conscription had made recruiting posters unnecessary – instead, raising funds for organizations such as the Red Cross or the YMCA caring for soldiers at the front became crucial. Unlike these two posters addressed either to potential soldiers or to civilians on the home front, the Shakespeare Exhibition poster could appeal to both men in khaki and the general public. The absence of a quotation and the overwhelming size of the coat of arms proclaim its singularity. Unlike most exhibitions throughout the country, the Red Cross Shakespeare Exhibition was more about Shakespeare the man and his status as 'national poet' than about his plays and poems.

The choice to include Shakespeare's coat of arms in a poster at this point in time suggests an attempt to provide material proof of his authorship. Shakespeare applied for a coat of arms on his father's behalf in 1596, but it has not been possible so far to establish whether this originated in his or his father's wish to improve the family's social prestige, damaged by financial troubles. In any case, it shows their upwardly mobile aspirations. The poster does not include the crest's motto *Non sancz droit* ('not without right'), which would have been particularly appropriate at a time when anti-Stratfordians, such as Delia Bacon, had made the authorship question popular. From the late nineteenth century onwards, the anti-Stratfordians had engaged the support of authors such as Mark Twain and George Bernard Shaw in an attempt to persuade public opinion that Sir Francis Bacon rather than 'the man from Stratford' was the true author of the plays of William Shakespeare. For the Baconians, one of the strongest arguments in favour of Bacon was his higher social rank and education, while Shakespeare's rural background and lack of university education played against him. Shakespeare's coat of arms iconically conveyed the poet's 'genteel' status and was clearly deemed appropriate while mobilizing Shakespeare for the war fund, because it offered veritable proof of his gentility and Britishness.

Drafting Shakespeare through the Red Cross to increase patriotic feeling was at the time regarded as the logical thing to do. In the opening pages of the Grafton Galleries exhibition catalogue, Shakespearean editor and critic Sidney Lee reminds the visitor that 'It is fitting to invoke in so urgent and so patriotic a cause the name of Shakespeare'.[3] After linking the 'quality of mercy speech' – delivered by Portia cross-dressed as lawyer Balthazar in *The Merchant of Venice* (4.1) – with the work of the British Red Cross, Lee considers that 'No student of his work needs to be reminded of the patriotic fervour which finds exalted expression in his pages', because 'Shakespeare is the national and imperial oracle' who 'is always helpful and cheering'. Lee gives as proof of this claim the Bastard's famous patriotic speech that closes *King John* ('This England never did, nor never shall, / Lie at the proud foot of a conqueror'; 5.7.112–13) and quickly resolves the tension between a local (British) and global (Empire) bard by stating that 'the sense of unity among the component parts of the British Empire is quickened by the common heritage of Shakespeare's thought and language'. Lee's preface to the Grafton Galleries exhibition is one of many instances of how Shakespeare and his works were enlisted during the First World War to raise patriotic enthusiasm at home or throughout the British Empire and also amongst both British and colonial soldiers at the front.

The Grafton Galleries Shakespeare Exhibition was also a direct product of the 1916 Tercentenary spirit, when the three-hundredth anniversary of Shakespeare's death was commemorated (an event that Monika Smialkowska also considers in Chapter 9 in relation to a gala held at the British Expeditionary Force camp in Calais). Everyone who had an item related to Shakespeare, whether folio, quarto, or early edition of some kind, seemed eager to exhibit it. There were exhibitions in most libraries in Britain and North America, but also in schools and private clubs. In England, there were important exhibitions in Oxford, in Stratford, in Manchester, and in London. Out of this Shakespearean fervour, the exhibition that possibly deserves most attention today in connection with the presence of Shakespeare in wartime is the British Red Cross Shakespeare Exhibition, arranged by actor-manager Martin Harvey as part of his programme of deploying Shakespeare's cultural capital for the war effort.

Although the exhibition's main aim was to honour Shakespeare's memory, it was also promoted as a war-fund charity show, given that revenue obtained from it (the entrance fee was one shilling) would be donated to the British Red Cross Society and the Order of St John of Jerusalem. The collaboration between Shakespeareans and the Red Cross during the First World War was well established by 1916. Harvey, in fact, had been very active during the Tercentenary year putting Shakespeare to work for charity, and had arranged a Shakespeare season in London for the benefit of the Red Cross.[4] He had volunteered to meet the expenses involved in bringing the exhibition to London on condition that the Red Cross would benefit from it.

The exhibition the poster advertises originated in the collection of 'pictorial Shakespeareana' (as *The Times* put it) curated by Robert Bateman, which had been on view at the Manchester Whitworth Institute in August and September 1916.[5] When the show was transferred to London, the number of exhibits was much enlarged with loans from different institutions, such as the Garrick Club, the Shakespeare Birthplace Trust, the Shakespeare Memorial Theatre at Stratford, and the London Museum. The original collection of prints and paintings included not only images of Shakespeare, his contemporaries, and his patrons, but also likenesses of Shakespearean players and portraits of Shakespearean editors, critics, and commentators. In London, this collection of pictorial Shakespeareana was expanded to accommodate other artefacts. Individuals provided not only paintings but private collections of tokens and medals. Actors lent costumes, including the gaberdine Irving used in his role as Shylock. Besides commemorative medals and theatrical costumes, there were props, models of theatrical sets and statues, and dubious Shakespearean relics (such as the signet ring and the brooch allegedly found in New Place).[6] The Grafton Galleries exhibition was so ambitious in scope that *The Times* described it as 'the most complete and interesting exhibition of Shakespeariana ever held'.[7]

The exhibitions arranged for the 1916 Tercentenary had, of course, multiple forerunners in previous shows of Shakespeareana, including the Shakespearean exhibits at the Great Exhibition (1851).[8] Before 1916, there were two other important occasions in which Shakespeareana was also exhibited: the Shakespeare Exhibition at Stratford's Town Hall for the 1864 Tercentenary and the 1912 Exhibition at Earl's Court. The 1864 Shakespeare Exhibition was a truly Victorian, Salon-type exhibition in which the visitor was confronted by a diverse collection of individual items, combining paintings (including twenty-eight portraits of Shakespeare) with the hagiographical display of supposedly Shakespearean relics, such as his jug, death mask, and walking stick.[9] The 1912 Earl's Court Exhibition was of a very different nature: it was Shakespeare's England rather than Shakespeare that was being exhibited to the world.[10]

The 1916 Tercentenary exhibitions took place at a time when the Bacon controversy was receiving diminishing attention, but it was still present enough to be material for cartoons and attract newspaper coverage. Behind the memorializing of Shakespeare modelled by these exhibitions at a time of war, one could detect an impulse to celebrate the national poet for patriotic purposes, leaving no doubt that the man from Stratford was the indisputable author of the plays and poems. A visitor able to see all four major exhibitions from the Tercentenary year (Stratford, Oxford, Manchester, and London) would have obtained a persuasive vision of Shakespearean authorship. Stratford presented him as a businessman and entrepreneur, Oxford as a published writer, Manchester as a reader and pupil at school, and London as a man of the theatre. The Rylands Library in Manchester used the presence of textbooks in the exhibition to point out in its catalogue the excellent level of schooling in early modern rural England. Stratford included in the exhibition the royal patent giving Shakespeare's company permission to put on plays on the stage. In Oxford, the Bodleian catalogue more explicitly separated Shakespeare's works from the listing of other exhibits by a line running across the page. The Grafton Galleries displayed the ultimate proof of authorship – Shakespeare's handwriting – by exhibiting a facsimile of Hand D in the manuscript of *Sir Thomas More*. It is perhaps significant that, for some, the most revelatory, exciting exhibit was the author's handwriting. *The Times*, probably unaware of the fact that it was a collotype and not the actual autograph, showed its wonder that this artefact was on display and tried to account for it: 'The name of the Red Cross has indeed a way of opening doors that are usually locked.'[11]

What makes the 1916 Tercentenary Shakespeare exhibitions distinctive is the fact that they took place at a time when the 'sacralization of culture' was almost complete. Harry Levine has shown how this process involved a change in the nature of museum exhibitions that followed 'a familiar pattern of development from the general and eclectic to the exclusive and specific'.[12] This transformation of museums from 'places of entertainment' into 'sacred precincts' was followed in the early decades of the twentieth century by the segregation of the collections and the imposition of order and hierarchy on the exhibits.[13] Stephen Greenblatt has extensively discussed another type of evolution in the cultures of exhibition, an evolution that moves from the central role played by *wonder* to the desire of achieving *resonance*. While wonder is the power of the object on display 'to stop the viewer in his tracks, to convey an arresting sense of uniqueness', resonance is the power the object displayed has 'to evoke in the viewer the complex, dynamic cultural forces from which it has emerged'.[14] Although, as he argues, a successful museum or exhibition should aim for both resonance and wonder, it is possible to trace a movement from the wonder cultivated by *Wunderkammers* or curiosity cabinets of the Renaissance with their display of natural curiosities, unusual and rare objects or unique and precious artefacts, to the inclination to prioritize resonance in the Jewish Museum in Prague or the Musée d'Orsay in Paris. A third element in the changing configuration of museums and exhibitions is the nature of the display space, which has evolved from the clutter of the Salon, where paintings lined the walls in *horror vacui* fashion, to the clinical isolation provided for each artwork by the white walls of the modern art museum.

Accordingly, what made many of the 1916 exhibitions different from previous Shakespeare exhibitions was a deliberate attempt at classification. Exhibits were grouped into sections and this was clearly signalled in the exhibition catalogues. The viewer was invited to see the objects on display through a certain sense of order, conferred to them by the curators. In this

context, the British Red Cross Shakespeare Exhibition was remarkable for
its unity of purpose and its chronological arrangement. The exhibition
invited the viewer to see the playwright's life followed by the afterlife of his
works. It offered an opportunity to become acquainted with the man from
Stratford who had become a man of the theatre and whose memory was
kept alive for centuries by editors, critics, and actors. The impulse behind
this exhibition was not simply to collect a handful of Shakespearean curiosities but to offer an integrated approach to the life of Shakespeare and
the plays' afterlives in the theatre through all the media afforded at the
time by artistic representation and visual culture: oil paintings, prints, and
photographs mixed with sculptures, medals, playbills, costumes loaned by
actors, props, and models of sets and theatres. This was pointed out by *The
Observer*: 'The purpose of the exhibition is to render it possible to visualize
the personality of Shakespeare by means of pictures, and to help present-day
students to grasp the incidents of his times, and the work of his expositors
in commentary or on the stage.'[15]

The unity of purpose of the Grafton Galleries exhibition was noticed
by *The Times*, which described it as a 'carefully classified and chronologi-
cally arranged exhibition'.[16] *The Observer* similarly stressed the hierarchy
imposed on the objects displayed: 'The exhibits will be arranged chrono-
logically, and will be divided into sections, dealing respectively with portraits, monuments, medals and so forth', a classification that was also
pointedly underlined in its title, 'The Shakespeare Exhibition: Historic,
Dramatic and Artistic'.[17] It was also established at greater length by Sidney
Lee's 'Introduction' to the catalogue: 'The aim of the exhibition is to bring
home to the visitor, pictorially and graphically, the most notable phases
of the national Shakespearean tradition.'[18] Even so, in the address given at
the private viewing that opened the exhibition, Lee stressed the element
of wonder the exhibits expected to arouse: 'Some of the objects here on
view have not been submitted to public exhibition before.'[19] The display
model of the set for Harvey's *Hamlet* in the 1916 Tercentenary season, a
production that many visitors for the exhibition may have seen live at His
Majesty's Theatre, was hardly a rarity, but the model of the set coexisted
with the signet ring and the brooch. The model aimed for resonance, but
the ring and the brooch – in spite of their questionable authenticity –
clearly meant to excite wonder on the part of the exhibition's visitors.

Overall, though, one can argue that resonance was the dominant
effect the Shakespeare exhibition was meant to elicit from its visitors. As
Greenblatt explains, resonance 'is the intimation of a larger community of
voices and skills, an imagined ethnographic thickness'.[20] The resonance of

the Shakespeare exhibition arose from its historical, chronological arrangement, as much as from its documenting the phases of Shakespearean performance. The 1917 Shakespeare Exhibition in London was, like the State Jewish Museum in Prague, not so much an exhibition of art objects valuable in themselves, as many were mezzotints of oil paintings or engravings, but a collection of artefacts gathered together with memory and commemoration in mind. The Grafton Galleries exhibition functioned as a memorial complex whose resonance today is partly due to the exhibition's venue and the associations it may have carried. Two weeks before the Shakespeare Exhibition, the Grafton Galleries had housed a show of official Canadian war photographs. This show of war photographs, which memorialized the presence of Canadian soldiers at the Western Front, has in turn been memorialized by a series of photographs kept in the Canadian National Archives, which allows us to see what the Grafton Galleries were like the week before the Shakespeare Exhibition was set up. The heavily decorated Edwardian interior contrasts with our experience of modern exhibition galleries, but the attitude of the viewers in one of the photographs, which includes civilians and HM King George V in his British Army uniform, conveys a moment of concentrated viewing experience similar to contemporary 'ways of seeing'.[21] If a museum, as Svetlana Alpers argues, is 'a way of seeing', then the Red Cross Shakespeare Exhibition of 1917 provided its viewers with a very contemporary viewing experience.[22]

The patriotic resonance generated by the exhibition, uniting national and imperial sentiment in a wartime context, as Lee put it in the catalogue, is documented by the contemporary press. On 19 January 1917, a journalist from the *Daily Mirror* shared his impressions at the preview with his readers:

> I turned in to the private view of Shakespeare exhibition at the Grafton Galleries. It is a real treasure trove for Shakespeare lovers, and the exhibits range from a model of the old Globe Theatre to an autograph letter of Miss Ellen Terry. A bill announcing the sale of Shakespeare's house at Stratford, dated 1847, hangs in the first room.[23]

Three days later, the same newspaper reporter was surprised to see First World War soldiers taking an interest in Shakespeare and reported,

> I looked in on the wonderful Shakespearean exhibition at the Grafton Galleries on Saturday. I was impressed by the large number of men in khaki who were studying the pictures and other memorabilia of the dramatist. A Canadian sergeant said: 'This show is great for me. I've been an amateur Shakespearean actor for years, and the portraits of the famous actors and the ancient programmes fairly fascinate me. I'm coming again.'[24]

As the words of the British journalist and the Canadian soldier suggest, the Red Cross Shakespeare Exhibition had a patriotic resonance beyond its function as a charity show for the war effort. Its emphasis upon a specifically *theatrical* Shakespeare, rather than a textual or British Shakespeare, provided a common cultural ground that non-British soldiers fighting on the Western Front could share with both British civilians and men in khaki. The Canadian sergeant, like many of the soldiers on leave who visited the Shakespeare Exhibition, could through their experiences with Shakespeare on stage identify with First World War discourses presenting the British involvement in the conflict as a chivalrous fight for democracy and civilization. The Grafton Galleries exhibition served to stress that Shakespeare and theatrical culture were part of the shared heritage that men in the trenches were told Britain and its allies were fighting to preserve.

Shakespeare needs no statue, proclaimed *Punch* in 1864.[25] Forty years later, the projected erection of a memorial to Shakespeare in London was still contested terrain. Opinion divided those who thought that London needed a memorial of Shakespeare that could equal the Walter Scott Memorial in Edinburgh, and those who thought that the best-fitting memorial was a National Theatre.[26] As memorials, the proposed statue and National Theatre were redolent of past cultures of commemoration, their roots clearly entrenched in eighteenth- and nineteenth-century commemorative practices. By the time of the 1916 Tercentenary celebrations, Shakespeare still had no statue and no Memorial Theatre in London, in spite of the joint efforts of the Shakespeare Memorial Committee and the National Theatre campaigners.[27] The Great War interfered with the plans of the merger of these two groups, the Shakespeare Memorial National Theatre Committee, making the raising of further funds or the erection of a building impossible in a city taken over by the fever of Kitchener's Army and the allure of the 'Great Adventure'. As is well known (and discussed by Ailsa Grant Ferguson in Chapter 8), the Tercentenary year ended with the site destined for a Shakespeare Memorial National Theatre turned into a YMCA hut for First World War soldiers on leave.[28]

If the Great War and the Tercentenary combined to make it impossible to provide a permanent site of memory for Shakespeare in London in the form of a statue or theatre, they did succeed in arranging another kind of non-permanent memorial through the Red Cross Shakespeare Exhibition, a show that pointed to what cultures of commemoration in general and retrospective exhibitions in particular were going to be like in the twentieth century. Unlike statues or memorial buildings, an exhibition is a movable, portable site of memory with a temporary existence, which may nevertheless be reproduced in a different location at a different time. As such, the 1917 Shakespeare Exhibition in London, with its origin in Manchester, was much more clearly inscribed in the cultures of commemoration of modernity than the failed attempts of the statue and the National Theatre. The importance of this exhibition both for studies of Shakespearean reception and for the study of commemorative practice lies in its contribution to the development of today's cultures of commemoration, as it constituted an intermediary step between the Victorian 'Salon' type of exhibition and the modern 'white box'. Despite the old-fashioned rhetoric of just war, patriotism, race, and universality that coloured other commemorative practices in 1916, and in spite of the patriotic and imperial rhetoric of the opening pages of its catalogue, the Grafton Galleries exhibition was a spearhead of modernity in the Tercentenary celebrations. Recruiting Shakespeare and his cultural capital as national poet in wartime contributed to this achievement.

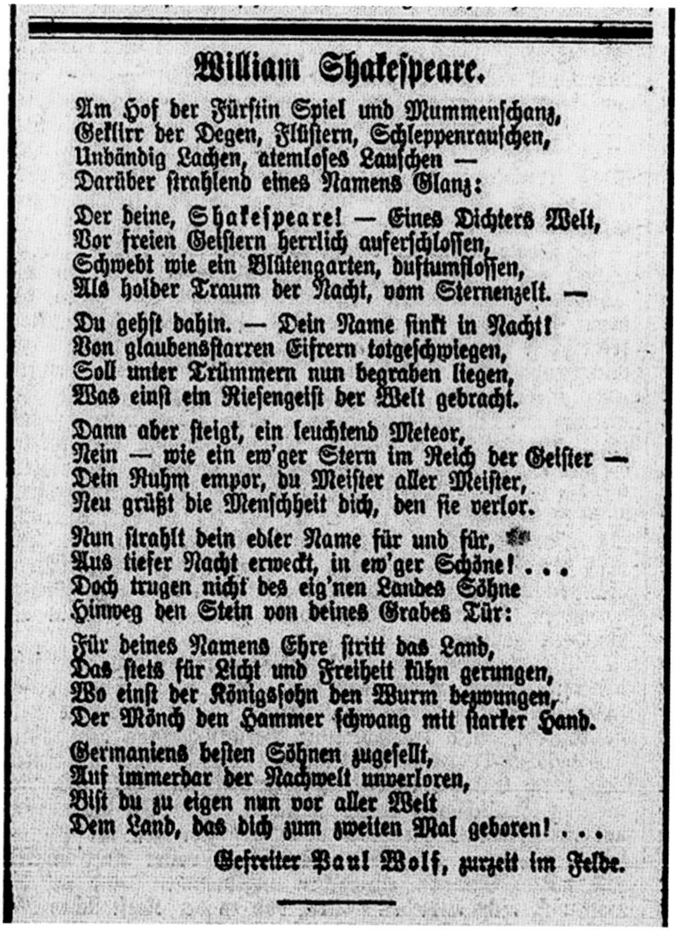

William Shakespeare.

Am Hof der Fürstin Spiel und Mummenschanz,
Geklirr der Degen, Flüstern, Schleppenrauschen,
Unbändig Lachen, atemloses Lauschen —
Darüber strahlend eines Namens Glanz:

Der deine, Shakespeare! — Eines Dichters Welt,
Vor freien Geistern herrlich auferschlossen,
Schwebt wie ein Blütengarten, duftumflossen,
Als holder Traum der Nacht, vom Sternenzelt. —

Du gehst dahin. — Dein Name sinkt in Nacht!
Von glaubensstarren Eiferern totgeschwiegen,
Soll unter Trümmern nun begraben liegen,
Was einst ein Riesengeist der Welt gebracht.

Dann aber steigt, ein leuchtend Meteor,
Nein — wie ein ew'ger Stern im Reich der Geister —
Dein Ruhm empor, du Meister aller Meister,
Neu grüßt die Menschheit dich, den sie verlor.

Nun strahlt dein edler Name für und für,
Aus tiefer Nacht erweckt, in ew'ger Schöne! ...
Doch trugen nicht des eig'nen Landes Söhne
Hinweg den Stein von deines Grabes Tür:

Für deines Namens Ehre stritt das Land,
Das stets für Licht und Freiheit kühn gerungen,
Wo einst der Königssohn den Wurm bezwungen,
Der Mönch den Hammer schwang mit starker Hand.

Germaniens besten Söhnen zugesellt,
Auf immerdar der Nachwelt unverloren,
Bist du zu eigen nun vor aller Welt
Dem Land, das dich zum zweiten Mal geboren! ...

Gefreiter Paul Wolf, zurzeit im Felde.

At the princess's court games and mummery,
Clashing of rapiers, whispering, the rustle of trains,
Boisterous laughter, breathless listening—
Gleaming above them the lustre of one name:

Yours, *Shakespeare!*—The world of a poet,
Marvellously revealed before free spirits,
Floats like a garden of flowers, suffused with scents,
As a fair nighttime dream of the starry firmament.—

You pass away.—Your name sinks into night!
Hushed into deathly silence by stiff-minded zealots,
Shall now lie buried under ruins
What once brought a gigantic spirit to the world.

But then rises, a shining meteor,
No—like an eternal star in the empire of spirits—
Your fame aloft, you master of all masters,
Mankind greets you anew, whom it had lost.

Now shines your noble name forever and ever,
Awoken from deepest night, in eternal beauty! …
Yet your own country's sons did not carry
The stone away from the door of your tomb:

For the honour of your name that country fought
That has always keenly struggled for light and freedom,
Where once the king's son subdued the wyrm,
And the monk swung his hammer with a forceful hand.

Delivered to Germania's best sons,
For evermore unforsaken for posterity,
You are now adopted before all the world
By the country that has given birth to you a second time!

Figure 11   Paul Wolf, 'William Shakespeare', published in the *Norddeutsche Allgemeine Zeitung* on 23 April 1916 (from Deutsches Zeitungsportal and translation by Marius S. Ostrowski).

CHAPTER II

Germanizing Shakespeare during the First World War

Marius S. Ostrowski

Paul Wolf's poem, entitled simply 'William Shakespeare', appeared on 23 April 1916 in the *Norddeutsche Allgemeine Zeitung* (Figure 11), nestled among Eastertide poetry in the paper's literary section, and accompanying reports of the sinking of the SS *Sussex* and clashes in Iraq and the Caucasus.[1] It was published as part of the lavish cultural celebrations in Wilhelmine Germany that marked the Tercentenary of William Shakespeare's death, which included an extensive roster of think pieces in all corners of the German press, performance cycles of Shakespeare plays dotted across the major cities of the *Kaiserreich*, as well as a flurry of books, commentaries, and sundry Shakespeareana. The publication of such a lurid paean to a foreign author might seem a somewhat unusual decision for a national newspaper even in a normal context. But it becomes an order of magnitude more remarkable given that it was published at the height of the First World War – two months into the Battle of Verdun, during the international outcry against unrestricted German submarine warfare, mere weeks before the Battles of Jutland and the Somme, when the war had already cost *c.* six million military deaths across all fronts – and that the author in question, Shakespeare, was held by the German *Kulturwelt* to be *the* greatest cultural export of Great Britain, with whom Germany was directly embroiled on the battlefield.

This apparent paradox is sharpened by the fact that its author, Wolf, is identified as a *Gefreiter* ('lance corporal') in the German Army serving at the front at the time of writing. Even more intriguingly, the *Norddeutsche Allgemeine* was one of the most significant conservative newspapers in Germany, the leading pro-government voice from before unification through to the late Weimar Republic – which meant that in the censorious atmosphere of the wartime *Kaiserreich*, Wolf's poem would have required an official stamp of approval to be published at all. So how are we to understand this curious vignette? How should we read its transparent attempts to fuse war with culture, to exalt the stoic courage of the German troops by blending it seamlessly with a purportedly elevated capacity for aesthetic understanding – in more-or-less explicit contrast to that of Shakespeare's 'own country's sons'?

In a narrow sense, this contribution from the trenches conjures a perfect microcosm of a highly idiosyncratic tone that pervaded German Shakespeareanism during the First World War. But more broadly, its message also represents a specific yet influential answer to a question that preoccupied the German wartime public right across the ideological spectrum. Was it possible to be a patriotic supporter of German national culture and still continue to enjoy the cultural artefacts produced by countries that were now Germany's enemies? Could any product of a specific culture 'rise above' the fray of national rivalries and grievances? Might any national culture claim a monopoly on 'its' exponents, authors and artists, poets, and musicians, or were some national 'greats' so great as to be the rightful common property of all of humanity? And, if the latter, who might these international 'greats' be, both those that Germany might borrow from its enemies, and those it should share with them in return?[2]

Of course, Germany was far from the only country confronted with this question. Acutely similar debates raged in the countries of the *Entente* as well, geared towards especially musical and literary output of Germanic origin. In general, a tide of nationalist boycotts swept through the populations of the belligerents on both sides. The 'headline' cases, such as royal and imperial families jettisoning their courtesy titles, foreign military honours, even their dynastic names, have proven enduringly familiar. But the same sentiment extended also to advertisers playing up the 'homegrown' goods they were hawking, from swiftly rebranded cognac 'in field post packaging' (Landauer & Macholl) and baking powders under the rubric 'Never again English cornflour!' (Dr Oetker) to blunt listings for 'German jackhammers, German steam cranes, German chains, German compressors, German automatic grabs' (Deutsche Maschinenfabrik A.G.).

But what distinguished the debate on the German side, at least in the eyes of its participants, was the idea that Germany was steering a more nuanced course between pre-war tolerance and wartime chauvinism than both its allies and enemies. While British orchestras were impetuously striking Ludwig van Beethoven and Richard Wagner from their repertoires, and Ottoman functionaries were organizing public burnings of books by authors from the *Entente* powers, the German *Kulturträger* ('doyens of culture') had, they insisted, found a way to reconcile the demands of patriotism with the imperatives of cultural good taste.[3]

For German intellectuals, the question of literature – prose, drama, and poetry – lay at the heart of this question, and the works of William

Shakespeare, in particular his plays, occupied the pinnacle of their concern. German literary tastes were fairly charitable towards foreign produce, especially where 'the classics' were concerned.[4] During the First World War, it was possible to find plays by Molière, George Bernard Shaw, and Leo Tolstoy, as well as (less controversially) Henrik Ibsen and August Strindberg, alongside classic fare such as *Faust* and *Götz von Berlichingen* by Johann Wolfgang von Goethe or *The Robbers*, *Intrigue and Love*, and *The Death of Wallenstein* by Friedrich von Schiller, and contemporary dramatists including Gerhart Hauptmann and Hugo von Hofmannsthal. But it was Shakespeare that prompted them to engage in their most intense soul-searching, exacerbated by the not insignificant coincidence that war broke out in the interstice between two major anniversaries of the Shakespearean calendar: the 350th anniversary of his birth in April 1914 and the 300th anniversary of his death in April 1916. Both focused the minds of the German *Kulturwelt*, forcing the German cultural *élite* to confront hitherto unquestioned perceptions of their relationship to Shakespeare and his literary output.

§

First and foremost, Germany's relationship to *der große William* emphasized his sheer canonical importance in 'civilized' (read: European) literature. For German literary scholars, Shakespeare sat between Aeschylus, Euripides, and Hans Sachs on the one hand, and Goethe, Schiller, Johann Gottfried Herder, and Gotthold Ephraim Lessing on the other; a rare foreign interloper in the smooth transition from classical antiquity to Germanic modernity. In the florid style of turn-of-the-century literary critics, comparisons to Shakespeare were as sought-after as those to Goethe or Schiller, especially regarding authors' and playwrights' grasp of history or the intricacies of the human condition – in both of which Germans strongly felt Shakespeare brooked few equals.[5]

One sign of Shakespeare's popularity was the Shakespeare-Gesellschaft, the premier home for all matters Shakespearean during the *Kaiserreich*. Founded in Weimar in April 1864, it soon grew to equal the parallel Goethe- and Schiller-Gesellschaften. It celebrated its 50th anniversary with great fanfare in April 1914, receiving donations of 500 *Reichsmark* (just over £3,000 in today's currency) from Kaiser Franz Josef of Austria as well as King George V of Great Britain, and marking the occasion with a guest lecture by Hubert Carter, an acclaimed member of the company at His Majesty's Theatre, London.[6]

But it is performances of Shakespeare's plays that offer the best indication of his popularity before and during the First World War. In true

Teutonic style, the Shakespeare-Gesellschaft kept meticulous accounts of Shakespeare-related statistics, which it published in its *Jahrbuch* in every second quarter. These included annual performance numbers for Shakespeare plays: from a high point of 1,133 performances in 1913, these almost halved to 675 performances in 1915 at the height of chauvinist fervour, but had recovered to 990 performances in 1917, and continued to rise till the end of the war.[7] Among these was a celebrated 'Shakespeare cycle' directed by the innovative Austrian impresario Max Reinhardt at the Deutsches Theater in January 1914. Although German critics were sometimes a little sniffy about Reinhardt's directorial style, which they saw as obscuring the intrinsic genius of Shakespeare's text in favour of production *als Selbstzweck* ('for its own sake'), this diffidence did not stop the Wilhelmine government from making full use of Reinhardt as an image-boosting tool once war broke out, sending him on extended tours of neutral countries in Europe in 1915–17 with a programme of Goethe, Lessing, Strindberg – and Shakespeare.[8]

Further, in the *Kaiserreich*, Shakespeare was clearly regarded as not only something to be watched but also a key source to be taught and studied. Reviews and opinion pieces were replete with asides about how important it was to *read* Shakespeare, in German or English, as 'the' way to fully understand his meaning – and get the most out of his plays in performance. This emphasis did not drop off once the war began. In the social-democratic women's periodical *Gleichheit*, itself often peppered with didactic Shakespearean dictums, the supplement *Für unsere Mütter und Hausfrauen* stressed the benefits of teaching children to read a core 'set' of authors, including Shakespeare.[9] In a similar vein, *Vorwärts*, the official organ of the Social-Democratic Party of Germany, carried advertisements for adult workers' education seminars at the Arbeiterbildungsschule in Berlin, which on 21 May 1916 listed two lectures by the venerable social-democratic theorist Eduard Bernstein on 'Ireland and England' and 'The Struggle over the Corn Laws in England', one by the leftist journalist Ernst Däumig on 'Mesopotamia and English rule in India', and one by the socialist poet Franz Diederich on Shakespeare and Miguel de Cervantes.[10]

Yet the German affinity for Shakespeare ran far deeper than simply acknowledging his literary importance – or, indeed, celebrating the long Shakespearean pedigree of the German cultural scene (see, for example, Amy Lidster's account, in Chapter 4, of Shakespeare's cultural importance in the German lands during the Napoleonic Wars).[11] Rather, the commentary of the time proposes an essential connection between Shakespeare and the German *Geist* ('spirit'). Perhaps the clearest pre-war expression of this came in 1911 with the literary scholar Friedrich Gundolf's *Shakespeare and the German Spirit*, which not only explored Shakespeare's role as a theatrical innovator and key figure in the intellectual history of rationalism, but also posited him as a direct precursor, even 'early adopter', of the core tenets of German Classicism, Romanticism, and *Sturm und Drang*.[12]

During the war, this profound German self-identification with Shakespeare reached fever pitch. As the Anglicist Ernst Sieper put it bluntly, 'they thought that they could rescue Shakespeare by summarily declaring him to be *ours*, to be *a German poet*!'[13] Hauptmann wrote that Shakespeare's dramas had become 'a national good' unlike those of 'any other German poet'.[14] A Cologne production of *Othello* in November 1914 received rave reviews along with the comment, 'For the audiences here, Shakespeare is not an Englishman, but a German classic.'[15] Critics recalled their first – often ostentatiously disappointed – encounters with the English *Geist* when they arrived in Britain before the war with 'a thankful heart full of that great German poet called Shakespeare', insisting that the Britain of today would be 'just as abhorrent' to Shakespeare as it was to contemporary Germans, so that 'our country should remain his *only true home*'.[16]

The flipside of this claim that Shakespeare had a unique connection to the German *Geist*, was, unsurprisingly, that other countries and peoples did not. German literary critics relentlessly disparaged the French theatre scene's unwillingness or inability to bring halfway decent performances of Shakespeare to the stage.[17] But they were also perfectly prepared to extend this snobbery towards Britain. The playwright Ludwig Fulda commented that Shakespeare had 'only accidentally been born in England', adding that 'perhaps we will have him ceded to us after the peace settlement'.[18] In response to the British government's declaration of book exports to Germany as 'war contraband', one critic argued in January 1915 that this would be ineffective, since 'we in Germany already publish and print everything of value in this [English] literature already':

> We have brought out your old texts in exemplary form, from *Beowulf* to the *Spanish Tragedy*. We were loving and devouring *our* Shakespeare at a time when you, with tasteless affectation, merely brought out the *Gems from Shakespeare* and thereby came to the wrongheaded belief that this coarse author could only be partially enjoyed.[19]

Similarly, on 23 April 1916, the *Berliner Börsen-Zeitung* began one of its Tercentenary comment pieces with the following vignette:

> A German was lingering in his library with an English guest. Among the rows of books, the Englishman spotted Shakespeare's works as well and

said: 'Oh, you know Shakespeare?' 'Certainly', came the reply, 'I have read all his works many times over and I believe I know the most important ones of them well. But of course my knowledge of Shakespeare will not be able to compare with that of an Englishman.' 'Oh, I have seen several of his plays in the theatre', retorted the Briton.[20]

Though readers should not generalize too much from this experience, the piece continued, 'it nonetheless remains the case that Shakespeare is interwoven with the intellectual history of no other people so intimately and indissolubly as that of Germany in the previous century and a half.'

This baffled resentment towards non-Germans' supposed lack of appreciation for Shakespeare spilled over into a more general culturally tinged hostility towards the people that *happened* (by some world-historical absurdity) to have produced the man himself. A particularly – to nationalist German ears – emblematic comment by the poet Heinrich Heine in 1838 was trotted out with cultish regularity in the wartime press, as for instance in February 1915 in the *Badische Landes-Zeitung*:

> I become depressed when I consider that he (Shakespeare) in the end is still an Englishman, and belongs to the most repulsive people that God in his anger ever created. What a repulsive people, what an unedifying country! How starchy, how homely, how self-absorbed, how narrow, how English! A country that the ocean would long since have swallowed up if it did not fear that it might cause upsets in its bowels … A people, a grey, yawning monstrosity, whose breath is nothing but stuffy air and deadly boredom … that island of damnation, smouldering with coal smoke, buzzing with machines, churchgoing, addle-brained England! Beneficent Nature never entirely disinherits her creatures, and while denying the English all that is beautiful and lovely, and lending them neither voices to sing nor any sense for enjoyment, endowing them perhaps only with living wineskins full of stout instead of human souls, she has awarded them in compensation a great piece of bourgeois freedom, the talent to comfortably make themselves at home, and William Shakespeare.[21]

Sentiments such as these led a few lone voices in the wartime wilderness to bemoan the 'pharisaic' ignorance that convinced 'many among us … that we Germans have given the English their Shakespeare, that through our deepening and life-preserving admiration we give him to them over and over again'.[22] Oskar Blum, writing in the socialist theoretical journal *Neue Zeit* on the proletarian dimensions of Shakespeare's works, went so far as to observe that Germans were not alone in their appreciation for the Bard, tracing the 'Slavic' and 'Romance' dimensions of Shakespeare's international presence.[23] But overall, these sentiments fell decidedly into a minority position.

§

In short, the dominant approach in early twentieth-century Germany towards Shakespeare and his works was to tread a confident, sometimes questionable, even outright graceless path between cultural appreciation and cultural appropriation. But how did this jealous adulation manifest in the specifically military context of the First World War? It did not, as might perhaps be expected, noticeably change *which* Shakespeare plays were performed – neither increases in works that could be given a jingoistic twist, nor decreases in those that were too obviously 'English' in character. According to the Shakespeare-Gesellschaft, *Hamlet*, *A Midsummer Night's Dream*, and *Twelfth Night* were consistently in the top five plays between 1914 and 1918, with *The Merchant of Venice*, *Othello*, *As You Like It*, and *The Winter's Tale* oscillating in and out of the leading spots.[24] While occasionally these performances were 'improved' through (often ad-libbed) war-related insertions, most fell squarely into the category of entertainment for a public that needed to be distracted from mounting war exhaustion. Shakespeare, in other words, was not enlisted for the German war effort, as he later would be by the Nazis during the Second World War (an issue discussed by Richard Ned Lebow in Chapter 18). Instead, the role of pro-military nationalist morale-boosting was reserved for more middle-of-the-road staples of the German stage repertoire, from Wagner's *Parsifal* and *Lohengrin* to Goethe's *Götz* and Schiller's *Wallenstein*, as well as explicitly nationalistic contributions by more minor playwrights such as Christian Friedrich Hebbel and Heinrich von Kleist.

Yet even if their output was not roped into Wilhelmine military policy, Germany's cultural institutions of Shakespeare-appreciation were certainly dragooned into supporting the *Kaiserreich*'s cause. Both Reinhardt and the philologist Alois Brandl, president of the Shakespeare-Gesellschaft, were signatories to the 'Manifesto of the Ninety-Three' of 4 October 1914, which declared the support of *das geistige Deutschland* ('the intellectual Germany') for the German invasion of Belgium, alongside luminaries such as the economist Lujo Brentano, composer Engelbert Humperdinck, chemist Fritz Haber, and physicists Max Planck and Wilhelm Röntgen.[25] Reinhardt, like some other signatories, later recanted his support when the brutality of the *Kaiserreich*'s war conduct became better known.

Shakespeare also helped 'keep troops going' during their horrific experiences in the trenches or out at sea. Descriptions of soldiers' quarters noted that they contained a smattering of important literary works, including the Bible and the works of Shakespeare.[26] On 6 August 1916, the *Frankfurter*

Zeitung recounted the heroic tale of the blockade-breaking merchant submarine *Deutschland*, which avoided detection while traversing the English Channel by resting on the sea floor. The submariners kept their spirits up by listening to Edvard Grieg's *Peer Gynt* on a crewmember's gramophone, drinking French champagne, and reading – Shakespeare.[27] Two days later, the same paper printed a letter from troops at the Somme thanking the Rhine-Main Association for Popular Education for their donation of English reading materials, including Shakespeare and Charles Dickens, which they commented was ironically the same language as that of British Prime Minister H. H. Asquith and then-Secretary of State for War David Lloyd George, who were the ones raining armaments down on them.[28]

The upshot of this semi-integration of Shakespeare as a *normal* presence in a society and among a population that gradually became ever-more disrupted by the *abnormality* of war led to the two following a somewhat surreal parallel course. The press kept up its brisk trade in gushing reviews of Shakespeare performances and cheery announcements of upcoming Shakespeare-related antiquarian auctions, planned performance cycles, and new publications. But where beforehand they were juxtaposed with relatively more mundane news items, they now shared the same pages as, for example, the brutal staccato of stenographic updates from the Oberste Heeresleitung ('Supreme Army Command'). 'Shakespeare Week' at the Königliches Schauspielhaus in Dresden was printed alongside battlefield reports from Verdun;[29] Reinhardt's first ever production of *Macbeth* at the Deutsches Theater accompanied the progress of the German submarine war;[30] a content summary of volume 53 of the Shakespeare-Gesellschaft's *Jahrbuch* appeared underneath a précis of the Polish bargaining position in the negotiations at Brest-Litovsk;[31] and eventually, a paean to 'Shakespeare's most personal drama', *Troilus and Cressida*, featured alongside reports of the Reich conference debates of the workers' and soldiers' councils on economic socialization during the early months of the Weimar Republic.[32]

Especially remarkable are the occasions where the two – war and Shakespeare – elided directly into one. This often took the form of German politicians, rulers, or military leaders using turns of phrase from Shakespeare to illustrate the strategic situation in which they found themselves. Wilhelm II notoriously quoted 'to be or not to be' when characterizing the war as an existential question for Germany,[33] while the *Frankfurter Zeitung* reported other diplomatic binds in similarly Shakespearean terms, quoting, 'Misery acquaints a man with strange bedfellows' (*Tempest*, 2.2.35),[34] and

> Who steals my purse, steals trash; 'tis something, nothing,
> 'Twas mine, 'tis his, and has been slave to thousands:
> But he that filches from me my good name
> Robs me of that which not enriches him
> And makes me poor indeed.   (*Othello*, 3.3.158–62)[35]

This habit was not restricted to the upper echelons of the German hierarchy. A 'war participant' convalescing in a field hospital described the 'tunnel warfare' of 1914–15 in bitter terms:

> For 'tis the sport to have the engineer
> Hoist with his own petard an't shall go hard
> But I will delve one yard below their mines
> And blow them at the moon. Oh 'tis most sweet
> When in one line two crafts directly meet.
>
> (*Hamlet*, 3.4.206–11)[36]

Shakespearean thinking and language, in other words, deeply coloured German society's experience of the war in all its forms, macroscopic and microscopic, grandly strategic and intimately personal.

§

All in all, Shakespeare survived the nationalistic tidal wave of the First World War relatively unscathed. Despite a brief dip of uncertainty in the early months of the war, as German intellectuals struggled to determine which of their erstwhile imported delights they could keep and which they should discard in favour of more local fare, Shakespeare's place on the Wilhelmine cultural menu settled fairly swiftly into a continued constant presence. The *Berliner Börsen-Zeitung*'s retrospective on Reinhardt's tenure at the Volksbühne from September 1915 to May 1918 noted that, of the fifty plays he brought to the stage in that time, eleven were by Shakespeare, well ahead of six by Hauptmann, four by Schiller, and three by Goethe.[37] In fact, a German theatregoer in November 1918 would have been essentially no less able to find a Shakespeare play to watch than one in August 1914. Having battled to 'adopt' Shakespeare, and rouse his legacy from its 'deepest night', 'Germania's best sons' were understandably loath to abandon what they saw as their signal literary acquisition – which, with no small irony, helped ensure Shakespeare's preservation for *German* posterity in precisely the way they claimed to have done for humanity at large.

Interior Coliseum Theatre, Dublin, after bombardment.

Figure 12   Postcard depicting five men posing amid the ruins of Dublin's Coliseum Theatre after the Easter Rising of 1916 (image courtesy of UCD Digital Library, from an original in UCD Library Special Collections).

CHAPTER 12

Readers and Rebels
Ireland, Shakespeare, and the 1916 Easter Rising

Katherine Hennessey

The photograph of Figure 12 illustrates the extent of the damage done to the Coliseum Theatre in Dublin during the Easter Rising of 1916. The image was taken from what was once the stage area, providing us with the perspective of an actor standing on the stage, looking into the house. The group of men front and centre stare back at the camera from what might well have been the first row of seats, as though they were audience members who have now become part of the spectacle, one posing with a hand raised to touch a twisted girder, another balanced precariously on a heap of rubble. The image, which became part of a postcard series commemorating the Easter Rising, serves as a striking reminder of the significance of theatrical performances in Dublin in the years leading up to the revolt, of the elements of theatricality and spectacle inherent in the Rising itself, and of the ways in which the collateral damage from the Rising and its aftermath struck cultural institutions and events, such as the Coliseum Theatre and Dublin's aborted commemorations of the Shakespeare Tercentenary. Yet, much as the postcard image shifts the expected theatrical perspective from that of an audience member looking at the stage to that of an actor peering out into the crowd, the void left by the destruction created a space for new invocations of Shakespeare in Ireland, shifting the focus from the plays themselves to their presumed effects on readers and spectators, and illustrating that where some cultural activists and commentators in Ireland assumed Shakespeare to be an anti-revolutionary icon, others found within his work an inspiration for rebellion and resistance.

Dublin's Theatres, the Easter Rising, and Shakespeare

The Coliseum Theatre was a grand building in both size and design: stretching the full length of a city block between Henry Street and Prince Street, with an entrance graced by neoclassical flourishes on a four-storey façade, an immense stage eighty feet wide by forty feet deep, and a seating capacity of three thousand, the Coliseum offered Dublin audiences theatrical performances as well as cinema screenings.[1] Yet its history was a short and mostly unhappy one, fraught by the increasing sociopolitical tensions that would culminate in the Rising. Before the theatre even opened, its owners angered local craftsmen by engaging British rather than local firms to carry out much of the theatre's construction and furnishing. The theatre's inaugural performance on 5 April 1915 was marred by Irish nationalist audience members' heated reaction to a rendition of a British war recruitment song.[2] And by the start of May 1916, after having been in existence for just over a year, the Coliseum was reduced to the piles of rubble and twisted girders depicted in the postcard image, a casualty of a conflagration ignited by the artillery bombardment of the General Post Office (GPO), which the rebels had commandeered as their headquarters, and which was located just to the east of the Coliseum on the same block.[3]

The ruins of the Coliseum were extensively documented in the period immediately after the Easter Rising. In photographs taken from slightly farther back, we can see additional elements like the remains of the proscenium that once framed the vast stage, and the building's collapsed roof. Other photos show the burnt-out shell of the façade at the theatre's entrance on Henry Street.[4] The image of Figure 12 was reproduced in a postcard series issued by Coleman's Printers in 1916, depicting the devastation of some of Dublin's most prominent landmarks, like the GPO and its neighbour on Sackville (now O'Connell) Street, the Hotel Metropole. Other printers, like Eason's and Valentine, issued their own series of post-rebellion postcards. Some of these juxtapose 'before' and 'after' images of streets and landmarks, while others depict British soldiers barricading streets and posing triumphantly with the rebels' captured flag. One particularly striking photograph, taken at night, shows huge conflagrations consuming Sackville Street, while heavy grey clouds of smoke and ash fill the air.[5]

In the months before the Rising, no one would have predicted that the commemorative souvenirs from Easter Week 1916 would include a postcard of a burned-out theatre. In fact, in early 1916 some Irishmen and women were planning to participate in a markedly different instance of theatrical commemoration: the celebrations of Shakespeare's legacy upon the three-hundred-year anniversary of his death. Members of the Dublin branch of the British Empire Shakespeare Society (BESS), a literary and amateur acting association, were rehearsing *Hamlet* and *Henry V* for performance at Dublin's Abbey and Gaiety Theatres, respectively. They had also organized a series of public events for the Tercentenary, including a February lecture on plot construction in *Hamlet*, accompanied by a programme of Shakespearean songs and recitations.[6] Their production of *Hamlet* premiered on 7 April, directed by Mary O'Hea, an Irish actor, singer, and librettist who had trained at the Lyceum in the West End under the great Shakespearean actor Henry Irving.[7]

BESS's pair of performances – the former widely acknowledged as Shakespeare's greatest play, the latter, his most patriotic – were likely intended at least in part as a show of allegiance to the British Empire amidst the turmoil of the First World War. Yet the engagement of the Abbey Theatre as the venue for the *Hamlet* performance highlights some of the paradoxes inherent in the staging of Shakespeare in Ireland: while the staging of *Hamlet* may have been envisioned by the BESS troupe as a paean to England and the British Empire, the members of the Abbey's resident company were supporters of (and many played key roles in) the Rising.[8] Abbey actor Seán Connolly, for example, was the rebels' first casualty, killed while leading an attack on Dublin Castle, a mere week after he had tread the boards at the Abbey in the lead role in the nationalist play *Under Which Flag?* by James Connolly, one of the leaders of the Rising.[9] Moreover, as Willy Maley points out, many key figures in the rebellion, such as Padraig Pearse, Thomas MacDonagh, and Ernie O'Malley, openly expressed their admiration for Shakespeare.[10] Douglas Hyde, who composed a widely acclaimed series of Irish-language plays in collaboration with William Butler Yeats and Lady Augusta Gregory as they worked to establish the Abbey Theatre, and who would eventually serve from 1938 to 1945 as the first president of an independent Ireland, spent part of 1916 composing an Irish-language poem for Israel Gollancz's *A Book of Homage to Shakespeare*, a Tercentenary commemorative collection of Shakespeare-inspired poetry and essays from writers around the globe. Hyde's poem depicts Shakespeare and his works as a redeeming counterpoint to Irish memories of English exploitation and betrayal (though, as Andrew Murphy notes, the English translation that accompanies the poem in Gollancz's text expurgates many of Hyde's pointed barbs).[11] Shakespeare's work was thus invoked on both sides of the Easter Rising – on one hand, as a patriotic icon in support of the British war effort, and on the other as a source of support for Irish nationalists' political and cultural aspirations.

Brush Up Your Shakespeare: *The Irish Times* Editorial

BESS's *Hamlet* ran for three nights at the Abbey, concluding on 9 April. A mere two weeks later, on 23 April 1916, Irish rebels were debating whether or not to mobilize in the wake of the capture of Roger Casement and the loss of the cache of German arms that he had hoped to smuggle into Ireland. Over the following days, *The Irish Times*, which had planned to run a set of Tercentenary feature stories throughout the week, instead found itself scrambling to cover an insurgent movement that had seized control of landmarks throughout Dublin and was declaiming, not Shakespearean soliloquies, but the proclamation of an Irish republic. On 27 April, a day after British authorities imposed martial law throughout Ireland, *The Irish Times* published an editorial that urged the populace to adhere dutifully to the restrictions. For those who wondered, 'What is the fire-side citizen to do with those hours?', the editorial suggested conversing with family, gardening, carrying out home repairs, and above all, reading Shakespeare: 'How many citizens of Dublin have any real knowledge of the works of Shakespeare? Could any better occasion for reading them be afforded than the coincidence of enforced domesticity with the poet's tercentenary?'[12]

   The editorial is rife with multiple levels of unintended irony. One obvious one is the suggestion that Dublin's residents should read Shakespeare while the Coliseum burned. Another is the euphemistic description of martial law as a tranquil period of 'enforced domesticity' in which to tend gardens and read by the fireside, in a city whose centre had just been shattered by violent armed conflict and artillery fire. A third, though perhaps less glaring, irony is the assumption that Dubliners have little to no 'real knowledge' of the works of Shakespeare. In 2010, Patrick Lonergan and Deirdre McFeely of the National University of Ireland Galway (NUIG) completed an online database cataloguing performances of Shakespeare's work in Dublin between 1660 and 1904 – that is, from the Restoration to the establishment of the Abbey Theatre.[13] The NUIG database contains a remarkable 4,698 entries (which, as the researchers emphasize, are drawn from incomplete documentary records, particularly in the seventeenth and early eighteenth centuries). In sum, over the three hundred years that separate Shakespeare's death and the Easter Rising, Ireland, and the city of Dublin in particular, were significant loci for the performance of Shakespearean drama. But perhaps most striking of the assumptions embedded in *The Irish Times* editorial is its implied connection between reading Shakespeare and acquiescence to the imposition of martial law, as though Shakespeare's works could inoculate the Irish public against rebellious tendencies (an assumption that Andrew Murphy also challenges through his account of Irish nationalist Michael Davitt's interest in Shakespeare in Chapter 6). The fallacy of this notion is illustrated by, among other things, the fact that at least one Irish rebel actually carried a copy of Shakespeare's work with him into the fray: Irish Volunteer Seosamh de Brún notes in his diary entry for 29 April that the nerve-wracking skirmishes and sniper fire eventually gave way to a calm that allowed him to read a segment of *Julius Caesar*, 'following', as he wryly notes, 'the advice of *Irish Times*'.[14]

De Brún's assertion that he was adhering to the editorialist's advice by taking his copy of Shakespeare with him to the line of fire is amusing, but its irony pales in comparison to his comments on *Julius Caesar*. He notes that it is his first Shakespeare play, and finds Cassius and Brutus an 'interesting study ... a beautiful expression of manly love, an ideal conception of the idea of the Brotherhood of man and free from cant or cheap political platitude'.[15] This evaluation suggests that de Brún had read the two characters' first exchange, which includes the celebrated lines in which Cassius describes his resentment of Caesar's increasing political power, against which courageous republicans should rebel:

> ... he doth bestride the narrow world
> Like a Colossus, and we petty men
> Walk under his huge legs and peep about
> To find ourselves dishonourable graves ...
> The fault, dear Brutus, is not in our stars
> But in ourselves, that we are underlings.   (1.2.135–41)

Such lines would have resonated with a young man like de Brún, who on 25 April had recorded in his diary his own and his fellow Volunteers' fervent patriotic readiness to set their own lives at risk in the Rising in order to achieve Irish independence: 'We now thoroughly realize our position and are becoming reconciled to it. We believe we are going to make a sacrifice. We offer it to god & our country.'[16]

But de Brún's evaluation of the two characters' friendship also suggests that the pressures of battle left him unable to read – or perhaps unable to fully concentrate on – the quarrel between Brutus and Cassius in 4.3, after the assassination of Caesar has left Rome not the glorious Republic of Brutus's aspirations but a divided nation, riven by civil war. It offers an uncanny parallel to Ireland's own history in the years subsequent to the Easter Rising, which saw the ravages of both the Irish War of Independence (1919–21) and the Irish Civil War (1922–23). In other words, the lessons that Irish readers might have drawn from Shakespeare in 1916 far exceeded what *The Irish Times* editorialist imagined.

1916 and Caroline Byrne's *The Taming of the Shrew*

A century later, in the summer of 2016, as part of the 'Wonder Season' planned by Artistic Director Emma Rice at Shakespeare's Globe Theatre,

Irish director Caroline Byrne chose to return Shakespeare to Ireland during the Easter Rising. Byrne set her production of *The Taming of the Shrew* in Ireland in 1916, simultaneously paying homage to the global Quadricentenary celebrations of Shakespeare's legacy and participating in the complex conversations then unfolding in Ireland around the hundred-year anniversary of the Rising, particularly those sparked by the 'Waking the Feminists' (WTF) movement.[17] WTF arose in late 2015, in direct response to the Abbey Theatre's announcement of its programming choices for the 1916 centenary under the title 'Waking the Nation', which promised the theatre-going public a challenging interrogation of prevailing narratives of Irish nationhood, but which effectively excluded Irish female theatre-makers from the programme: 90 per cent of the plays chosen were authored by men, and 80 per cent of the slated directors were male. Irish theatre-makers Lian Bell and Maeve Stone and *Irish Times* columnist Úna Mullaly notably protested the gender imbalance of the Abbey's programme and the marginalization of women in the Irish arts, paralleling a public debate that had already begun regarding the unfulfilled promises of the 1916 Proclamation of the Republic. Famously declaimed by Padraig Pearse from the steps of the GPO in the midst of the Easter Rising, the Proclamation specifically addressed itself to 'every Irishman and Irishwoman', and asserted that the new Republic 'guarantees ... equal rights and equal opportunities to all its citizens' – a guarantee that, as Irish activists for equality and inclusion pointed out in the run-up to the centenary, had not been borne out in Ireland in the subsequent century, even after the nation achieved independence from Britain.

By setting *The Taming of the Shrew* in 1916, Byrne simultaneously confronted the long history of misogynistic interpretations of Shakespeare's play and the unresolved issue of gender inequality in Ireland.[18] Her production cast female actors in many of the male roles, including Grumio, Tranio, and Biondello, and cut the partial framing device in Shakespeare's play, the 'induction' featuring drunken wastrel Christopher Sly, replacing it with a song sung by lead actress Aoife Duffin, who played Katherina. Byrne developed the lyrics in collaboration with dramaturg Morna Regan, and they entitled the piece 'Numbered in the Song', after the line from 'Easter, 1916', Yeats's poetic elegy for the leaders of the Easter Rebellion, in which Yeats refers to a participant in the Rising with the line 'I number him in the song'. Though the poem begins with an allusion to Irish nationalist activist Maud Gonne, Yeats never mentions her by name, while he does specifically cite the names of four male leaders of the Rising at the poem's conclusion – a choice which epitomizes the erasure of the contributions of female activists like Gonne within the subsequent historiography of the Rising. In Byrne's production, conversely, the female lead gives voice to the opening lines, a passionate plea for equality that sets the tone for the action that follows: the struggle to 'tame' the feisty Katherina becomes a metaphor for the suppression of female contributions to the story of Easter 1916 and for the ways in which the 1937 Irish Constitution enshrined gender inequality, as for example in Article 41, which prohibited divorce and stressed the importance of women's 'life within the home'.[19]

Though Byrne's production had moments of levity, overall it depicted Petruchio's attempts to control his unwilling bride in strikingly grim terms, as instances of physical deprivation and psychological abuse visited upon a woman who clearly has no legal recourse nor socially accepted means of protest.[20] Only at the very end of the production, when Katherina begins to reprise 'Numbered in the Song' from a kneeling position, does Byrne's Petruchio seem to acquire a sense of shame at her abject submission. Moved by the lyrics, Petruchio tries to lift Katherina up, but instead she pulls him down with her. They remain kneeling for several bars as the entire cast takes up the lyrics to 'Numbered in the Song', and then the pair eventually rises to their feet together, suggesting, though not conclusively, that their relationship may continue on a more equal footing.

As Declan Kiberd has noted apropos of *The Irish Times* editorial, had Dublin's citizens followed the editorialist's advice to stay home and read Shakespeare, 'what they would have read about is Caliban's insurgency against Prospero, or Hamlet trying to put an end to a merely bureaucratic elite. They would have read, in fact, the story of their own Revival.'[21] Whether we look at the Easter Rising of 1916 or contemporary attempts to grapple with its fractured legacy, we find Irish writers, artists, and rebels not only reading Shakespeare's work but challenging and reinventing it, deploying his plays to express their own sociopolitical perspectives and concerns, as illustrated by Caroline Byrne's 1916-set production of *The Taming of the Shrew*. The Coliseum and much else were destroyed in Dublin in 1916, but the complex legacy of Shakespeare and the Easter Rising continues.

Figure 13   Production photograph from Maggie Smales's all-female *Henry V* (Upstage Centre, 41 Monkgate, York, 2015) (photograph by Michael J. Oakes).

CHAPTER 13

Forgotten Histories

The Barnbow Lasses in Maggie Smales's Henry V
(Upstage Centre, 41 Monkgate, York, 2015)

*Amy Lidster and Sonia Massai (LM) in
conversation with Maggie Smales*

LM: Could you tell us what is happening in this production photograph (Figure 13) and why you chose this image to start our discussion?
For this all-female production of *Henry V*, I developed a narrative frame within which the women workers of a local munitions factory during the First World War would enact the play. Drawing on a construct of Shakespeare often utilized to layer different worlds and make interesting juxtapositions, the notion was that the women would be exploring their own understanding and feelings of war from their distanced perspective. I wanted to explore the paradox that this devastating conflict ravaging the lives of millions also offered women opportunities and agency that would previously have been inconceivable.

The moment captured in the photograph is the key moment of transformation as we move from the narrative frame into the play. The women workers have arrived on shift (at the same time as the audience) and have been busy filling shells and singing their Barnbow Lasses song when a supervisor delivers a parcel to one of them (played by Claire Morley). The shop floor falls silent. The package confirms the dreaded news of the loss of a missing loved one and contains his military jacket. An act of solace ensues as a fellow worker urges her to don the jacket, prompted by a shared tacit notion that somehow by wearing his jacket she would be comforted.

What you can see in the photograph is what follows this moment. It is an event of transformation. In a foreshadowing of Henry's later speech in Act 4 Scene 1, when he is disguised as a common soldier and reflects on his role and the clothes of kingship, the jacket invests her with the authority it represents.

Not only does she receive the role through the wearing of the jacket but it is affirmed by those around her. There is a collective recognition of the transformation. No longer are they bearing witness to the grief of a colleague but beholding their leader, and they endow her with authority over them. This is represented by the piling rod that just moments ago was being used to ramrod toxic dynamite into shells and is now being offered as a mace of kingship. The transformation is a collective act and the workers have become subjects. A range of emotions and identities can be identified across the factory floor as Claire's Barnbow Lass enactment of Henry's reign begins.

At this point the play started. The lines of the prologue's Chorus were shared amongst the women as they asked the audience to imagine, as much as imagining for themselves, where they are now and what is happening within the world of their play. By this the audience also became complicit in the idea of the enactment.

LM: Why did you choose those distinctive red caps for your production and can you describe the role they played in this transformation?
The caps were styled to match those worn generally by munitions workers – although the ones worn by workers at the Barnbow factory near Leeds were not red. That idea came from a research visit I made to the Imperial War Museum. There, in a case all on its own, was a bright red factory cap. I knew immediately that I would use it as part of the design for my production.

They are a crucial prop within the play as they mark the change from factory worker to soldier: the women tuck them under their shoulder tabs to enhance the sense of a military uniform. Later, in the closing moments of the play, as the company as Chorus deliver an Epilogue that comments on the futility of war, the women who had all been casualties of the factory explosion removed their caps and placed them on the stage floor. As they left the space, all that remained was an image like that of a poppy field. It was important for me that the fate of the lost lives of women should be seen alongside those spoken of in the play and those of soldiers commemorated by the poppy. Throughout, the Barnbow women are always present and, at significant moments, their fictive personae bleed through as they speak the lines of the play. The audience is invited to share in their experience of enactment.

LM: Why was it important for you to set your production in the Barnbow munitions factory? What kinds of stories about conflict did you want to tell or recover?
In my original pitch to direct the first all-female cast for the York Shakespeare Project, I proposed the idea of *Henry V* through the eyes of women during the First World War, because the period was so inextricably linked with the changing role of women in western society.

This conflict afforded women of all ranks of society agency, a voice, financial independence, and a level of self-determination that could only have occurred through the absence of large numbers of men and the need for the everyday wheels of society to continue to turn. It put women in control of their whole domestic environment and gave them opportunities to have employment, to earn and keep their money, to control their finances, and to engage in pastimes that were previously forbidden or not thought of as feminine. For example, there were many local rugby and football teams which, sadly, were disbanded at the end of the war with the return of the men. For the duration of the conflict, they lived a very different life in almost every way. So there is a striking duality here: on the one hand, it was the most appalling time to be living through with fear ever present, but at the same time, many women were living an emancipated life that they could only have dreamed of before the war.

Whilst researching the occupations that women took up, I discovered there had been a very large munitions factory nearby. The Barnbow factory outside Leeds employed a staggering 16,000 people – 93 per cent of whom were women. They were recruited from a wide surrounding area, including our City of York. Special tracks were laid to run trains to transport the workers, some of whom had addresses that were only a few streets away from where we were to be performing.

Unsurprisingly, given the poor working conditions, there were many explosions in these factories. The explosion at Barnbow left thirty-five dead and many more injured and horribly maimed. Through the Barwick-in-Elmet Historical Society, I found stories such as that of a reclusive great aunt who had spent her years in front of the stove with a towel over her head. She was ashamed of her disfigurement. Today, a memorial to those who lost their lives in the factory explosion of 1916 can be found tucked away in York Minster, but the story at the time was considered unhelpful for morale and went unreported. Here was a story to recover – a story that belonged in York, but spoke to our realization of the contributions and sacrifices of women. I was now as committed to the retelling of their story as to that of Shakespeare's play.

Just as the recruits in Henry's army offered a place in history in exchange for their self-sacrifice, the Barnbow women must have recognized the irony and duality of their situation. The working women were provided with very little in the way of protective equipment. They were dealing with toxic chemicals, including cordite, which turned their skin yellow (hence the nickname 'canaries') and caused lung problems. They would easily have identified with the vulnerability of their counterparts in the play. At all times, the audience would be seeing the Barnbow Lass playing her role. As Shakespeare is exploring kingship through the character of Henry, so the Lasses are exploring the war itself and their place within it.

LM: Transformation seems to be a concept at the heart of your production – as it is in *Henry V* itself. How did you respond to Shakespeare's interests in the transformative power of conflict and how did you repurpose this idea in your production?

I wanted to emphasize that wartime brings about a collective transformation. Using the Barnbow Lasses narrative conveyed the notion that this is an ensemble production demonstrating that everyone undergoes a transformation during conflict. It is as much about the experiences of all the factory women as it is about Claire in her dual role as Barnbow worker and Henry V. They had conferred power to her that made them collectively responsible.

When Henry is trying to legitimize his claim to France in Act 1 Scene 2 by asking the Archbishop of Canterbury, 'May I with right and conscience make this claim?' (1.2.96), Claire pointedly addressed the whole company. She was seeking their consent: 'Is this what you want me to do?' This was not in any way to show Henry as weaker than in other interpretations, rather to show that leaders are the product of a collective will. They derive their authority from those around them. I think we all recognize this as a pertinent issue. Deeply controversial leaders such as those we know of today are an example of the power that is invested in them by voters, the people who have endowed that individual with seemingly limitless authority. Later, once the campaign has begun, Henry delivers his rallying speech to the troops outside Harfleur. The soldiers were ready to be whipped up – it was transactional, not one-way. Shakespeare provides us with a range of characters' responses that we explored using the women and their own stories.

It is evident from the way in which *Henry V* has been produced and utilized at various times that, throughout the play, there are questions either implied or spoken that offer scope for many directorial choices. These questions were at the heart of our approach. They culminate in the horror of the Battle of Agincourt, which in our production coalesced with the explosion at the factory.

LM: Could you talk a little more about that moment and its overall impact on the reception of your production?

That was the hardest bit to work on – to get it to work both as Agincourt and as the explosion at the factory. As we know, Shakespeare shied away from including full-scale staged battles, relying mostly on reports and scenes around the edges of the field of battle. I pursued this idea – that the absence of full-scale battle offers opportunity, rather than the opposite, and gives us a chance to utilize the imaginations of the audience. We worked on building the emotions of the women within their roles as the dawn of battle approaches. They know they are arriving at the climax of events and the imminent danger they are in. Through the use of sound (which I should mention was an important element throughout the production, both through the use of voice in song and recorded music), a crescendo provided the sense of battle and explosion. A large H-shaped structure made of ladders, which was part of the factory set, fell dramatically forwards, creating a sense of destruction. Through the haze it could be seen that most of the women had fallen. The eerie moments following were the only time in the production that I added to the text. As Claire read the list of those fallen in the battle, she continued adding the names of the Barnbow women who perished in the 1916 explosion. As she did so, the woman bearing that name rose and left the stage.

From this moment on, there was a colder atmosphere. The price of going to war was being counted. The enactment became more of a set of circumstances that must be played out to their conclusion. Questioning and enquiry ceased. Political consequences, retributions, and reparations were to be made. The women resignedly played their parts almost by rote. They no longer recognized themselves. Finally, following the last Chorus which was spoken by the youngest of the women, last seen as Montjoy, each company member laid their red cap on the stage in an act of remembrance of those lost in the widest sense against the soundtrack of Karl Jenkins's 'Te Deum'.

LM: Your production was staged a few years after the withdrawal of troops from Iraq. Did this contemporary wartime context inform your aims or production decisions?

There had been quite a fashion for setting Shakespeare inside our contemporary lives, and I wanted more distance. I often think you get a sharper view of current affairs and contexts when you are not looking directly at them. Perhaps in a similar way, Shakespeare gave his audience *Henry V*, rather than a play about the Nine Years' War in Ireland. I think the metaphor becomes more powerful when you detach the story from what we know. For my production, it was the female experience of war that particularly drove it and that, of course, has huge resonance with contemporary situations. I hope it spoke to the fact that accounts of the strength and endurance of women during conflict are still overlooked.

LM: How did audiences respond to your production and did you feel you were successful in inviting a different kind of reflection on *Henry V* that drew attention to the female experiences of war?

As we prepared the production, we encountered considerable local scepticism – and even unhelpful press – that focused on the perceived novelty of a bunch of women doing *Henry V*. As it turned out, our audiences saw beyond such banalities. They became immersed and invested in the women's stories. It was reviewed as 'moving, political and potent' (by Charles Hutchinson in the *York Evening Press*), as well as being named 'York Play of the Year for 2015'.

Our production was not just significant as an all-female production but because it invited a different perspective on the play and cast a spotlight on the neglected history of the Barnbow women during the First World War. I'm very pleased to see that there have been more all-female productions since and that a lot of things have changed in the past seven years. There's been a new monument erected on the site where the Barnbow factory once stood and a musical called *The Barnbow Canaries* toured the North. I'm really proud that we were part of this process of remembrance and that casting attitudes have changed.

COUNCIL OF WAR AT THE SIEGE OF TROY

Nestor	Mr. John Garside
Agamemnon	Mr. Arthur Ridley
Ulysses	Mr. Robert Speaight

Figure 14   George Whitlaw, 'Council of War at the Siege of Troy', 12 October 1938,
Punch, or The London Charivari (reproduced with permission of
Punch Cartoon Library/TopFoto).

CHAPTER 14

'Now Good or Bad, 'tis but the Chance of War'
Counter-Punching against Appeasement

Robert Sawyer

The cartoon of Figure 14 shows Shakespeare's Greek war council in *Troilus and Cressida* as staged in Michael Macowan's 1938 modern-dress production, in which the council was conceived as a modern high-level cabinet meeting, with Agamemnon, Nestor, and Ulysses played by Arthur Ridley, John Garside, and Robert Speaight, respectively. Since one of the most noted aspects of this production was its contemporary costuming, the drama and the cartoon provide a striking immediacy for the viewer about the twin themes of love and war in Shakespeare's play and in their own lives. In *Punch* magazine, the cartoon, titled the 'Council of War at the Siege of Troy', shows all three characters seated around a table 'on comfortable folding chairs' with a large military map in the background.[1] James Joseph Christy described this moment in the production as follows: 'Civilian amenities were observed; Ulysses cleaned his pince-nez, prepared a whiskey and soda for Agamemnon [and] cigars were passed round.'[2] Others thought Speaight 'resembled a professor called from the classroom to the conflict'.[3] Indeed, throughout the play, their elegant civilian clothes depicted them 'as cosmopolitan men of the world who would be more at home on the yachts of armament kings' than at some military headquarters.[4] The overall effect seemed to distance them from 'the immediate military milieu of the Greek camp'. Some observers even suggested that 'they were in some way connected with economic powers behind the military effort'.[5]

The women of the play were similarly modernized, but the use of modern dress for their roles was satirized by reviewers, who did not think it worked as effectively. According to one reviewer, Cassandra's 'black velvet evening frock made [her] dwindle from a frenzied prophetess to a young lady with fits'.[6] A review in *Punch*, alongside George Whitlaw's cartoon, agreed, dismissing Cressida as 'the girl who did not want to go home', and concluding that the 'love-scenes, which should be the most independent of costume or setting in fact suffered most' through the modern dress version.[7] Moreover, Cressida's 'swift inconsistency in the Greek camp with Diomedes', claimed the *Punch* review, 'did not emerge as the important part of the play it is plainly intended to be'.[8]

The cartoon illustration by Whitlaw underscores Macowan's modernization of *Troilus and Cressida* and the topicality of his production. After studying at the Glasgow School of Art, Whitlaw (1887–1959) joined the *Glasgow Evening News*. During the First World War, he served in the Tank Corps and, after the Armistice, he worked for *Punch*, where the cartoon above appeared on 12 October 1938. Perhaps due to his service in the First World War, Whitlaw was chosen to add illustrations to a review of Macowan's innovative modern-dress production of *Troilus and Cressida* when it premiered at the Westminster Theatre in London on the evening of 21 September 1938, just hours before Neville Chamberlain's second visit to Germany in an attempt to avert war. In fact, in the same issue of *Punch*, there are numerous cartoon and graphic illustrations alluding to the political and military tensions that characterized the immediate pre-war period, along with nine separate mentions of the so-called 'Peace Treaty', historically referred to as the Munich Agreement. For example, in a two-column 'Letter to the Editor', entitled 'Peace After the Storm', the correspondent complains that Mr Chamberlain's treaty 'finally convinced Herr Hitler that he could gain more for himself by absorbing the Czechs with bluster than by destroying them with bombs: and he has got that gain'.[9]

A survey of this single issue's contents reveals how the threat of impending war was a key focus for the editors of the magazine. On page 404, for instance, there is a poem entitled 'What Have You Done to Me, England?' that ends with a consolation line between two lovers – 'But, oh, they signed the Peace!' – with the title in this context ironically criticizing the Munich Agreement. Just below this poem is a short piece called 'Fishing Notes', where the writer, in a sort of dramatic monologue, states, 'I too have fished. I know the dampness and the emptiness. I see M. Chamberlain fishing all night and catching nothing.'[10] Two pages later, a half-page cartoon of a woman in her bedchamber adjusting her new gasmask sits above a lyric called 'Song of Peace', which declares,

It's peace!
The gas-masks are distributed;
It's peace!
Ten millions are contributed.
We've dug up lots of trenches in everybody's garden,
We've commandeered the Underground without your leave or pardon.[11]

The song ends with '[w]e're going to use diplomacy for every strained relation … to live on friendly terms with each and every nation – / And we've just completed all our plans for swift evacuation / It's peace, It's peace!' Overall, this song critiques a sense of the naïve optimism, capturing the futility of political machinations underlying the negotiation of peace and solidifying, instead, the impending threat of war.

The following page is taken up by a full-size cartoon, called 'Four's Company', depicting Hitler, Mussolini, Daladier, and Chamberlain, and the four are toasting 'all together' under a portrait of Edvard Beneš, and claiming, paradoxically, 'Well, before we go on, here's to Self-sacrifice!'[12] And just ten pages before the Whitlaw cartoon, printed under a cartoon of a diplomat holding a copy of the Munich Agreement, which allowed the German annexation of the Sudetenland, the caption reads, 'H'm – As Sir Philip Francis would have said in 1801, "It is a peace everybody is glad of, though nobody is proud of."'[13] The connection between the ongoing appeasement of Hitler by Chamberlain could not be mistaken.

This issue of *Punch* reflects its characteristic brand of political and social satire. *Punch*, from its birth in 1841 as a British weekly magazine, had never hesitated to satirize most social classes, from the elite to the labouring workers. The magazine was partly responsible for the modern usage of the word 'cartoon' and its illustrations more often than not packed a 'punch'.[14] Co-founded by Henry Mayhew and the engraver Ebenezer Landells, with Mark Lemon co-editing with Mayhew, it was originally subtitled *The London Charivari*, a reference to a similarly sarcastic, humorous magazine in France entitled *Le Charivari*. The main title 'Punch' was inspired not only from the famous English puppet of Punch and Judy fame, but also from Lemon's joke that 'punch [is] nothing without Lemon'.[15]

Although other satirical journals, such as *Fun*, initially competed with *Punch* for readership, it veered away – by the early twentieth century and the outbreak of the First World War – from its more subversive origins, and it fell in line with other print media of the time by emphasizing a patriotic stance. By this time, however, it was a national institution. It continued to thrive financially and to influence British society by using humour as a protection against its sometimes unpopular ideas. Indeed, two of its editors – John Tenniel and Bernard Partridge – were awarded knighthoods during the war, mainly for the political cartoons they printed. Although it acquired a reputation between the wars as 'a magazine produced by schoolmasters for schoolmasters', it sold well until the late 1980s, but then it limped along until 1992, when it temporarily closed down. Revived by an Egyptian businessman in 1996, it shut down again in 2002.[16]

It would not be too overstated to describe the issue containing Whitlaw's cartoon, at the height of *Punch*'s popularity in the interwar period, as 'an assemblage'.[17] In graphic narratives, as Lisa Diedrich points out, such texts 'share a preoccupation with exploring how subjects come into being in relation to experiences and events that are both ordinary and extraordinary, such as childhood, war, illness, trauma, shame, stigma, love and hope'.[18] The cartoon I noted in the *Punch* issue of the four political leaders ('Four's Company'), as well as the Whitlaw image, do what any graphic assemblage attempts to do: whether as a cartoon panel or, in this case, a single image, the artist attempts to capture or 'freeze one segment in what is in reality an uninterrupted flow of action' – for our purposes, the Whitlaw image for the Macowan play, and the others for the 'flow of action' leading up to another world war.[19] In the rest of this essay, I argue that Whitlaw's cartoon, in fact, points to 'an uninterrupted flow of action' between the cartoonist's take on Macowan's production and Macowan's take on Shakespeare's *Troilus and Cressida*, and that the cartoon and the production in turn connect this specific mobilization of Shakespeare to the 'flow of action' in the political and military spheres that led to the outbreak of another global conflict. The extent to which this type of mobilization of Shakespeare impacted public opinion can only be partly reconstructed from the archival evidence available to us, but it shows that Shakespeare occupied a central role within the debate that accompanied the events leading up to the outbreak of the Second World War.

§

Shakespeare's play addresses, among other themes, the notion of true love and virtuous behaviour, while employing the Trojan War as the backdrop for the story of Troilus, the youngest son of King Priam, and his attraction, and possibly true affection, for a Trojan woman named Cressida, whose father, Calchas, has defected to the Greek side. The play goes on to interrogate issues of conquest bound up in both physical battle and sexual wooing: honour, fidelity, degree, and so forth. Yet, the play's focus on the element of 'Injurious time' (4.4.41) may be the most compelling theme, and it was certainly the main concern highlighted by Macowan's contemporary setting.

Macowan's three-act version of *Troilus and Cressida* seemed to many, as we shall see, a production imbued with the resonance of contemporary events. According to a story Macowan liked to repeat, when he and his associates were passing by Buckingham Palace after the second performance of the play, they noted crowds of people cheering Chamberlain. It was the night when Chamberlain believed he had secured the now-notorious 'Peace in our Time'. In a later interview about this moment, Macowan claimed that 'all he could think of was how glad he was he had done the play the way he had, and that Thersites' line, "a burning devil take them!" [5.2.192–3] kept running through his head'.[20]

Besides the use of modern dress, Macowan's incorporation of direct addresses to the audience, particularly in relation to the character of Thersites, helped him ground this production in its contemporary context. While Thersites' voice in the play almost always belongs to a sour, cynical character, Macowan further defined this character by portraying him as a war journalist – a 'mordant, maggoty product of New Grub-street', claimed Ivor Brown.[21] Such a portrayal, and Macowan's decision to assign him the Prologue, strengthened his connection with the audience, his 'function as a reporter soliciting the sympathy' of the spectators or the 'fair beholders', as he flatteringly calls them at line twenty-six of the prologue.[22] In Macowan's own words, he cast Thersites as an 'embittered and cynical kind of narrator, who would guide the audience and comment on the action'.[23]

While other Shakespearean directors had recently employed modern dress for their productions (Barry Jackson, most notably), I would argue that others had used their contemporary costumes to facilitate access to and understanding of Shakespeare's play, while Macowan used modern dress for political purposes. This specific use of modern dress, which was in turn adopted by later directors of this play, was noted immediately by critics for its ability to make Thersites' character come alive.[24] For instance, Desmond MacCarthy felt that Thersites was 'much more *real* than [he] had ever been before' (emphasis in original), so that the character was reanimated, his bitter sarcasm seeming like an appropriate condemnation of the sabre-rattling taking place simultaneously in both the Westminster Theatre and in the accelerating levels of aggression threatening to take place in Europe.[25]

The militaristic reading and currency of the production were also shaped by a contemporary art exhibition: the display of Pablo Picasso's painting 'Guernica' – the most prominent testament to the brutality of war on a civilian population – at the nearby Whitechapel Art Gallery only a week into the show and on the same day as the Munich Agreement was signed. Intended to raise funds for the rebels resisting Franco's troops in the Spanish Civil War, the painting had toured a number of towns in England, including Oxford, Leeds, and Manchester, before arriving in London.

The timing of the exhibition in London is significant: some critics drew attention to the fact that 'theatergoers [could] see the painting in the afternoon and Macowan's meditation on the disillusions of war in the evening'.[26] Also noteworthy are details that the painting shares with Macowan's production. For example, the seemingly dismembered soldier, located below the central image of the gored horse in Picasso's painting, seems to be grasping an ancient, broken sword, while the multiple daggers, which replace the tongues screaming and streaming from the mouths of the horse, the bull, and the five grieving women, represent another time-less weapon of war. I suggest that the swords and daggers in the painting, not unlike those used in the Trojan–Greek conflict, collapse ancient and modern warfare, a prominent feature of Macowan's production as well.

Contemporary military machines of destruction, such as the German Junkers JU-88 bombers, are also invoked in both painting and produc-tion. By riddling his production with the noise of machine guns and of anti-aircraft fire, Macowan used sound as well as sight to collapse historical time into the present tense of his production. In turn, these aural and visual effects connected his production with the strafing and carpet bombing of the Basque village. Picasso's monochromatic palette of grey, black, brown, and white (which was unusual for him) is similarly echoed in the background design of Macowan's production. According to Frances Shirley, designer Peter Goffin's sets used 'skeletal frameworks against a dark backdrop to sug-gest contemporary locales', and the production also incorporated binoculars, battle-field telephones, and long lengths of barbed wire surrounding some scenes.[27] I would add that the flaring lighting and dark background in the production may have also been influenced by stark and realist photographs reprinted in newspapers and newsreels taken from current battle zones.

In Macowan's production, however, even though the background appeared monochromatic in most scenes, the warriors looked like colour-ful tin soldiers, more decorous than deadly. Shirley claims that the Greeks wore 'pale blue' uniforms, while the Trojans wore 'British Khaki'.[28] Working from production notes and a personal interview with Macowan, Christy instead claims that the Greeks wore 'gray-green' uniforms and the Trojans wore 'sky blue'.[29] Whatever shade of blue or grey Macowan's Greeks wore in this production, he admitted in an interview that there was to be 'a faint suggestion of German about them', what he called a 'little hangover from the First World War'.[30] In any case, Macowan argued that neither side – the Greek/German nor the Trojan/British – was portrayed positively, as both 'were considered morally wrong in their espousal of war: one was consciously cynical, the other, thoughtlessly pugilistic'.[31]

Macowan's vision for this production, which had clearly been inflected by his assessment of the events that led to the outbreak of the Second World War, was crystallized by Thersites' role as a mordantly omniscient narrator. Taking neither side, he mediated between three levels of signification, all influenced by a sense of time and timing: the actor performing in real time before the audience, the contemporary historical context, and the classical past represented in the play. Macowan's production was also one of the very first to have both Pandarus and Thersites onstage simultaneously during the final scene. This directorial choice makes sense for a number of reasons. As Matthew Greenfield observes, 'the bastard Thersites speaks from a cosmopolitan, extranational perspective', one that allows him to root 'alternately for the Trojans and the Greeks' during the 'climactic battle' scene in part because his 'illegitimacy liberates him from the ideological claim of the nation, whose central trope imagines citizens as brothers'.[32] Macowan's Thersites also spoke in front of the curtain during some scene changes. Played in this manner, this character evoked the play's 'power to disturb' settled notions of any kind, particularly 'nationalism's narratives', so often broadcast on the new 'wireless' and proclaimed in large type on numerous newspapers.[33]

To conclude, one could therefore argue that the Whitlaw image with which I began, with its depiction of fashionably dressed ambassadors and neatly pressed and uniformed commanders, captured Macowan's cynical but clear-sighted assessment of the devastating roles that key figures in Shakespeare's Troy and on the world stage were about to play in the unravelling of any sense of order on a global scale.

Figure 15   Signed photograph of Fay Compton and John Gielgud at Kronborg Castle, Elsinore, 1939 (Odense Bys Museer/Holger Damgaard).

CHAPTER 15

'Precurse of Feared Events'
A Pre-War Hamlet at Elsinore, 1939

Anne Sophie Refskou

A photograph (Figure 15) shows a man and a woman in front of a stone wall – a wall that bears a portrait, also in stone, of William Shakespeare. The wall is old and weathered, while Shakespeare's portrait is smoother and marble-like. The portrait looks as if it might have been inspired by the Martin Droeshout engraving that adorns the title page of the 1623 First Folio and perhaps also by Shakespeare's funerary monument in Holy Trinity Church at Stratford-upon-Avon with the addition of the quill in the right hand. Underneath the portrait is some text, just legible, which gives us a clue to where the photograph was taken. The writing in Danish tells us that 'in the Renaissance Shakespeare rewrote the fate of one prince Amleth, who lived in Jutland before the Viking age and whose story had first been written down by Saxo in the Middle Ages'. Shakespeare's version, the text further claims, attached Hamlet's fate to 'this castle, thereby securing eternal fame for the Danish prince and worldwide recognition of the name of Elsinore'.

The photograph, taken at Kronborg Castle in the Danish town of Elsinore (Helsingør), north of Copenhagen, is set in a gilded frame indicating that it too would have hung on a wall at one point and was perhaps considered an object of some historical or personal value. The chipped frame and the small brown stains on the glass, on the other hand, suggest that such value has decreased, or that the story told by the photograph has receded into the past without someone finding it necessary to reframe or restore it. The man and woman are dressed in mid-twentieth-century fashion, the woman in a day dress, the man in a light jacket and tie. His two-toned shoes give off a hint of debonair stylishness. On the ground in front of the stone plaque with Shakespeare's portrait is a large wreath recalling those usually laid at memorial monuments, and the woman holds a bouquet of flowers, which she may be about to lay next to the wreath. Her gaze is directed towards the wreath and her expression is serious, while the man looks over her shoulder and out of the photograph. On the yellowed border inside the frame, two signatures reveal their identity: 'Fay Compton' and 'John Gielgud, Hamlet, Kronborg, 1939'.

In the summer of 1939, shortly before the outbreak of the Second World War, John Gielgud's production of *Hamlet* played at Kronborg Castle, with Gielgud in the title role and Fay Compton as Ophelia. In this essay I want to suggest that the photograph of Gielgud and Compton – this slightly faded image in its tired frame – is a repository for several meanings and resonances that link Shakespeare to a deeply tense moment in European history. Cultural artefacts or objects that we label as 'pre-war', especially ones that represent human subjects, put us, as later historical subjects, in a strange position. We want these figures from the past to convey certain feelings of foreboding ahead of the catastrophe that they are yet to experience and can therefore only gesture at in uncertain and indirect ways. The photograph of Gielgud and Compton does not speak directly to us of what was about to happen. Nor does the photograph seem to invite any emotional empathy from us as viewers with what we imagine its subjects might feel. If anything, it seems to warn us of the dangers of projection and inference involved in interpreting the material past from our own standpoint.

However, 'war' is nonetheless present in the photograph. Not just because of hindsight but because the photograph performs and participates in acts related to what Irena R. Makaryk, drawing on influential scholarly engagement with the 'spectrality' of theatre, calls '"ghosting", repetition, memory, recycling, and "double-vision"'.[1] These are useful concepts, Makaryk argues, when interpreting Shakespeare's cultural presence during this conflict, partly because 'Shakespeare's "return" in the Second World War was "haunted" by the extensive uses of his plays in the first'.[2] The First World War might also make a 'haunting' appearance in this photograph, as I will seek to show; but more importantly, the concepts Makaryk invokes provide a framework for discussing the larger set of events of which the photograph is part – events that seem to involve acts of '"ghosting", repetition, memory, recycling, and "double-vision"' to an extraordinary degree.

'Precurse of Feared Events'

The Renaissance castle of Kronborg in Elsinore, built in the early 1580s, has a long-standing association with Shakespeare's setting for *Hamlet*. It is a site that inevitably produces a kind of double-vision for the

Shakespeare-orientated visitor when the play's fictional setting is projected onto the historical buildings. Like other such sites that claim a connection with Shakespeare's plays – 'Juliet's house' in Verona, for instance – Kronborg's fame relies on Shakespeare's imagination rather than on its historical, material presence, but this has not diminished the castle's attractiveness for tourists. In the 1930s, a cooperative of stakeholders, which included the Danish Tourist Association, had precisely this attraction factor in mind when they initiated a tradition that persists to this day: outdoor *Hamlet* performances in Kronborg's beautiful quadrangular courtyard by theatre companies invited from abroad.[3]

The first of these performances, in 1937, was by the Old Vic company directed by Tyrone Guthrie and starring Laurence Olivier and Vivien Leigh as Hamlet and Ophelia. It was followed in 1938 by Gustaf Gründgens's German-language *Hamlet*, with Marianne Hoppe as Ophelia and an ensemble from Berlin's state theatre, and the year after by Gielgud's production. Prior to opening at Kronborg on 6 July 1939, Gielgud's production had been the last show at the Lyceum in London before the intended closure of that theatre. As it happens, it also became the final *Hamlet* to play at Kronborg for some time, because a few months later, on 1 September, Adolf Hitler invaded Poland and declarations of war on Germany followed from Britain and France. By spring 1940, Denmark was occupied by Nazi Germany, and German troops were stationed at Kronborg. For the next five years, the castle's visitors would not be famous actors from abroad attracting the excited attention of the locals but uniformed soldiers guarding the entrance and installing anti-aircraft guns on the ramparts.

These events were of course unforeseen both by Gielgud and the actors who performed in Kronborg's courtyard in 1939 and by the audiences who watched them, but knowledge of Nazi Germany's increasingly aggressive behaviour and the international conflict clearly hung heavily in the air. The opening scene of a *Hamlet* performance at Kronborg always produces an interesting negotiation between fiction and reality – both for actors and for audiences – as Shakespeare's 'Elsinore' meets its geographical/material double. But of the many *Hamlet* performances that have taken place at the castle it is hard to imagine one where the opening scene would also be so poignantly resonant with historical reality as in Gielgud's production. The play famously opens with a nightly meeting between two guards whose mutual fearful jumpiness is captured in Barnardo's 'Who's there?' and Francisco's quick retort, 'Nay answer me. Stand and unfold yourself' (1.1.1–2). We soon learn the cause of their anxiety: the appearance on previous nights of the ghost of old king Hamlet on the platform where they watch. But we also learn that the Ghost's appearance is somehow inextricably linked to fears of an approaching war. Not only does the Ghost appear to the guards and Horatio in a 'fair and war-like form' (1.1.47), prompting them to remember the dead king's military achievements in the past – 'Such was the very armour he had on / When he th'ambitious Norway combated' (1.1.60–61) – but its appearance is interpreted by them as the sign of a new war. As Horatio explains, young Fortinbras of Norway is amassing an army and preparing an invasion of Denmark to regain the lands and honour lost by his father to the Danish king in the past. Barnardo concludes that the Ghost's appearance must signify this impending invasion and Horatio reinforces that interpreta-tion by invoking 'the most high and palmy state of Rome' (1.1.113), where shortly before the assassination of Julius Caesar similar signs and omens would appear:

> And even the like precurse of feared events,
> As harbingers preceding still the fates
> And prologue to the omen coming on,
> Have heaven and earth together demonstrated
> Unto our climatures and countrymen.   (1.1.121–25)

The Arden editors of the play, Ann Thompson and Neil Taylor, note that, because Barnardo and Horatio's lines from 112–25 are printed only in the second quarto text of *Hamlet*, some editors have argued that Shakespeare did not intend them to remain in the play and that they do nothing to advance the action.[4] But Thompson and Taylor also add that John Gielgud firmly believed that these lines were necessary to create suspense for the audience between the first and second appearances of the Ghost in the scene. It therefore seems reasonable to assume that, given their resonance in 1939, rather than being cut, they would indeed have been included in performances of Gielgud's *Hamlet* at Kronborg and perhaps prompted actors and audiences to absorb the deep anxiety of the scene into their own present. Moreover, much of the anxiety and foreboding produced by the scene comes not just from the characters' knowledge of an impend-ing conflict but also from their futile attempts to ascertain their worst fears: 'If thou art privy to thy country's fate / Which happily foreknowing may avoid, / Oh speak' (1.1.133–35). The characters, in other words, are suspended in a particularly tense moment between one war and the next, in which the memory of the past serves as forewarning but does not pro-vide any form of certainty. In his book on Shakespearean scholarship and cultural production during the years between the two World Wars, Robert Sawyer looks to another moment of suspension in *Hamlet* to conceptualize the interwar era: the closet scene in Act 3, midway in the play, which he argues, 'looks back to the past even while trying to focus on the future, all captured in an infinite moment in the dramatic present'.[5] To Sawyer the closet scene presents an all-too-brief moment of lull in the play, before tragic events resume and escalate, which helpfully parallels the temporal experience of the interwar years, when there was both hope that a new war might be prevented and increasing frustration that it might not. At Kronborg in the summer of 1939, that period and any hope that it might have held were coming to an end. The threat for Denmark was not from Norway in the north, as in Shakespeare's play, but from the border that Jutland, the peninsula that forms a major part of Denmark's geography, shares with Germany to the south. Although Denmark and Germany had signed a treaty of non-aggression in May 1939, Denmark's geographical position as a stepping stone towards Norway (where the Germans could both acquire ice-free harbours to control the North Atlantic and thwart any British/French countermeasure) made it vulnerable to an invasion that it had no military means to resist. Indeed, when Germany invaded with a surprise attack in the early hours of 9 April 1940, Danish resistance only lasted a few hours, and most Danes woke up to find that their country had been occupied without any signs of fighting.

The anticipation of fearful events at Kronborg in 1939 might also have been accentuated by recent local memories: many of those welcoming Gielgud's company would have seen the German performance of *Hamlet* the previous year, which had not only been uneasily framed by the presence of Hitler's photograph in the printed programme but also by the unannounced arrival at the show of Hitler's minister and designated successor, Hermann Göring.[6] Hitler's photograph appears to be the result of some diplomatic tip-toeing around the fact that the previous year's programme for the Old Vic production had included photographs of the British Queen Consort Elizabeth and the Danish King Christian X as joint patrons. Hitler did not join the Danish king as patron in 1938, but his photograph (on the page following that of the Danish king) signals a certain political anxiety on the part of the organizers.[7] The German visit to Kronborg had not gone unnoticed in Britain either, judging by references to it in the British newspapers that later covered Gielgud's visit. The correspondent for the *Daily News*, Lionel Hale, wrote home about the reception of the English players in Elsinore, comparing the warmth they encountered with the reception of the German players the previous year: 'Whether for

political or other reasons, they have won a popularity not so warmly given
to the German company which last year played "Hamlet" at Kronborg
Castle', while his colleague from the *Daily Herald* was more explicitly
antagonistic in his comparison:

> When John Gielgud and his company do "Hamlet" at Elsinore this week
> they will perform in the castle courtyard where, not long ago, Goering sat in
> the front row, to watch a similar performance. Grundgers [*sic*], the German
> actor, with whom Goering's wife used to act, was playing Hamlet there,
> and not nearly such a success as Laurence Olivier had been during his visit.
> So Goering went along to give the German actor a hand. Not even that
> drew the crowds.

The fact that Kronborg hosted two English and one German *Hamlet*
in the three years immediately before the Second World War looks like
an extraordinary intersection of cultural and world politics. Another
chapter was being written in the long-standing 'battle' between England
and Germany over national-cultural ownership of Shakespeare, a battle
which, as scholars, including Ostrowski in this collection (Chapter 11),
have demonstrated, was fought vehemently during the First World War,
when Shakespeare was appropriated for propagandistic purposes by both
nations.[8] In this context, Kronborg – a site powerfully associated with
the (fictional) origins for *Hamlet* – takes on the appearance of a new
'battlefield', where the English and the Germans might once again stake
their respective claims to 'our' and '*unser*' Shakespeare, repeating the
conflicts of the past. It was hardly a coincidence that Gielgud's visit took
place under the auspices of the newly founded British Council, whose
chairman, Lord Lloyd, wrote a message in the printed programme emphatically stressing the cordial relations and even the common ancestry between
Britain and Denmark. In this cultural and political conflict, Denmark was
still treading on diplomatic eggshells, hoping to stay neutral in relation to
both Britain and Germany – or to an extent, at least. The British newspapers that reported the much warmer welcome received by the British
players might have been exaggerating, but Danish reviews of Gielgud's
performance were certainly enthusiastic. The printed programme contained a welcome from the Danish prime minister, Thorvald Stauning,
which reads as a carefully neutral response to Lord Lloyd, but it is followed
by a warmer welcome in the form of a poetic 'prologue' in both Danish
and English written by the Danish writer Tom Kristensen. I have argued
elsewhere that Kristensen's prologue appropriates lines from Gertrude's
welcome to Rosencrantz and Guildenstern in Act 2 of Shakespeare's play
and recontextualizes the implied urgency of those lines to fit the present

moment.⁹ Kristensen's words seem to convey – in a cleverly veiled manner – the fearful dilemma that was felt by some, if not all, Danes at this
moment:

> Welcome, John Gielgud and your actors, welcome! Moreover that we much
> did long to see you, the need we have to use you did provoke our hasty
> sending. Something have you heard of Hamlet, Prince of Denmark's trans-
> formations and of the manifold interpretations which have confused us and
> confuse us still.¹⁰

Not only does Kristensen repeat Shakespeare's words, but the prologue
also brings the concept of repetition – 'the manifold interpretations' and
allusions to their memory – into play with a potentially political message.
As described in one of the Danish national newspapers following Gielgud's
premiere on 6 July, Kristensen's words were also performed as an actual
prologue to the performance itself, spoken on the stage by the popular
Danish actress Else Skouboe.¹¹ Some in the audience would undoubtedly
know that plans had existed for a *Hamlet* production featuring Skouboe as
Ophelia together with Leslie Howard to be performed in 1938 and that the
German players had in fact been invited when those plans fell through.¹²
What is interesting to observe here is how artists and artistic production
supply the diplomatic discourse and find alternative ways to express what
is politically sensitive and therefore impossible to verbalize explicitly. This
easily overlooked diplomatic role of the arts during the interwar years
brings us back to the photograph of Gielgud and Compton.

The event captured in the photograph was the unveiling, on 8 July, of
the portrait-plaque of Shakespeare by the Danish artist Einar Frank-Utzon,
which took place as part of the English visit. The unveiling was witnessed by
the Danish interior minister and the British minister to Denmark and
punctuated with speeches by the official dignitaries as well as by Gielgud and
the Danish author Karen Blixen, who became close friends after the visit.¹³
The stone plaque was placed near the main entrance to the castle, pointedly
making Shakespeare's presence at Kronborg more 'material' than it had
ever been before. Its purpose was to serve as a memorial to Shakespeare,
which explains much of what goes on in the photograph: Gielgud and
Compton are engaged in an act of commemoration signified by the wreath
and the flowers. A commemorative gesture at a site that only holds a fictive connection with Shakespeare might look slightly misplaced or unmoti-
vated, unless of course the motivation was something that the photograph
does not reveal directly. At a glance the photograph's subject – two famous
actors celebrate Shakespeare's contribution to Kronborg's fame – is perfectly

neutral. But a closer look, combined with the contextual description above, turns the photograph into a 'performance' of interwar cultural diplomacy in which Shakespeare provides the occasion for subtly political manoeuvres on the part of both the Danes and the British visitors. Shakespeare's presence in the photograph is not neutral either, because it recalls political uses of Shakespeare during the previous war. Moreover, the 'commemoration' of Shakespeare here is also an act that repeats or 'ghosts' another kind of more familiar commemoration: the kind that would have been performed at memorials for fallen soldiers of the First World War. And, at the same time, it uncannily predicts future commemorations for those who would fall during the Second World War. In other words, the photograph offers several kinds of 'double-vision' of Shakespeare and 'war' through a complex act of 'ghosting, repetition, memory, and recycling', which also makes it representative of the whole set of events that included Gielgud's *Hamlet* performance at Kronborg.

'Horatio and Laertes Are Both in the Army'

On 6 March 1940, Gielgud wrote a letter from London to Karen Blixen in Denmark. Asking her to remember him to his 'many kind friends in Copenhagen', he ends the letter with 'Horatio and Laertes are both in the army, but Jack Hawkins is coming with me to the Vic to play Edmund in King Lear'.[14] Glen Byam Shaw, who played Horatio at Kronborg, joined the Royal Scots in 1940, serving in Burma, while Harry Andrews, who played Laertes, had joined the Royal Artillery as early as October 1939. By 1941, Jack Hawkins, who had doubled as the Ghost of Hamlet's father and Claudius, had joined the Royal Welch Fusiliers. Marius Goring, who doubled as First Player and Osric, joined the British Army in 1940 and later the intelligence staff of SHAEF (Supreme Headquarters Allied Expeditionary Force). John Robinson, who opened the play as Marcellus and ended it as Fortinbras, was in the Reconnaissance Corps and took part in the 1944 D-Day landings in Normandy. Gielgud and George Howe, who played Polonius, joined ENSA (Entertainments National Service Association) and toured extensively to provide British troops with entertainment. When some of these actors returned to their careers after the war, it was to play soldiers and officers in 1950s war films. Jack Hawkins, who as the Ghost had embodied the foreshadowing of 'feared events' at Kronborg in 1939, became one of post-war cinema's most popular portrayers of military characters – yet another instance of the resonant relationship between war-themed fiction and wartime reality explored in this essay. And at Kronborg, the *Hamlet* performances would recommence in 1946, fittingly with a visit from Denmark's Nordic neighbour, Norway, a country that – taking on a role rather different from the one given it by Shakespeare – had also endured, and survived, occupation by an unwelcome army. To Denmark the Norwegian visit represented a strengthening of Nordic bonds after the war. But Danish prime minister Knud Kristensen, like his pre-war predecessor, welcomed the players in the programme, while acknowledging that their visit also served as a reminder of the difference between Norway's coherent resistance to Nazi occupation and the relative indecisiveness of official Danish policy – an indecisiveness that Kristensen characterizes as 'Hamlet-like' in the 1946 programme. Shakespeare's pre-war role at Kronborg continued in this way to evolve in a post-war context through acts and patterns of continuously resonant repetition that extended far beyond the castle walls.

Figure 16   Photograph of the Old Vic Travelling Theatre Company in Trealaw,
Wales at the Settlement Hall (1941) (Reproduced by permission of the Imperial War
Museum, IWM D 5658).

CHAPTER 16

But What Are We Fighting For?
Shakespeare, Economics, and the Arts in Wartime Britain

Ros King

A photograph (Figure 16), taken in 1941, shows a large hall in Trealaw in the South Wales coalfields in use as a feeding centre for destitute families. In the background, members of the Old Vic theatre company, director and actor Lewis Casson (in the dark suit), and stage manager Paul Smythe (kneeling) are setting up for a performance. Their tour of Euripides' *Medea* and George Bernard Shaw's *Candida* starred Dame Sybil Thorndike (married to Casson) and was underwritten by CEMA, the Council for the Encouragement of Music and the Arts, established by the government in late 1939 to bolster morale and preserve British culture. Other photographs in this Ministry of Information series show Casson in an old furniture van transporting scenery and costumes past colliery pitheads, Thorndike encouraging miners to come to the show, and actors sharing a meal with the family they were staying with.

The poverty on show in this photograph marks the economic and social failure of early twentieth-century Britain. Most of the population had no more than a basic elementary education and there was severe unemployment. The school leaving age had been raised to fourteen in 1918 but attempts to raise it further had failed. The wartime coalition government commissioned William Beveridge to investigate, and his report, recommending reform of education, health, and social security, would be published in 1942. Various voluntary organizations were trying to fill the gaps. The Workers Educational Association had been offering evening classes since 1903. The Educational Settlements Association, sponsored by the Rowntree Trust, offered classes in economics, psychology, and literature; craft training in pottery, dressmaking or cobbling; clubs for drama, music, even Morris dancing, although they were dismissed as the 'slums of adult education' by W. E. Williams, co-founder of Penguin Books, Secretary to the Institute of Adult Education, and responsible for 'Art for the People' touring exhibitions in the 1930s. It was John Maynard Keynes, the economist, art collector, founder of the Cambridge Arts Theatre, and Chairman of CEMA (1942–46) who, in trying to solve the problem of balancing supply and demand without incurring either inflation or unemployment, began, obliquely at first, to make an economic case for arts funding. After all, ancient Egypt had invested in pyramids, and the Middle Ages in 'cathedrals and dirges'.[1]

Shakespeare at the Old Vic

Still regarded as antithetical activities, the Old Vic had been feeding the bodies and minds of working-class people in South London since 1880, when Emma Cons had reopened the old Coburg Theatre as the Royal Victoria Coffee and Music Hall. Morley College's evening classes soon opened backstage, and there were concerts of operatic excerpts. Cons's niece, Lilian Baylis (1874–1937), who had inherited the building, started performances of Shakespeare shortly before the First World War, while West End theatres turned to revue and light entertainment. Baylis, who was convinced that nothing but 'the best' was good enough for 'my people', began staging whole seasons of Shakespeare plays, covering the absence of male actors away at the front by employing women, including Thorndike, for leading male roles.[2] Post-war, the opportunity to play several Shakespearean roles in a single season was attractive to both male and female actors, who worked at the Vic for very much less than they could command in the West End.

The celebration of Shakespeare's birthday was an Old Vic tradition, but Baylis marked the tercentenary of the publication of the 'First Folio' in 1923 by mounting a cycle of the complete canon of Shakespeare plays, some of which were rarely or never performed at that time. Subsequently, her trustees' purchase of the rundown Sadler's Wells theatre, in an equally unfashionable area of London north of the river, gave her opera and ballet companies (the latter led by Ninette de Valois) their own home, and allowed more space for Shakespeare at the Vic. There were school matinée performances, and the company also began to tour. Thorndike reports Baylis as saying, 'London isn't *all* of England … the grimy, ugly places in the north, all the poor darlings working so hard in the smoke … that's England too … and don't you actors forget it.'[3]

An indomitable and god-fearing woman, Baylis's focus was on serving her audiences (she gave the same no-nonsense helping hand to the inhabitants of the St Giles leper home in Essex). Seats were cheap and houses were generally full. She might sometimes fall out with those she employed, but the opera and ballet companies she founded, the visibility of the Old Vic as a home for Shakespeare, and the ethos she inspired of the arts as a public good survived her.

The contrast with conventional theatre-going was stark. A collection of cartoons by Pont, *The British Character*, reprinted from *Punch* magazine, takes a gently satirical view of middle-class life. One, entitled 'Love of Arriving Late at Theatrical Productions', shows the view from the back of the stalls in a West End theatre; everyone in evening dress. Two late-comers have caused an entire row to rise from their seats, completely blocking the view of the stage. Other examples of British character in the collection range from 'Strong tendency to become doggy' to 'Importance of not being Intellectual'. A forward by novelist E. M. Delafield pulls no punches: 'every Englishman is an average Englishman: it's a national characteristic', and being average, he will enjoy the cartoons 'without having to think'.[4]

In 1938, 'thinking' might have involved: reflecting on the Munich agreement, by which the League of Nations had agreed to Hitler's annexation of the Sudetenland area of Czechoslovakia; remembering the failure of sanctions to prevent Mussolini's invasion of Abyssinia (1935) or Japan's invasion of Manchuria (1932); or the ongoing civil war in Spain. One might be worried that there was not a single bomb shelter in London and that, in contrast to Hitler's militarization of the Rhineland, the country was unprepared for war. Hitler could requisition and compel, using the rewards of *Kraft durch Freude* ('Strength through Joy') with its offer of gymnastics for all, and cheap holidays for star workers. Most of the newspapers, like many in the government, were in favour of appeasement, thinking that Hitler would calm down and come round, but cheap paperbacks – Penguin 'Specials' at 6d each, and books from the Gollancz publishing house – argued the opposite case in detail, and were devoured by the public. A Gollancz initial print run of 50,000 was not uncommon.[5] A compelling novel, *Little Man, This Now* by XYZ – Frank Tilsley, later a scriptwriter for the BBC cop show *Z-Cars* – tells the story of a decent, ordinary German family getting sucked into the structure of Nazi society, and reminds readers that there were many middle-class English visitors to Germany in the 1930s, who thought Mr Hitler's social experiments quite 'marvellous'.[6]

When war broke out in September 1939, fears that London would be bombed, briefly caused the closure of all London theatres. Kenneth Clark, director of The National Gallery, packed up the pictures and sent them to a disused slate quarry in Wales for safe keeping, but he wanted to keep the building itself from being requisitioned for war work and readily agreed to pianist Dame Myra Hess's suggestion that the gallery should mount daily lunchtime concerts. Her inaugural concert on 10 October was announced on the BBC and a crowd of 1,000 people queued up to be admitted at one shilling per head. A variety of artists, each paid an expenses-level fee of £5, gave a total of 1,968 concerts throughout the war.[7]

Clark also instituted the War Artists Advisory Committee, designed partly to ensure that there would still be practising artists by the end of the war. Thirty-six men and one woman were given full-time contracts to paint and draw the war effort at home and abroad, with 100 on short-term contracts and works purchased from 264 others. In a separate initiative, the Pilgrim Trust (a philanthropic organization set up with funds from the American oil baron Edward Stephen Harkness) commissioned artists to record Britain's buildings and landscapes in case of their destruction by enemy action. *Recording Britain*, the resulting collection of 1,500 paintings and drawings (cottages, castles, pubs, windmills, and a teashop), is now held by the V&A.

W. E. Williams supported the Royal Naval War Libraries with sacksful of Penguins at cost for ships at sea, the size of the sack matching the size of the vessel and, in 1940, was made founding director of the Army Bureau for Current Affairs (ABCA). This remarkable, and controversial, organization trained officers in teaching techniques so that they could spend an hour a week during working time leading discussions with their troops. ABCA also supplied stacks of short booklets fortnightly to each unit so that discussions would be well informed. Many of these were illustrated (often by radical political artist James Boswell) to aid reading comprehension. Army units also encouraged servicemen and women to produce their own 'wall newspapers'. The initial argument was that men would fight more effectively if they knew why (for instance) they were in a certain theatre of war, but topics for discussion later included careers guidance for post-war life. Winston Churchill, however, thought soldiers should be fighting, not debating. Politically, he was probably right. ABCA's activities are often credited with facilitating the Labour landslide in the general election of 1945.

CEMA was inaugurated during the first winter of the war, when Lord Macmillan, head of the Ministry of Information and chairman of the Pilgrim Trust, invited Lord de la Warre, President of the Board of Education, and Dr Thomas Jones, former secretary to the Cabinet Office and secretary of the Pilgrim Trust, to a meeting. The result was an offer of a grant of £25,000 from the Trust, dependent on match funding by both government departments. CEMA's aim was to bring the best of arts and culture to churches, halls, and factory canteens across the country, although ENSA (Entertainments National Service Association) was already entertaining the troops, had a larger budget, and later also supplied symphony concerts to factory workers.

Afterwards Jones recorded gleefully that de la Warre had had visions of a post-war celebration led by the Board of Education, with barges containing performers from the Vic and the Wells sailing down the Thames from Whitehall to Greenwich, while Macmillan was pleased at the prospect of employment for artists. 'Supply and Demand kissed', he quipped.[8] Jones expected to be the CEMA general secretary, but all three were soon superseded.

The Old Vic in Burnley

When the Old Vic was bombed and Sadler's Wells requisitioned as a hostel, the theatre and ballet companies moved to the Victoria Theatre in Burnley, north of Manchester. From a small office in what the company's then director Tyrone Guthrie (1900–71) described as 'a quaintly decayed slum building', they organized tours to the north of England and Scotland, as well as South Wales – all areas of high unemployment – with short runs at the New Theatre in London. They opened in January 1941 in Lancaster with Shakespeare's *King John*, directed by Guthrie with dancers from the ballet company. Performers included Casson (Pandulph), Thorndike (Constance), and their daughter Anne Casson (young Arthur). The programme noted that for too long London had 'owned altogether too much of the cultural life of the country' and that 'one of the most important and encouraging symptoms of the current turmoil' was the spreading of art and culture through 'a wider area of the land, and a wider range of the people'.

Reviewers generally applauded the simple touring set (curtains, with heraldic devices), the blazing red costumes for the British, and blue for the French:

> … by an ingenious use of mime and the principles of ballet, by effects of grouping and lighting, by the sweep and fall of banners, by formalized attitude and gesture … the producers convey the full impression of the impact of great events and make the play throughout not only exciting but beautiful to watch.[9]

And audiences cheered the play's closing couplet, 'Nought shall make us rue / If England to itself do rest but true' (5.7.117–18).[10] This is not an uncommon reaction, although the structure of the play allows us to question what

England's 'truth' might be; the Bastard who says the line can never become king, even though he is the most suited for the role.

By 1942, the Old Vic had a permanent company based in Liverpool, and was touring *The Cherry Orchard* and *The Merry Wives of Windsor*. The funding they received was minimal but the programme for *Merry Wives* at the Preston Hippodrome assiduously states, 'These performances are given with the goodwill and assistance of C.E.M.A .... C.E.M.A.'s policy is "The Best for the Most". C.E.M.A. believes that nowhere is this policy better realised than in its specially arranged tours of the Old Vic.'

The CEMA Film

This sixteen-minute film by the Strand Film Company for the Ministry of Information, entitled *CEMA*, credits five people equally as its authors: Charles de Lautour, Alan Osbiston, Dylan Thomas, Desmond Dickinson, and Peter Scott.[11] Their roles are not specified, but the first four had careers as a director, Oscar-winning film editor, writer, and cinematographer, respectively. Scott, the wildlife artist and conservationist, had studied art in Munich before the war, competed in the Berlin Olympics (1936) as a sailor, and was the inventor of naval camouflage. Apart from the first speaker (R. A. Butler, then president of the Board of Education), none of the individuals or places in the film is identified by name. But the film's snippets of dialogue in juxtaposition with its images and sounds are telling. There is a sense of purposefulness and promise, a spring awakening, with artworks and people all 'on a journey' together.

It begins with stirring music over the title credits. Then a jaunty tune played on a flute introduces a Chaplinesque figure who proceeds to paste a CEMA poster on a hoarding. It advertises 'Plays, Music, Paintings' in towns across the country from Aberystwyth to Kilmarnock. Then, face-to-camera, Butler explains what the initials C-E-M-A stand for: it is 'a war-time inspiration, bringing the best to as many people as we can, to cheer them on to better times'. Yet he looks uncomfortable, playing with his pencil and regularly glancing down to his notes. He came from a patrician family and was married to the daughter of Samuel Courtauld, the millionaire art collector. Maybe he is not convinced about art for the people or, given the tensions in the cabinet, that this is a good career move. He continues in voice-over as the film cuts to the CEMA operations room. A woman, possibly Mary Glasgow, CEMA secretary, or Gladys Crook, who was responsible for booking artists, the so-called 'music travellers', takes a phone call. Posters advertise the current programmes of work. In a neighbouring office (both offices have vases of spring flowers), another woman brings a book to a man sitting at a table. He grabs it eagerly and turns the pages. It is the orchestral score for Tchaikovsky's first piano concerto. We hear a snatch of the piano chords as they modulate key in the middle of the first movement. Clearly, there is a plan. The man, as will become apparent later, is Reginald Jacques, founder and conductor of the Jacques orchestra and CEMA's Director of Music.

Cut to the Jacques Orchestra tuning up for a lunchtime concert. The audience files in expectantly past a military policeman. Four young boys run up to the door after the concert has started and happily mime approximations to the instruments they hear, a flute and viola. Back in the office, a man pins little flags into a large roadmap showing the names of the shows they are sending out: *Merry Wives* in Burnley, *The Cherry Orchard* in Kingston-upon-Hull, the Philharmonic Harp Trio just outside London. The lines of the map crossfade to fruit tree branches; *The Cherry Orchard* becomes cherry blossom. The camera 'travels' to the quintessentially English music of Vaughan Williams's arrangement of 'Greensleeves', coming to rest on the parish church of Chalfont St Giles. Two lads dressed in khaki, insignia of the 3rd Infantry Division on their arms, hurry up the path and open the door. The church, identifiable from its distinctive medieval wall paintings, is packed with people in their Sunday best. The concert has already begun, and in an echo of the Pont cartoon, the pair slide sideways along a row to their seats. A man rises crossly to remonstrate, but a hand from someone behind him touches him briefly on the shoulder and he sits down.

Afterwards, bare twigs and more blossom give way to a training camp, with soldiers operating a field gun. Then another English landscape with factory buildings and tall chimneys: Burnley. Trumpets and side drum introduce a poster for 'Shakespeare' by the Old Vic company. A group of actors, and rather more stagehands, are preparing for the production of *Merry Wives*. Shakespearean dialogue forms the soundtrack to manual work. In the auditorium, a cleaner stops to watch the rehearsal. A child playing the page boy announces Mistress Page, but from the proscenium door, Esme Church, the play's producer, marches on looking and behaving not unlike Baylis, who, Thorndike remembered, would often stride out of her office behind the stage at the Old Vic to give advice. She wags her finger at him: 'Oh, no, no, no, no; much more excited; say it as if you were announcing the invasion, and louder, much louder.' It may be Shakespeare, but it is made part of ordinary people's lived experience.

Cut to armoured vehicles tearing across a field, and then to a crowd visiting an art exhibition where the walls are tightly hung with a range of contemporary pictures in different styles: a flowering tree ('Oh that's a nice one, I bet it's in Devon'), abstract ('What is this, the chamber of horrors?'), figurative, and one of recent bomb damage around St Paul's. The aquiline-featured gallery lecturer Eric Newton (designer of religious mosaics for his father's firm of Oppenheimer and for *Peer Gynt* at the Vic in 1935, art critic of *The Manchester Guardian*, and a regular lecturer on the BBC in the 1930s) engages a stocky man wearing a military cap badge in his lapel, who asks bluntly, 'What's the point of all this 'ere art? Pretty pictures don't win anything.' It is a familiar objection. Newton looks at him quizzically, but responds patiently, 'We all know what we're fighting against, but don't you think we sometimes forget what we're fighting *for*?' He goes on: 'We've *got* to fight, because if we didn't, we wouldn't be free; free to work, to play, to listen, to look at what we want.' He then explains to one young woman that he likes a picture because its lines 'take you on a journey'. The film cuts back to Burnley's Victoria Theatre. The house is packed; civilians, servicemen in uniform, some teenagers, all laughing enthusiastically as Mrs Ford and Mrs Page fool Falstaff and bundle him into the washing basket.

The final section of the film takes place in a factory canteen. All the planning has come together, including the transportation of an orchestra and a Steinway concert grand piano to this inauspicious hall. Reginald Jacques announces that they are going to play the first movement of the Tchaikovsky concerto. There is the same mix of audience reactions as in the art gallery: some stare in wonder and rapt attention, some in bemusement. One man ostentatiously rolls and licks his cigarette paper. But the thunderous piano chords underscore a collage of images from the factory floor: whirling machine lathes and the hammering of riveters. The palette becomes very dark. The war work is going on all through the night. Finished bombs and shells pile up in their thousands; racks are filled with rifles; a procession of tanks rolls past and onto flatbed railway trucks.

The Ministry of Information would no doubt have been satisfied by the dramatic shots of munitions production and the suggestion that art was somehow enabling greater output. But there is a more nuanced, Keynesian story. Modest financial support of the arts allows a repurposing of existing plant (canteens, underused theatres), and facilitates the circulation of money in the economy by creating both employment in a range of jobs (cleaners and backstage crews as well as performers) and consumption (concert-, theatre-, and gallery-going). This is economic activity that doesn't involve physical goods and is therefore outside the boom-and-bust cycle of ordinary capitalism. It contributes both to wealth production and to life enhancement[12] – just as fighting the war is about being free both 'to work' and 'to look at what we want'.

Aftermath

Rather than forcing art, including Shakespeare, into a mould in the service of the government as was happening in Nazi Germany (discussed by Richard Ned Lebow in Chapter 18),[13] the range of educational and artistic ventures epitomized by the Old Vic gave the people, despite bombing and devastation, opportunities for participation. As Keynes observed when the announcement was made that CEMA would become the Arts Council, 'The arts, owe no vow of obedience.'[14]

The Council was inaugurated in 1945 with an annual grant from the treasury (£235,000 in the first year). Keynes had died suddenly, and the barrister Sir Ernest Pooley became the chair, although most of the members were practising artists or arts administrators. Of the people mentioned above, Casson was knighted and served on the Council with Clark, Williams, and Vaughan Williams. Hess, de Valois, and Jacques served on the Music Panel; Guthrie on the drama panel; and Courtauld on the Art panel. Mary Glasgow served as Secretary. There were committees for Scotland and for Wales. But while its first annual report celebrates the work of CEMA in bringing art to places that had never experienced it before, the new focus was once again on the capital. With two sets of opera and ballet companies housed in London (the Royal, and Sadler's Wells), the funding structure sowed the seeds for future controversies. There was, they claimed, a shortage of suitable buildings outside London to house plays and symphony concerts. The Council helped secure the Bristol Old Vic theatre and the London Old Vic, but the Victoria Theatre Burnley closed in 1955 with a production of *Hobson's Choice* – 'a Lancashire play, about Lancashire people, by a Lancashire author'. It had been acquired for an extension of neighbouring Woolworths and was demolished.[15] Eighty years on, with many working people turning to food banks, and arts education in decline in British state schools, we still need to answer the question, 'What's the point of all this 'ere art?'

BATTLE SCENES AT POWERSCOURT

MOVIE cameras are clicking on the green slopes of Powerscourt Estate these days as shooting on "Henry Five" gets under way.

Yesterday, writes an *Irish Times* reporter, I watched hundreds of gaily caparisoned war steeds of the Agincourt period bear their chainmailed, steel-helmeted soldiers in stately silhouette across the crest of a slope, while Director Laurence Olivier, who is seen on horseback in picture above, megaphoned instructions from the midst of the executives clustered around the cameras. The scene was stirring, impressive to both the historic and dramatic sense of the onlooker, and, at the same time, incongruity came with the realisation that these were Irishmen, directed by Britishers, playing the parts of Frenchmen, in the middle of Co. Wicklow.

A chat with Associate Producer Dallas Bower revealed many interesting sidelights on film-making, and showed what a large part Irish industry and Irish craftsmen are playing in this production. The "prop" chain-mail, which used to be imported from Germany, and is made of woven cord aluminium-painted to produce highlights, has been manufactured by the blind in various Dublin institutions. Of the 800 Irishmen employed as "extras," a large proportion are unemployed L.D.F. men, and they are feeding well for the duration of the film, as their weekly food bill per man is £3 17s., and they eat exactly the same food as directors and "stars."

The list of "strange occupations" must be enlarged to include rabbit hole-fillers. There are ten of these at Powerscourt, permanently employed at the job of filling-in the rabbit holes which appear daily, and which would be dangerous to the horses.

Expert electricians are to heighten the effect of the technicolour by using six 300-amp arc-lights to produce shadows, light, and shade—in broad daylight!

In the camp itself, in which no timber was used constructionally, on the suggestion of the Department of Industry and Commerce, asbestos sheeting was substituted. Only two of the buildings are concrete and permanent.

Ex-Galway and Lancashire Plate winner veteran jockey Jack McNeill is among the riders, as well as Joe Mitchell, the well-known amateur rider. The 165 horses used—most of which were sold by their farmer owners only after the heavy spring work—consume 10 barrels of oats a day and 35 cwt. of hay.

Figure 17   Front page of *The Irish Times*, 16 June 1943
(reproduced with permission of The Irish Times / Bridgeman Images)

CHAPTER 17

Henry V *and the Battle of Powerscourt*

Edward Corse

In the middle of the Second World War, on 16 June 1943, the front page of the *Irish Times* ran with the headline 'Battle Scenes at Powerscourt' (Figure 17). Below the headline was a picture of the British actor Laurence Olivier posing on horseback in front of a Technicolor movie camera with the rolling Irish countryside behind. The article explained that Powerscourt, a large estate in County Wicklow in neutral Eire, was to represent Agincourt, the site of the famous battle of the Hundred Years' War; and Olivier was both director and star of the new film adaptation of Shakespeare's 'Henry Five'. The unnamed journalist described what they saw:

> The scene was stirring, impressive to both the historic and dramatic sense of the onlooker, and, at the same time, incongruity came with the realisa-tion that these were Irishmen, directed by Britishers, playing the parts of Frenchmen, in the middle of Co. Wicklow.[1]

The journalist was keen to highlight the Irish contribution to the film-ing of *Henry V* and, despite Eire's neutrality, was not shy of referenc-ing the wartime context. For example, the chain-mail, which was actually 'woven core aluminium-painted to produce highlights', could no longer be imported from Germany and so instead was 'manufactured by the blind in various Dublin institutions'.[2]

The Irish contribution was not just limited to the props. Eight hundred locals appeared in the film as extras and the journalist claimed that 'a large proportion [were] unemployed LDF men'.[3] The LDF, or Local Defence Force, was essentially Eire's home guard, a part-time auxiliary semi-military force in existence to aid Ireland's defence against invasion. The LDF num-bered over 100,000 members in 1943 and it is often regarded these days, perhaps unfairly, as the Irish equivalent of a 'Dad's Army'.[4] The article outlined that there were 165 horses being used for the battle scenes with famous veteran jockeys and 'well-known amateur' riders joining the fray, including Jack McNeill, a previous winner of the Galway and Lancashire Plate, and Joe Mitchell. The horses used were largely farm horses, sold by the farmers to the filmmakers after hard work in the spring.[5] The journalist went on to describe some of the more unusual roles needed for the filming, including ten 'rabbit hole-fillers'. They were also amused to discover that, despite the filming taking place in broad daylight in June, 'expert electricians' were needed to brighten the Irish climate to create shadows and 'heighten the effect of the technicolour'.[6]

This essay explains how and why, in the middle of the Second World War, Olivier ended up in County Wicklow to film *Henry V*. Much previous analysis has focused on the film and its impact and reception, and perhaps the practical benefits of filming in a war-free country. However, little previous research has been completed on how the filming process fitted into wider Anglo–Irish relations and the British wartime propaganda efforts in the 'Emerald Isle' led by the British press attaché, John Betjeman. This essay explores how, despite a censorship regime being in place, Olivier's presence in Eire was too big a story not to be reported in various ways in the Irish press, bringing the Irish population into contact with a wider but subtle British message in their fight against the Nazis.

Early in the war, which in Eire was known as 'the Emergency', the Taoiseach (prime minister), Éamon de Valera, declared Eire's neutrality. From a military point of view, this status was often regarded in London as a potential 'back door' into Britain. This fear was reinforced by the fact that a German Embassy operated in Dublin throughout the hostilities. Anglo–Irish tensions were, as a result, strained, but not just because of the war. Relations were far from positive as memories of the Irish War of Independence (1919–21), the Irish Civil War (1922–23), and Partition were still very raw (see also Katherine Hennessey's discussion of the Easter Rising in Chapter 12). The Irish people were often regarded by the British authorities as 'hostile'.[7]

Nevertheless, London and Dublin knew that their interests were closely intertwined because of geography. Both countries relied upon the Atlantic convoys from North America for food – a point that British Prime Minister Winston Churchill was keen to emphasize in a speech in November 1940.[8] If Britain fell to the Nazis, Eire would likely fall too and be directly subject to the whim of Hitler. The war affected the whole island of Ireland. When Belfast was bombed heavily on 16 April 1941, de Valera despatched firefighters to help, and the bombing caused many refugees to flee over the border to Dublin.[9] Therefore, despite being formally neutral, de Valera's government recognized Eire's position and made a number of concessions to London, which included providing Britain with weather reports and other intelligence about the movements of Axis shipping as well as enabling the overflying of Eire airspace. All of this helped Britain's war effort and maintained Eire's freedom. One official at the Irish Department of External Affairs even noted, 'We could not do more if we were in the war.'[10]

Despite this secret collaboration being in Eire's interests, there was also recognition in Dublin that because of historical, but recent, Anglo–Irish conflict, the news the Irish population received needed to be carefully managed, and that a paramilitary organization, namely the Irish Republican Army, needed to be suppressed. A system of censorship was therefore introduced to control the media. 'The Censorship', an organization formally known with a capital 'C', was established to oversee this work as well as intercept letters and other forms of communication. Donal Ó Drisceoil has studied 'The Censorship' in detail and describes its measures as 'more rigid and wide-ranging than those imposed in most other countries, particularly other neutrals'.[11] For the British, having made the secret accord with de Valera, there was perhaps no need to pump Eire full of British propaganda. Certainly, there was recognition that poorly considered propaganda would have made things more difficult for Anglo–Irish relations. It was still felt in London, however, that a British voice was needed in Dublin, given the German Embassy was fully active and its exploits had to be countered.

In the Irish capital there was a 'UK Representation' – essentially an Embassy in all but name – in which John Betjeman, later Poet Laureate, but at that time press attaché, was tasked with overseeing British propaganda attempts to influence Eire. Betjeman had joined the Films Division of the British Ministry of Information (MoI) under Jack Beddington in 1940. Beddington and Betjeman had known each other prior to the war when Beddington had been Head of Publicity at Shell and Betjeman was working for *The Architectural Review*. They had developed the 'Shell Guides' – a pioneering and successful set of publications that helped Britons explore Britain in a way that was not possible before the motorcar.[12] After Betjeman's posting to Eire they corresponded regularly, with Beddington often trying to bring Betjeman back to work for him.[13]

Betjeman was a charming and charismatic member of the Representation. He often signed his letters 'Sean Ó Betjeman' and inserted them with various Irish Gaelic phrases. He was considered just the type of character needed to bring the Irish people into a more sympathetic mindset.[14] Betjeman was not in full control of events, however, and there were big issues such as Partition, which realistically he could do nothing to solve.[15] Similarly, he could not control the British press and the views expressed about Irish neutrality. British newspapers were sold in Eire and one infamous cartoon in the *Daily Mail* showed de Valera riding a donkey inscribed with the words 'Neutrality at any price' and holding a placard saying 'No Bases for Britain'.[16] Although there is an argument that these opinions actually strengthened de Valera's position within Eire – and that a strong de Valera, enabling that secret collaboration, was good for Britain – it certainly did not make the Irish feel more pro-British.[17] If the Irish people were to become more sympathetic to Britain, Betjeman needed a much more nuanced campaign.

Betjeman concentrated his efforts in three broad areas. First, he sought to win over the Catholic authorities to the British way of thinking. He befriended Cardinal MacRory, Catholic Primate of All-Ireland, drew attention to papal encyclicals that expressed dissatisfaction with the Nazis, and arranged for the British Catholic *Universe* publication, which carried stories of Nazi persecution of Polish Catholics, to be distributed in Eire.[18] Second, he sought to find ways of utilizing Anglo–Irish trade for propaganda purposes. Most Irish international trade was conducted through Britain and businessmen were asked by Betjeman to make it clear that 'Eire's future was inextricably bound up with the survival of the British Empire'.[19] The third method employed was to promote cultural contacts between the two islands. This is how Olivier came to be in Eire. Betjeman had been working for a couple of years to try to 'stimulate requests from Irish theatrical companies for English actors'. He also worked with the British Council, effectively the British government's cultural propaganda agency, to arrange visits by British theatrical companies to Eire.[20] Audiences wanted to see famous actors and artists, and these visitors could avoid 'The Censorship' by giving opinions through uncensored word-of-mouth, both off-stage and off-camera.[21] There were nevertheless risks. In July 1941, 'The Censorship' intercepted a letter from the British Council to the Gaiety Theatre in Dublin that proposed performances by Sybil Thorndike and Lewis Casson 'for good-will propaganda purposes'.[22] Perhaps as a consequence of this interception it was agreed in August 1941 that 'occasional visits' were suitable, but a flood of visitors would ruin the whole plan.[23]

Meanwhile, on the other side of the Atlantic, Olivier had been in Hollywood at the outbreak of war. There are suggestions that he stayed there at the beginning of the war at the behest of Churchill and film producer Alexander Korda, who may have been working for the Special Operations Executive in the USA. The reality is not clear, although it does seem likely that Olivier was at least playing an indirect propagandistic role in keeping Americans positive about Britain's plight.[24] In any case Olivier returned to Britain, via Lisbon, in late 1940 and served in the Fleet Air Arm.[25] Whilst he was largely kept away from major acting opportunities, he recalled that he was asked to carry out various 'propaganda' duties, '[f]rom village hall to Albert Hall', to help with recruitment, often using the *Henry V* quotation 'Once more unto the breach' to end his speeches.[26]

Italian film producer and owner of the Two Cities film company Filippo del Giudice, who had fled his home country before the war, felt Olivier was underutilized and made representations to the MoI. He argued that Olivier should direct and star in a large-scale patriotic film, namely *Henry V*, to boost the British people's morale.[27] Olivier described del Giudice as 'the moving force behind the project'.[28] The play is all about overcoming challenging odds and there was an obvious parallel between 1415 and the preparations for the forthcoming invasion of France. Olivier recalled that he was 'summoned' by Beddington, whom he described as the 'sidekick for the Minister on any question which concerned show-business propaganda'. Beddington requested that Olivier undertake two films for the British cause. The first, *The Demi-Paradise*, was aimed at improving the image of the Russians amongst the British public. The second, as del Giudice suggested, was *Henry V*.[29]

As Kevin Ewert has pointed out, although Olivier had played the character of King Henry prior to the war, the wartime *Henry V* inevitably needed to be 'heroic, stirring, patriotic, straightforward'.[30] Or as Jack Jorgens puts it, *Henry V* would be 'a blend of history and storybook romance, a tribute both to the glories of the English Elizabethan and Medieval past and to Englishmen in 1944'. It was most definitely conceived as a propaganda film, and as Jorgens states, there would be deliberate substitutions – D-Day for Agincourt; Germans for French; Nazi atrocities against the Jews for the killing of boys in the English camp.[31] One commentator has described *Henry V* as 'a contemporary war film in fancy dress'.[32] There was clearly no direct overlap between the circumstances of the Hundred Years' War and the Second World War, and no comparable position to neutral Eire in the former. However, the overall messaging was clear enough: both were a patriotic fight between right and wrong.

Most of *Henry V* could be filmed in a studio, and this took place at Denham Studios in Buckinghamshire. However, filming the Battle of Agincourt, which could not be played out at scale on stage but deemed essential for cinema, would require a big open space not readily available in wartime Britain. As Olivier's biographer, Anthony Holden, noted, finding a suitable filming location for the battle proved a problem. He stated, 'Where in Britain of 1943 could Olivier find an expanse of open countryside, uncluttered by pylons, the sky free of the vapour trails of Spitfires and Messerschmidts [*sic*], on which to re-create an unspoilt fifteenth-century landscape ...?'[33] More importantly, perhaps, Britain was short of youthful manpower to play soldiers in the re-enacted battle, as so many were fighting as soldiers in real battles in North Africa and elsewhere. Eire and Irishmen were the perfect answer. This is where the two sides of this overlooked story come together. Beddington was able to draw upon his pre-war friendship with Betjeman to negotiate with the Irish authorities and facilitate Olivier's journey to County Wicklow.[34]

Olivier was just the kind of visitor that Betjeman was after – famous and charismatic – and his presence in Eire was bound to create interest. The considerable translocation of equipment (including the only Technicolor camera in Europe)[35] from Britain, the need for hundreds of local horse riders for the battle, and the physical closeness of the filming to Dublin all meant that the news was hardly going to be kept quiet.

Olivier arrived in Eire some time ahead of the filming for a reconnaissance visit. There are reports of him staying in Dublin on 3 April 1943 when the *Irish Times* mentioned him in passing in an article about a Royal Hibernian Academy exhibition, but with no explanation given for his presence.[36] It did not take long before news of the film preparations became public, and speculation about the details abounded. On 14 April, Powerscourt was mooted as a potential location.[37] Finally, three days later, a big splash made the front page of the *Irish Times* – 'Big Film to Be Made in Wicklow' – in an article that contained a lot of details about how the filming was to take place and the preparations that were underway.[38]

Over the next few weeks Irish newspapers carried a story almost every day about different elements of the preparations, ranging from the arrival of horses to the need to make the scenes look more like October than June (given the historical date of the battle), as well as changes in terrain and the removal of obstacles.[39] The whole Irish press seemed to be obsessed with the filming in a similar way to the *Irish Times* article that opened this essay. One Irish journalist even gave a history lesson about Ireland's role in the years preceding Agincourt.[40] Articles continued to highlight the Irish contribution: that the art director, Carmen Dillon, was an 'Irish girl'; that 'young Irish artists, some of them members of the Dublin School of Art, had been engaged to paint exterior sets, shields for the warring armies, etc'; as well as, of course, the importance of the Irish horses and horsemen.[41] The *Waterford Standard* proudly reported that a number of the county's horsemen would be 'called up' as trick riders and farriers in a style reminiscent of a real war report – 'Waterford is providing it's quota [*sic*].'[42] Olivier himself was reported to be at Powerscourt before the end of May.[43] It was not just the journalists who were getting excited about the events, much of the population of Dublin were reported to be 'besieging' the site weeks before the filming actually took place.[44] It really was becoming the event of the year in County Wicklow and a major boon for Anglo–Irish relations.

Once the filming began, articles kept coming with references to Olivier's daily routine – the 'hardest working man' on set – and the challenge of the Irish weather, which made 'a couple of minutes' usable celluloid a good day's work'.[45] The scale of the operation was staggering. Roger Lewis, in his biography of Olivier, aptly noted that '[m]aking the movie was a military campaign … Olivier was now in command of hundreds of people, hundreds of horses, the cookhouse, latrines, wardrobes and props.'[46] There was no way the filming could have been done on stage, in a studio, or for a low budget. Olivier was putting everything into the battle for dramatic effect.[47] A number of observers have drawn parallels to the works of the Soviet filmmaker Sergei Eisenstein, who was a key player in the Soviet propaganda armoury in its early years.[48] It is not hard to see why.

The practical steps required to recreate the battle made it a real drama for the population of Eire. The battle lasts only ten minutes in the film. Olivier was in Eire to film it for six weeks, pumping £80,000 into the local economy – over £3 million in today's money.[49] The *Midland Counties Advertiser* believed that horsemen from that area were 'with comrades from every county in Ireland' and therefore the financial benefit was spread far beyond County Wicklow itself.[50] Olivier also took time out to participate in local events, alongside his filming commitments. For example, the *Wicklow People* recorded that he had arrived for a dance event at Woodbrook Opera Hall near Bray on 23 July to draw tickets for a raffle. All of these side events helped drive up interest and sympathy for Britain's plight.[51]

De Valera even came to Powerscourt on 18 July, bringing his daughter and son, Máirin and Terry, and a score of dignitaries. It was reported that they 'were received by Lord and Lady Powerscourt, and chatted with Mr Laurence Olivier, the producer, whom they saw directing a skirmish scene between English and French forces in the wood. The Taoiseach displayed a keen interest in the outfit, and remained there nearly three hours.'[52] De Valera reportedly told Olivier that he 'had a really pleasant afternoon', despite having to watch the English win.[53] Olivier had reached the key decision-maker on the island as well as making an impact on the people of Wicklow, Dublin, and the surrounding area – all at a time when the tide of the real war was turning in Britain's favour. The filming therefore was a sign of increasing confidence in the Allies in multiple ways, metaphorically as well as in reality – something that the Irish people and de Valera could not fail to notice. Even after the filming, a number of newspapers reported the sale by auction on 28 July of one hundred horses that had taken part.[54] Another auction followed of 'a large quantity of valuable building materials and camp equipment used in connection with the making of "Henry V"', including ladders, timber, concrete, boilers, drainpipes, and tent pegs.[55] All of this kept interest in the film going for some time.

The 'Battle Scenes at Powerscourt' article in the *Irish Times* was just one of a wave of articles that explored a multitude of aspects and angles of the filming of *Henry V*, bringing knowledge of Olivier's presence near Dublin to a wider audience. These articles are significant as they demonstrate an ingenious way to avoid 'The Censorship' and provide subtle political messaging through an ostensibly non-political subject, and a result of Betjeman's wider plan to improve Anglo–Irish relations. Betjeman left Eire in August 1943 having facilitated a major success in bringing Olivier there, and *Henry V* into existence. His successor as press attaché was Reginald Ross Williamson, who had been historical adviser for *Henry V*, and so the connection to the film continued. Ross Williamson continued the work Betjeman had started and expanded the role of British propaganda in Eire as 'The Censorship' began to wane and it became more obvious that the Allies would win the war.[56]

One final twist of interest to this story is a letter from Olivier to Betjeman on 8 December 1944. Olivier had provided complimentary tickets to the premiere of *Henry V* at the Carlton Theatre in London on 27 November, but Betjeman had not attended. From the letter it is clear that

'Beddie', as Olivier called Beddington, had kept Betjeman away on other work. What is also clear is how close the relationship had become between Olivier, Betjeman, and Beddington, and how appreciative Olivier was of Betjeman's help.[57] By the time of the premiere, D-Day had come and gone, and *Henry V* landed in a different setting to the one in which it had been filmed. During the filming, Shakespeare had helped improve Anglo–Irish relations. Now he played a role in consolidating British morale for the final push to Berlin.

Figure 18   Production photograph from *The Merchant of Venice*, directed by
Lothar Müthel (Vienna, 1943) (© Ullstein bild / Getty Images).

CHAPTER 18

Unser Shakespeare *in Nazi Germany*

Richard Ned Lebow

The image of Figure 18 is from the notorious Nazi staging of *The Merchant of Venice* in 1943 at Vienna's Burgtheater, directed by party member Lothar Müthel and starring Werner Krauss. The production 'mobilized' Shakespeare's play through textual, staging, and acting choices to make it conform as far as possible to National Socialist ideology. One critic approvingly described Krauss as having

> A pale pink face, surrounded by bright red hair and beard, with its unsteady, cunning little eyes; the greasy caftan with the yellow prayer shawl slung round; the splay-footed, shuffling walk; the foot stamping with rage: the claw-like gestures with the hands; the voice, now bawling, now muttering – all add up to a pathological image of the East European Jewish type, expressing all its inner and outer uncleanliness, emphasizing danger through humor.[1]

The play was widely reviewed, not only in Vienna, but throughout the Reich and in occupied cities as well. This effort to place reviews, and to distribute this photograph of Krauss to go with it, indicates that the Nazis thought they were producing high-value propaganda. The reviews applauded Krauss's portrayal of Shylock and his success in conveying the repulsive nature of Jews. The production's portrayal of Shylock, and Jews in general, as low, ugly, comic figures has been read as a significant departure from the prominent 1940 propaganda films *Jud Süß* (Süss the Jew) and *Der Ewige Jude* (*The Eternal Jew*), both of which presented Jews as clever, powerful, scheming, and dangerous because of their coordinated efforts to control the world.[2]

During the Second World War, Shakespeare was 'drafted' by multiple combatants. In Germany, Italy, and Japan, government-supported efforts were undertaken to make Shakespeare compatible with national culture and supportive of these regimes and their political goals. This process went furthest in Germany, where he was referred to as *unser Shakespeare* (our Shakespeare), furthering a cultural appropriation that had emerged much earlier and is discussed in Marius Ostrowski's contribution to this collection (Chapter 11).

Within the context of this new conflict, the mobilization of Shakespeare in Germany generated greater tensions than it did anywhere else.

The Nazis could not ignore or suppress Shakespeare without alienating members of the educated middle classes. But to present him on stage involved directors and actors, many of whom were not friendly to the Nazis. Shakespeare also posed a more fundamental conundrum for the Nazis. Playwright David Edgar rightly observes that 'Theatre invites – indeed requires – the audience to empathize'.[3] Shakespeare's plays do this, of course, but also encourage audiences to look beyond and above the divisions between protagonists and resist unalloyed support for either side. They problematize personal, religious, and national conflicts just as they do violence and war. They encourage audiences to distance themselves from, if not downright reject, the narrow nationalist identity and dehumanized ways of treating 'others' that the Nazis sought hard to legitimate. Theatre, and Shakespeare especially, created a powerful source of dissonance, but to suppress either would acknowledge the low-brow and anti-cultural nature of the Nazi movement. This essay is about how the Hitler regime recognized and struggled to cope with this tension.

Nazi Theatre

The Nazis were drawn to theatre as a means to arouse national and 'racial' consciousness.[4] They also offered theatre as evidence that they and the Germans were producers of the best exemplars of western culture. For example, drawing on the high valuation of Shakespeare as a German 'national treasure' that had been emerging since the nineteenth century, some insisted that Shakespeare was better in German than his original tongue and, when Britain declared war on Germany in September 1939, the propaganda ministry decreed that Shakespeare was a German author.[5] The Nazis not only supported theatre in Germany but subsidized German theatres in most of the countries they occupied.[6] Despite their professed support, theatres suffered grievously under the Nazis. Jewish actors, directors, and staff were fired and most went into exile, although a Jewish theatre was allowed in Berlin until 1938.[7] Anybody thought to be a communist was arrested. The transformation of the Kammerspiele of Munich was typical. Under the leadership of Otto Falckenberg since 1917, it was renowned for its avant-garde productions of Strindberg, Shakespeare, and early Brecht. Falckenberg was arrested and later released due to the direct intervention of Hitler. During the War, he was allowed to perform *Hamlet*, *Midsummer Night's Dream*, *Macbeth*, *Twelfth Night*, and *The Merry Wives of Windsor*. After the War, he was arrested by the Americans because Hitler had spoken highly of him, quickly released, but not allowed to return to the theatre.[8]

In May 1933, Goebbels told a convention of theatre directors that in the future German drama was to be 'heroic', 'steely romantic', 'unsentimentally direct' and 'national with grand pathos'.[9] Rainer Schlösser, Reichsdramaturg (chief theatre advisor) of the Propaganda Ministry, attempted to impose Goebbels's preferences on the country's public playhouses, and later on the private ones. He insisted that there would be more indoctrination, fewer plays by non-German authors, an end to naturalism, individualism, expressionism, experimentalism, and of modernism in its other forms.[10]

In the pre-war years the major cleavage in the theatre community was between the proponents and opponents of Weimar experimentalism.[11] Those opposed were conservative, nationalist, right-wing, and receptive to the Nazis, or at least willing to play along with them to gain the upper hand over their adversaries. The Weimar experimentalists, many of whom were Jewish, were quickly purged, as were all kinds of other Jews and half-Jews in the theatre world.[12] The fault lines that now emerged were between the new Nazi-supported establishment and the larger theatre community and educated public. The latter conceived of theatre as a form of *Kultur* that should be above and outside of politics.[13]

Most theatre Intendants (directors), even the most conservative ones, had little interest in propaganda pieces stressing heroism and communalism. Many did not approve of purging Jewish actors and staff. A few Intendants privately supported their Jewish colleagues, even hiding them or helping them to escape.[14] Others pleaded unsuccessfully with Schlösser to let them keep Jewish composer Felix Mendelsohn's musical accompaniment of *A Midsummer Night's Dream* on the grounds that it was so beautiful and that audiences expected to hear it.[15]

Many Intendants waged a quiet but largely ineffective resistance. Beginning in the late 1930s, Gustav Gründgens, Heinz Hilpert, Jürgen Fehling, and Falckenberg openly defied regime preferences. This was made possible by the artistic bankruptcy of the Nazi regime, its fragmented political authority, and the desire of middle-class German audiences for good theatre.[16] In practice, however, Intendants still had relatively little room for manoeuvre. At the outset of the Nazi takeover, directors could go into exile but usually at the price of their careers. Actor skills were not readily transportable. Few of Germany's top actors spoke English well enough to perform successfully in Britain or the USA. If they stayed in Germany, they had to reach an accommodation with the regime. They had some wiggle room at the outset because Hitler was keen to demonstrate the Nazis' cultural bona fides. Once war began, this goal receded in importance and officials became more intrusive in their management and more ideological in their demands. At least openly, actors and directors were forced to perform plays and parts they would otherwise have rejected.

Shakespeare and the Reich

The two major theatres in Berlin, both known for remarkable Shakespeare productions, fared surprisingly well at the outset with their Shakespeare productions because they too had a friend in high places. Hermann Göring genuinely liked the theatre and protected it in his capacity as Minister President of the State of Prussia. He desperately needed a qualified director at Berlin's Deutsches Theater to replace the Jewish Max Reinhardt. He appointed Heinz Hilpert despite his wife's Jewish ancestry.[17] Gustav Gründgens, a popular actor, known to be gay, and certainly no Nazi, was appointed director of the Berlin Staatstheater. The previous year he had played Hamlet wearing a blond wig and had provoked controversy.[18] Once in exile, Klaus Mann wrote that Gründgens – they were good friends – played Hamlet in a manner suggestive of a neurotic Prussian lieutenant.[19] Despite the criticism and informant reports of Gründgens's sexual preferences, he retained Goebbels's favour.[20]

In 1937, Gründgens invited Jürgen Fehling to produce *Richard III* at the Staatstheater. Werner Krauss performed the role of the Duke of Gloucester, not as a Nordic hero, but as a dark, evil, and daemonic figure, and one, moreover, with a limp, which may have been intended to evoke Goebbels. Clarence's assassins were dressed in a black uniform suggestive of the SS.[21] All theatres, however, soon came under increasing pressure to participate in Goebbels's anti-British propaganda campaign and encouraged to do this through their Shakespeare productions. From April to December 1941, all British literature became *strengst verboten* (strictly forbidden) and Shakespeare productions and a Shakespeare festival in Vienna were cancelled.[22] Hitler later overrode Goebbels's order that theatres could perform only one Shakespeare play each season.[23]

From 1942, the number of Shakespeare performances declined precipitously. Still, throughout the twelve years of the Nazi dictatorship the only playwright performed more than Shakespeare was Schiller. Goethe and Schiller were condemned by Nazi ideologues for their individualism.[24] Shakespeare's comedies remained acceptable, although *A Midsummer Night's Dream* was less appealing to Intendants and audiences once Mendelsohn's music was banned. Among the tragedies, *The Merchant of Venice* remained in the repertoire because of its anti-Semitism, but some productions presented Shylock in a manner intended to evoke sympathy for its villain.[25] The same happened with

Othello, with its Moor transformed from a Black African into a lighter-skinned Arab noble.

The Nazi party was not monolithic but included diverse strands of opinion. Some officials and intellectuals rejected Shakespeare on the grounds that he indulged in irony and created highly individualist characters who were at odds with the more communal and serious nature of German *Kultur*. In 1940, dramatist Kurt Langenbeck published a manifesto, *Wiedergeburt der Tragödie aus dem Geist der Zeit* ('Rebirth of Tragedy from the Spirit of the Time'), to this effect. He wanted the regime to support Greek tragedy instead of Shakespeare. He provoked strong opposition within the theatre community. Those in favour of Shakespeare came up with arguments to make him supportive of Nazi ideology. They maintained that he was a 'Nordic visionary' whose individualist characters nevertheless submitted to the state in his tragedies and to the social order in his comedies. Many of his tragic heroes, moreover, were 'Germanic heroes' in their display of strong leadership and single-minded focus on their goals. Julius Caesar, Coriolanus, and Ulysses were cited, but also Macbeth, Richard III, and Hamlet. German Shakespeare enthusiasts proposed a new hierarchy of 'Heroic Plays' (*Julius Caesar, Coriolanus*), 'Nordic Tragedies' (*Hamlet, King Lear, Macbeth, Richard II*), 'Racial Dramas' (*The Merchant of Venice, Othello, The Tempest*), and 'Comedies' (*Twelfth Night, Winter's Tale*).[26]

One of the biggest problems about Shakespeare for the Nazis was that his Jewish characters could be viewed sympathetically. The Propaganda Ministry nevertheless decided that *The Merchant of Venice* could be a useful vehicle to propagate hatred of Jews.[27] In his table talk, Hitler is reported to have described Shylock as 'a timelessly valid generalization of the Jew'.[28] More recent research on German theatre indicates a more complex picture. In the first few years of National Socialism, *The Merchant of Venice* was performed less often than it had been in the Weimar Republic. It continued to decline and in 1941 reached an all-time low of only three performances.[29]

The Merchant of Venice can readily be presented as an anti-Semitic propaganda piece. However, Shylock is a complex character and, although acting unreasonably, does so out of anger at the way he has been treated by Christians. His Jewish daughter Jessica weds the Christian Lorenzo, a sharp violation of Nazi racial laws. Various solutions were proposed, all of them involving changes in the plot and rewriting the long-standing and generally revered Schlegel–Tieck translation. Author and translator Hermann Kroepelin proposed that Jessica listen to her father and not marry out of her faith.[30] Rainer Schlösser suggested making Jessica Shylock's Christian foster child.[31] In July 1940, Schlösser submitted a memo to Goebbels in favour of a revised version of the text and urged its widespread performance on the grounds that it 'would actually be able to support our fight against the Jews'.[32]

The Propaganda Ministry insisted on further changes that portrayed the conflict between Christians and Jews as racial, not religious, in character. Their biggest change in the text was to delete Shylock's famous speech: 'Hath not a Jew eyes? Hath not a Jew hands, organs, dimensions, senses, affections, passions? …' (3.1.46–47). The intent was certainly to keep the audience from feeling any sympathy for Shylock or regret about his destruction. They may also have wanted to distance the regime and its theatre from a long history of Shakespearean productions in Germany in which Shylock and other problematic characters were given strong performances and became vehicles for questioning dominant cultural practices.[33]

With Goebbels's approval, *The Merchant of Venice* was performed in Berlin in 1942 and in several provincial cities. These performances coincided with the deportation of German Jews to death camps in the east. The Berlin production was set in the Venetian ghetto and featured Georg August Koch as Shylock. He portrayed Shylock as a stereotypical Jew, wielding his knife and looking forward to using it with glee against his Christian adversary. Critics were on the whole favourable although some objected to the stature still given to Shylock and the 'inappropriate' element of comedy in the play.[34] None of these critics made any reference to the fate of contemporary Jews, although they all knew what was happening. Actress Inge Stolten noted in her diary that this juxtaposition was even more evident to everyone in Minsk, where the German theatre performed the Schlösser version of the play at the very moment the Jewish ghetto in the city was being liquidated. The programme baldly noted the contemporary relevance of the play.[35]

As argued at the beginning of this essay, the most notorious production of *The Merchant of Venice* was in Vienna at the Burgtheater in 1943. Baldur von Schirach, the Nazi governor of Vienna, commissioned the performance to celebrate that the city had become *Judenrein* (free of Jews). The director was Lothar Müthel and the famous actor Werner Krauss played Shylock. His portrayal is said to have differed little from his performance of the same role in Berlin in the 1920s for Max Reinhardt. But the context was very different as the Holocaust was under way and Krauss was now associated with anti-Semitism in the eyes of the audience because he had previously starred in the viciously anti-Semitic Nazi propaganda film, *Jüd Süss*.[36] Krauss was nevertheless far from a committed Nazi. In Berlin he had protected his Jewish friend Carl Zuckmeyer. When it became unsafe, Krauss accompanied him on the overnight train to Prague. He returned the next day to perform the role of Hamlet in Göring's theatre.[37]

Müthel retained Shylock's famous monologue that dramatizes the similarities in physiology and sentiment between Jews and Christians, but deleted all references to Jessica's Jewishness. He had it hinted that she might not be Shylock's natural daughter but did not transform her into Shylock's foster child. He cut Antonio's request at the end of the trial scene that Shylock be baptized in keeping with the Nazi position that Shylock is evil because of his ethnicity, not his religion.[38] On 15 May 1943, Müthel explained his concept of the play in a local newspaper, the *Neues Wiener Tagblatt*. He cited several German 'scholars' in support of his claim that *The Merchant of Venice* is a comedy and Shylock a stage villain. He is a 'cunning, dangerous, polluting, simpleton … a mischievous idiot who is dispensed with'.[39] Müthel insisted that he was restoring the traditional staging of the play that had been falsely reinterpreted as a tragedy by Jews, beginning with Heinrich Heine.[40] Krauss insists that Müthel instructed him to portray Shylock as a comic character but that he decided to represent him 'as really stupid but nevertheless cunning'.[41]

The interesting and unanswerable question is how Viennese audiences reacted to the Nazi production. For a century, Shakespeare's plays had been staged in Germany in ways that foregrounded the complexity of characters and their values. The Nazis' production of *The Merchant of Venice* represented a sharp departure from this practice. Did audiences recognize its retrogression? Did they note any shift in the portrayal of Jews from threatening to pitiful? Did knowledge of the destruction of the Viennese and other Jewish communities deter decent people from attending a play and performance intended not only to legitimize but celebrate it? Did those who attended realize this connection, or care about it? Did some perhaps revel in it? We will never know.

Conclusion

We have become increasingly aware that Shakespeare means very different things to different people. His works have been read and produced over the centuries in dramatically different ways. *The Merchant of Venice* accordingly serves as a kind of Rorschach Test that tells us something about the people who produce and act in the play and their audience. I have used it this way to illuminate the perceived threat and opportunity that it posed to the Nazis. They saw real costs in banning it and sought to exploit it as anti-Jewish propaganda, but had to take liberties with the text in order to do so.

The Nazi production discussed in this essay must, however, be put in historical perspective. While on the one hand, Shakespeare's Shylock broke to some degree with anti-Semitic theatrical conventions of the day, so evident in Christopher Marlowe's *The Jew of Malta*, on the other hand, those conventions re-emerged in the 1600 quarto edition – especially its title page, which quite luridly described the 'extreme cruelty of Shylock the Jew towards the said Merchant, in cutting a just pound of his flesh' – and were similarly reflected in the 1623 First Folio's presentation of *The Merchant of Venice* within the 'Comedies' section. Shylock would later be humanized by Charles Macklin, who in 1660 presented him as a complex figure rather than a comic scapegoat. Nevertheless, George Granville's 1701 adaptation adds new lines to intensify our revulsion at Shylock.[42] Most modern productions of *The Merchant of Venice* emphasize Shylock's humanity. They foreground the best and worst qualities of his character. Presented this way, Shakespeare's play celebrates human resilience, just as successfully as it depicts prejudice. The Nazi production discussed here was a regression to an earlier epoch and, like the regime more generally, a rejection of all Enlightenment values.

Figure 19   Production photograph from *The Shylock Play*, Act 2, Scene 21, Belmont
Garden. From left: Portia (Miranda Pleasence), Sarah (Ruth Posner), Antonio
(Rod Smith), and Bassanio (Jonathan Woolf) (photograph by Sam Jacobs,
reproduced by permission of Tony Brown).

CHAPTER 19

Framing the Jew
Julia Pascal's The Shylock Play
(Arcola Theatre, London, 2007)

Amy Lidster and Sonia Massai (LM) in conversation with Julia Pascal

LM: Could you tell us what is happening in this photograph (Figure 19) from your production of *The Shylock Play*, which you adapted from Shakespeare's *Merchant of Venice* in 2007, and why you chose this image to start our discussion?

The photograph encapsulates major elements of the production. It has four focal points. In the top-left corner, Portia watches the central stage image where Antonio leans into the kneeling Bassanio. Almost imperceptible in the shadows stands one of two courtiers in a white ruff. The dominant action is the playful movement between Antonio and Bassanio. From the way Antonio inclines towards his lover, it is clear that he is in thrall to Bassanio. Portia looks on without judgment. Her majestic gown denotes wealth and status. The most discrete presence, centre frame, is that of a white-haired onlooker, Ruth Posner, who plays the role of Sarah.

Costuming reveals multiple time periods. Designer Sam Jacobs dresses Portia in Norman Hartnell-style 1950s couture. This may be the New Look, but it also carries the old antisemitic prejudice of an earlier Elizabethan age because distinct time periods are connected through the opulence of the fabric: Empire in Elizabethan England suggested new wealth as did the 1950s New Look, where the generous cut of a woman's skirt promises an opulent post-war British society. The choice of design is politically meaningful. Two male figures in doublet and hose endorse the glorious Elizabethan legacy evoked by Portia's costume.

I also chose this photograph because it captures the key role of Sarah, played by actor and former dancer Ruth Posner, née Weissberg. Theatrical tradition mainly presents the 'stage Jew' as a repulsive male. Jewish female characters are almost totally absent from the English canon. Posner's presence upends centuries of Jewish female absence and counters the commonplace representation of grotesque stage (male) Jews. Posner is central to the photograph and to the production as the character of Sarah, which also partly represents Posner's own story. Her fictive persona – a modern-day visitor to the Venice Ghetto happening on a dress rehearsal of *The Merchant of Venice* – accuses Christian society by challenging Shakespeare's text. Sarah's interventions are multiple, as she gets sucked into the narrative. She is both spectator and intruder. Her discrete interruptions critique a script historically praised as the epitome of Christian mercy and justice to unearth its inherent racism. Ruth/Sarah crosses the invisible frontier between *The Merchant of Venice* and its fallout over the centuries. She questions the value of repeated production as I question my own reasons for confronting the text itself. As she puts it, 'It's the Shylock Play! … I wish it had never been written.'[1]

LM: Could you explain how this layering of historical time via Sarah's character relates to your vision for the adaptation as a whole?
My defining vision for this reworking of *The Merchant of Venice* is the creation of Sarah. I was educated to read this play as a philosemitic text. It is not. The title from the first quarto edition of 1600 gives away a clear reading: '*The excellent Historie of the Merchant of Venice. With the extreme cruelty of Shylocke the Jew towards the saide Merchant, in cutting a just pound of his flesh*.' My version interrogates centuries of crude Jewish representation. Posner disturbs the plot device indicated in the quarto edition's logline. Shylock is no longer alone. There is another Jew from across the centuries with whom he touches fingers as they cross the stage at the end of the production. The solitary presence of the moneylending Jew is fractured by the presence of an older Jewish woman who is sympathetic to the Jewish male who could be her son.

The presence of Ruth/Sarah also provokes the audience to consider the importance of acting. When eleven-year-old Ruth escaped the Warsaw Ghetto in 1942, she changed her name and religion to survive. As she says, 'I had to act to save my life' (p. 19). The Venice Ghetto of 1516, Shakespeare's play of 1596, and the Warsaw Ghetto of 1942 all intersect. This multi-temporal framing of the text suggests political injustices that reach back across centuries of western European history.

I also made other additions to Shakespeare's plot lines. Shylock is a widower. Historically, the Jewish community would have arranged his remarriage, particularly as he has a motherless daughter. The maternal absence in the play inspired me to write scenes between father and daughter to deepen their relationship. Shylock and Jessica celebrate shabbat and generational differences are exposed. Jessica, half-seduced by Catholicism, questions Hebrew scripture. She challenges her father. 'The Bible is full of cheats. Why do you quote it?' (p. 28). At other times silent action reveals bonding. Shylock hems Jessica's coat. On the Venetian sunny rooftop, he bleaches Jessica's hair with lemon juice so that she might conform to European concepts of fair beauty. Shylock tells Jessica, 'I love you Jessica. More than my life. Do you know that?' (p. 41). The invented character of Sarah becomes a quasi-mother/grandmother when she interacts with Jessica across the centuries. Sarah tries to dissuade Jessica from eloping with Lorenzo, warning 'he wants you for your money' (p. 47). The attraction-repulsion impulse between Christianity and Judaism is suggested in several ways. When Jessica follows the Catholic street procession, Sarah follows in a fruitless attempt to prevent Jessica's conversion. There is an irony here, as the audience has heard how Ruth Weissberg pretended to be a Catholic in order to survive the Nazis.

LM: The layering of historical and fictive time led to a similar layering of the performance space, which in turn defamiliarized key moments in the play, including the 'Trial Scene'. Could you tell us a bit more about how Ruth/Sarah's presence affected its dynamics?

A crucial decision in staging the 'Trial Scene' was the placing of Sarah as silent observer in the gallery. The acting ensemble became a Venetian antisemitic crowd and everyone was so close that audiences could feel the mob's breath. Proximity to antisemites and silence in front of them might have suggested complicity. This positioning was crucial to suggest a dance of Jew-baiting. This moment echoed the thuggery of an earlier physical attack on Shylock that I added to the original plot line. Within the Court, which pretended impartiality, Jew-baiting was therefore legitimized. But several layers of witnessing prevented it. Most important was Sarah, who stood before the crowd, accompanied by Jessica. Antonio, Bassanio, and Shylock occupied the central area. Between these parties stood the Duke and the moving figure of Portia disguised as a lawyer. When the mob hurled antisemitic abuse at Shylock, they were observed by Black British actors who were part of the original ensemble. Their gaze added yet another dimension by critiquing white supremacy and racism. It also connected Jews and Blacks. Within Shakespeare's England, both were exploited and today they both remain at the heart of difficult histories for Europeans to own and acknowledge as their own.

In short, I confronted the 'Trial Scene' rather than rewriting it, but I added Sarah and Jessica to it. As Sonia Massai writes in her preface to *The Shylock Play*, 'Sarah and Jessica function both within and beyond the fictive boundaries of the courtroom' (p. 8). Massai also notes its blurring boundaries and interconnected fields of vision, where 'separate, discrete categories – history and fiction – and separate, discrete temporal layers – the long history of European antisemitism and the recent ravages of the Holocaust' are firmly rooted within the production's aesthetic (p. 9). I allowed Shakespeare's ludicrous plot to play out. To deny the truth of the Blood Libel cancels an important chapter of European history. But the framing of it, from a silent Shoah survivor, added a comment that I hoped would upend the power of the Old Lie.

LM: Which aspects of Shakespeare's *Merchant of Venice* lent themselves most naturally to your vision for the adaptation? And were there any points of resistance, where Shakespeare's take on religious, cultural, and ethnic/racial diversity jarred with your own?

Despite the addition of Sarah and Jessica, major points of resistance still occurred for me during the 'Trial Scene', because the scene is an accumulation of centuries of literary Jew-hatred. The generic image of the Jew wielding a knife before a Christian breast is pornographic. But to remove it from the text is to demolish the play. The crux of the problem for me is that Shakespeare's central motif is rooted in a vicious lie. That Jews are murderers, longing for Christian blood, conflicts with kashrut laws. It is a fantasy that has fuelled antisemitism since the birth of Christianity. Indeed, Jewish law dictates that, if an egg contains even a tiny speck of blood, it must be discarded. Therefore, the concept of Shylock wanting to cut a pound of flesh from Antonio's body is specious. Shakespeare clearly knew nothing about Jews. There were Christian scholars who did know about Jewish law: Shakespeare did not consult them. But the play has been produced so many times, with Shylock at its centre as the representative 'Jew', and, as we know in our own 'post-truth' society, the repetition of lies tends to validate them. The image of Shylock, with his knife pointing at Antonio's breast, is the apotheosis of that lie. That is why I did not rewrite Shakespeare. That is why the 'Trial Scene' remained central to my production. However, I felt uneasy, being myself a Jew, as I attempted to subvert stereotype because I too was allowing Shakespeare's repetition of this calumny. My revenge against the centuries of Jew-hatred was to add Posner as Sarah. She represents a double-layering of Ghetto upon Ghetto, which takes us straight to Treblinka.

LM: What would you say was the most important function of the frame that you devised to re-present *Merchant of Venice* to a twenty-first-century audience? Did you hope that audiences might, through your adaptation, return and review their own perspectives

on the Second World War and the stories that are told (or often left untold) in dominant war narratives?

It is difficult to make any assumptions about the effect of one's work on audiences. I wanted to transmit the text through the lens of Jewish artists and I hoped that this would be understood.

My intention was to overlay the text by casting two Jewish performers who understood it through their own lived histories; in particular Posner's war experience. I am not convinced that many members of the audience understood why Posner was inserted. The reason for this is that most British audiences, who are not Jewish, know nothing of how Jewish history has been expunged from the national narrative. British school children do not learn about the importation of Jews by the Normans to fulfil the hated role of moneylending, the English pogroms between the eleventh and thirteenth centuries, the expulsion by royal decree in 1290, and the subsequent failure to cancel Edward I's banishment of all Jews.

Black Lives Matter has provoked an interrogation of the way British history is taught, but there has been no parallel Jewish Lives Matter movement or change to the curriculum. In 2017, a decade after this production, a BBC study showed that over a quarter of the population held antisemitic views.[2] This figure had almost doubled by 2021 according to an *Independent* survey showing that 45 per cent of UK adults 'hold antisemitic views'.[3] In our own antisemitic historical moment, taking on *The Merchant of Venice* was not an easy task and I see the 'Trial Scene' as a literal trial that I forced myself to undergo. I did not seek to educate the audience but rather to wrestle with the play as a British-Jewish theatre practitioner. It would have been naïve of me to think that I might change attitudes. British antisemitism is an insidious undercurrent. My most important intervention was the framing of the play through Posner's gaze and the casting of a virile Shylock. Both were unrecognizable as symbols of defiance to most audiences as they had no idea what was being defied. It is rather as if audiences were to watch an anti-apartheid play without knowing what apartheid was.

In answer to your question, I therefore doubt that my production prompted audiences to rethink their perspectives on the Second World War. Without an understanding of how 'The Jew' was demonized in medieval Christendom up to, and beyond, the twentieth century, there is unlikely to be a shift in attitudes towards modern-day Jews. *The Merchant of Venice* was produced in Hitler's Germany over fifty times between 1933 and 1939.[4] The stereotyping of Jews, even down to their depiction as rats, was a vital premise to Jews being gassed as 'vermin'. Similarly, the success of Jewish stereotypes within the zeitgeist of English culture before

Shakespeare wrote *The Merchant of Venice* meant that his Shylock was part of an established and recognizable literary tradition. The Second World War's annihilation of Jewish life and culture is endemically linked to European, institutionalized antisemitism. British people know that this war was not fought to defend the Jews. In Guernsey, Jersey, Alderney, and Sark, where Nazis occupied British soil, the absorption of the Nuremberg Laws into British Law and the betrayal of the Islands' Jews by the collaborationist authorities remain mainly unknown. I believe that huge ignorance around Jewish experience of antisemitism in Britain and Europe means that a radical production of *The Merchant of Venice* can do little to change centuries of prejudice. In fact, knowledge about destruction of Europe's Jews has largely disappeared and is replaced by new forms of antisemitism masked, in many cases, by anti-Zionism. The jump from Shylock to the antisemitic cartoon of engorged Jewish bankers in Mear One's 2016 East End London street mural, endorsed by Jeremy Corbyn as leader of the Labour Party, shows that antisemitic stereotypes are still central to British popular culture.

LM: Were you surprised by how reviewers, critics, and scholars responded to *The Shylock Play*?
In her review essay, Massai responded with a clear understanding of the dramaturgy's spatial, thematic, and political levels. The press response was less informed. In *The Evening Standard*, Fiona Mountford wrote, 'If only Pascal had ... written a play *about* The Merchant of Venice. It seems initially she has, as elderly Sarah chats with her tour guide ... [but] just when this is shaping up, the rest of the cast bounces on ... and poor old Sarah can [only] sit – and sit – and spectate.'[5] Mountford sums up new dialogue about contemporary Italian antisemitism, Zionism/anti Zionism, Ruth/Sarah's flight from the Warsaw Ghetto, and the gassing of her parents in Treblinka, as 'chat'. She patronizingly reduces a Shoah survivor to 'poor old Sarah'. For *The Guardian*, Lyn Gardner was unable to register the centuries-long terror regime of the Inquisition, as she myopically critiqued the production for 'making Shylock the victim of demented Catholics'.[6] Gardner and Mountford, who may well have benefited from reading for higher-education degrees, nonetheless went through the narrow, English curriculum, where Chaucer and Shakespeare are lauded as humanist authors rather than the transmitters of racism. Their reviews reveal ignorance of the larger historical and political landscape. Neither registers the power of the embodied Shoah as represented by Posner, the concept of the virile, New Jew and the direct line between empire, slavery, and exiled

Africans selling their wares on the European street, who were also part of the new frame I devised for this production. Kevin Quarmby, writing for *Rogues and Vagabonds*, did watch it through a Jewish lens: 'Pascal', he wrote, 'has created a new character for this adaptation, one which is fascinating in its own right ... The visceral implication of this act of enforced voyeurism is the history that accompanies Posner's performance.'[7] Rivka Jacobson similarly noted that 'Pascal's treatment of Shylock introduces an interesting and stimulating insight in this production. The dramatic ploy used is a play within a play, an effective device if the audience eventually manages to appreciate the thematic links.'[8] Many were resistant to these thematic links. Just as Black history has been mainly invisible to the white gaze, similarly Jewish history is invisible to British viewers. As recent surveys show, Jews remain a difficult minority for British society. Therefore a production that connects Shakespeare's play to contemporary antisemitism via the Holocaust is bound to anger and disturb those who see Jews as privileged, dangerous, and always as outsiders.

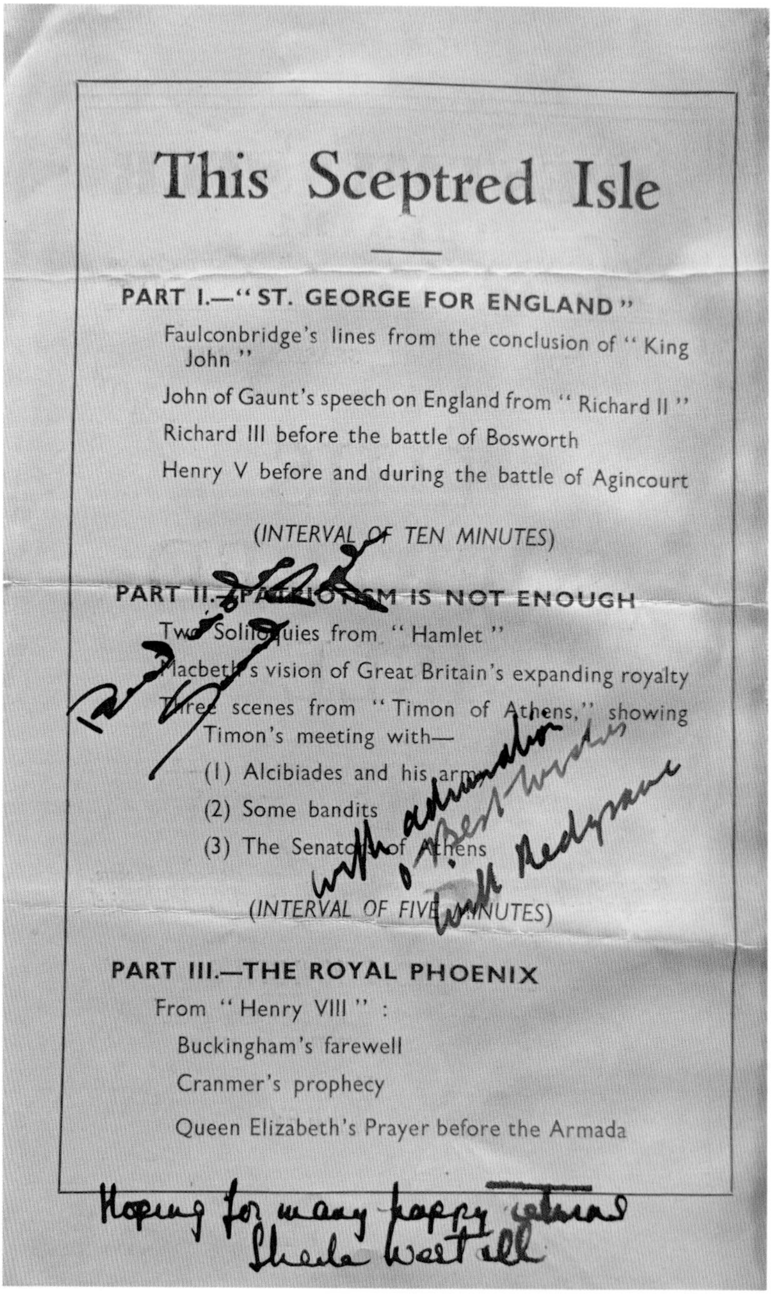
This Sceptred Isle
PART I.—" ST. GEORGE FOR ENGLAND "
Faulconbridge's lines from the conclusion of " King John "
John of Gaunt's speech on England from " Richard II "
Richard III before the battle of Bosworth
Henry V before and during the battle of Agincourt
(INTERVAL OF TEN MINUTES)
PART II.—PATRIOTISM IS NOT ENOUGH
Two Soliloquies from " Hamlet "
Macbeth's vision of Great Britain's expanding royalty
Three scenes from " Timon of Athens," showing Timon's meeting with—
(1) Alcibiades and his army
(2) Some bandits
(3) The Senators of Athens
(INTERVAL OF FIVE MINUTES)
PART III.—THE ROYAL PHOENIX
From " Henry VIII " :
Buckingham's farewell
Cranmer's prophecy
Queen Elizabeth's Prayer before the Armada
Best wishes Will Redgrave
Hoping for many happy returns
Sheila Westall

Figure 20 G. Wilson Knight's copy of the programme of 'This Sceptred Isle' (Westminster Theatre, 21–26 July 1941), with autographs of stage manager Sarah Peple, actor Will Redgrave, who supplied 'voices off', and well-wisher Sheila Westall, possibly the author of *The Galmart Affair* (1977) (from George Wilson Knight scrapbook (S 650.8F), reproduced with the permission of the Library of Birmingham).

CHAPTER 20

G. Wilson Knight's 'Royal Propaganda' in 'This Sceptred Isle' (1941)

Reiko Oya

In a scrapbook in the possession of the Wolfson Centre for Archival Research, Library of Birmingham, there is a programme of a Shakespearian revue that ran from 21 to 26 July in 1941 at the Westminster Theatre in London (Figure 20).[1] The show, entitled 'This Sceptred Isle', was a stage adaptation of a small book that Shakespeare scholar G. Wilson Knight (1897–1985) had published under the same title a year earlier. Knight not only arranged the scripts but played all the main parts, while other dramatic characters were either 'imagined' or 'done by voices off'.[2] Eminent actor Henry Ainley came out of retirement to read the commentaries as prepared by Knight.

The programme reproduced here was Knight's own copy, inscribed, apparently on the opening night, by the show's stage manager, Sarah Peple, actor Will Redgrave, who supplied some of the off-stage voices, and a well-wisher, Sheila Westall, possibly the author of *The Galmart Affair* (1977). Billed as a 'Dramatisation of Shakespeare's Call to Great Britain in Time of War', the presentation featured such warlike set pieces as 'This England never did, nor never shall, / Lie at the proud foot of a conqueror' (*King John*, 5.7.112–18) and John of Gaunt's 'this sceptred isle' oration (*Richard II*, 2.1.40–68).[3] Also included were scenes from *Timon of Athens* and *Henry VIII*, which Knight, in defiance of the critical tradition, regarded as Shakespeare's masterpieces. To him, *Timon* offered 'a terrible warning to Great Britain' when the play's misanthropic protagonist 'denounces wholesale the decadence and miserly greed of man's so-called civilisation',[4] while Cranmer's prophecy of the golden age of Queen Elizabeth (*Henry VIII*, 5.4.14–55) was 'as fine a statement as we shall find in any literature of that peace which the world craves and for which Great Britain labours'.[5] Ainley's recitation of the queen's prayer before the Spanish Armada provided a finale to the show.

The makeup of the programme seemingly supports Michael Taylor's observation that Knight was 'a propagandist of Shakespearean good cheer'.[6] Indeed, since the outbreak of the Second World War, the scholar had been engaged in what he called 'Royal Propaganda', running a flurry of book and stage projects to support Britain's war effort, by 'using Shakespeare to define the meaning of the Crown, for us, today' (*RP*, p. 66). They were 'purely personal adventures' with no governmental support, but Knight was convinced of Britain's imperial destiny and of the central importance of Shakespeare ('a national prophet') in it.[7] He decided to 'press on', and arranged the Westminster production, thinking it 'necessary to plant this particular poetic statement at this particular time, in the nerve-centre of the Empire' (*RP*, pp. 19–22).

'This Sceptred Isle' was, in fact, hardly a typical piece of British war-time propaganda, considering that its creator was a great fan of Nietzsche, whose ideas were appropriated by Nazism. Knight's books on Shakespeare, *The Wheel of Fire* (1930), *The Imperial Theme* (1931), and *The Crown of Life* (1947) in particular, were spattered with references to supernormal persons and supermen as the cleansing force in a corrupt society. Knight loathed the 'mental atmosphere' of contemporary Britain and was indeed attracted to 'that dark enigma of National Socialist Germany' itself.[8] In effect, he launched the 'Royal Propaganda' for a nation he was not proud of. The remaining pages of this essay will explore Knight's thinking behind the programme of 'This Sceptred Isle' to clarify how the admirer of Nietzsche and Nazism created a polemics of patriotism with recourse to Shakespeare. Indeed, Knight's interpretation of the playwright directly informed his wartime assertion about the centrality of the Crown and Britain's imperial destiny.

Wolfit and Knight

In both its purpose and structure, Knight's Westminster production echoed the legendary 'Selections from Shakespeare' (also known as 'Lunch Time Shakespeare'), which Donald Wolfit had staged at the Strand Theatre in 1940. The actor-manager and his company braved the air raids and performed excerpts from Shakespeare over a hundred times, and 'Civil Servants, typists, journalists, factory workers and students all packed themselves eagerly into that oasis of light and entertainment'.[9] There were, however, important differences between the two ventures. To begin with, Knight failed to replicate the predecessor's popular and critical success. Wolfit's show generated a 'finest hour' myth by playing in the middle of the Blitz and by playing Shakespeare. According to Zoltán Márkus, these two exertions were deemed 'equally audacious' by contemporaries.[10] 'This Sceptred Isle' also staged Shakespeare in wartime London but met with a lukewarm reception. Knight's audience was appreciative but thin. The reaction from 'the intelligentsia' lacked warmth. The reviewers were blind to the production's purpose and only picked on the oddity of 'a professor acting while an actor lectured' (*RP*, p. 38). The only significant exception was the review in *The Times* (23 July 1941), which had reservations about Knight's acting but registered that 'the whole unusual production firmly establishes his conception of Shakespeare as the poet and prophet of a free and virile people'.[11] After the London run, Knight tried to 'interest cinema-land' in the venture, to no avail. An amateur company, the St Cross Players, toured a modified version of 'This Sceptred Isle' at several venues in England. But that was all.

Unlike its predecessor, 'This Sceptred Isle' operated on a precarious financial base. 'Lunch Time Shakespeare' was supported by the Council for the Encouragement of Music and the Arts and was protected against losses. Knight sought funding from the Ministry of Information, convinced that he 'was handling stuff of importance'. Nothing came of it (*RP*, p. 20). The scholar incurred personal loss even after Sir Archibald Flower, chairman of the Shakespeare Birthplace Trust and one of the sponsors of the production, reimbursed him to the extent of the guarantee.

Most crucially, the two wartime productions were based on different assumptions about both British society and Shakespeare. To Wolfit, 'Shakespeare represents more than anything else the fighting spirit of the country' and 'Only the best' – meaning Shakespeare – 'is good enough for people who are striving and enduring as Londoners are today.'[12] 'Lunch Time Shakespeare' alluded to war by performing the rousing prologue to *Henry V* and the short scene from *Hamlet* with Fortinbras and his army marching to war against Poland (4.4), but the audience preferred songs from *As You Like It* ('Blow, blow, thou winter wind', 2.7.174–97), *Twelfth Night* ('O mistress mine', 2.3.33–38; 'Come away, come away, death', 2.1.49–64), and *Two Gentlemen of Verona* ('Who is Sylvia?', 4.2.37–51).[13] It probably did not matter: Wolfit was offering the 'right entertainment for the lives people are living in London now', with Shakespeare guaranteeing the production's patriotic intent. The actor-manager was clearly proud to be British.[14]

Knight had a different view. When the war started, the 'mental atmosphere of England was not healthy', as the rise of Hitler culminating in the invasion of Poland in 1939 'had put many people in a defeatist mood'. Knight's native country was wrapped in darkness in a way reminiscent of Shakespeare's Danish prince in his inky cloak: 'I recall many bitterly ironic remarks characteristic of the Hamlet-like mood in which many worthy Englishmen at that time saw England, and themselves' (*RP*, p. 4). Knight did not register any 'fighting spirit' in either England or in Shakespeare's famous tragic hero.[15] Rather, he was in awe of the 'satanic virility' of Nazi Germany, as contrasted with Britain's 'indecision, self-deception, and national not-being'.[16] Knight's wartime appropriation of Shakespeare was driven by his frustration with Britain, not Germany.

Knight 'Interprets' Shakespeare and Britain

Today, Knight is best remembered for his early publication, *The Wheel of Fire*, which promoted a 'spatial' poetics and extolled sympathetic 'interpretation', as opposed to judgmental 'criticism'.[17] He played a crucial role in the shift to Modernist approaches to reading texts and released Shakespeare studies from the narrow focus on such 'temporal' elements as plot and character development.[18] For all the originality and lasting value of his critical insights, Knight has often been regarded as (in his own words) 'a kind of wild Caliban ignorant of the rudiments of scholarly disquisition'[19] – and not without cause. According to Northrop Frye, who was Knight's colleague at Toronto University for several years, the English-born Shakespearian 'gave the impression of not knowing a Quarto from a Folio text, certainly of caring even less'.[20] Knight's 'interpretation' of individual plays was often eccentric, if not entirely untenable. His characterization of Hamlet as 'the ambassador of Death' and Claudius as 'the typical kindly uncle, besides being a good king' are just two examples of his critical aberrations.[21] Also, while it is perfectly respectable for Shakespeare scholars to appear on stage, they tend not to go so far as to publish a book of photographs, like Knight's *Symbol of Man* (1979), and pose half naked in it while impersonating Shakespearian roles. The idiosyncrasy of his wartime activities was only to be expected. As he saw it, European societies in the 1930s were badly in need of a purifying scourge. His autobiographical novel, *Atlantic Crossing* (1936), recorded the dark years that witnessed widespread poverty, aggressive dictatorships, and the approach of world war:

> The great cities of Europe are to-day paralysed by fear. As fanged beasts they watch jealously each other's tentative movements, grasping each its own possessions, exposing their teeth and sharpening their claws, and from

time to time a low growl tremors their world cage. Such beasts, you think, should never have been caged together. Fear is now our best reasoning, prevision of danger our first ideal, and national hatred the main solidification of internal love.[22]

Among the 'beasts', Knight particularly resented his native land, not Germany. In fact, he admired how Germans and Italians under fascist regimes 'think less of freedom and more of service', when in Britain 'youth takes suicidally to drugs in reaction to a murderous and vision-thwarting society'. He also acknowledged 'an undeniable fascination about the Nazi programme, for state, continent, or world, offering as it does a place for everything and everything is in its place'.[23] His ostensibly jingoistic books, such as *The Olive and the Sword* (1944), were 'undertaken in no spirit of triumphing patriotism: it was rather a searching for patriotism; a searching for a possible way of thought, scale of values, and source of power' (*RP*, p. 4).

Knight's 'Royal Propaganda' was likewise a deliberate, strategic campaign. He was intent on 'enlisting the purifying powers of great drama, and especially Shakespeare, as a means to national rebirth and social guidance' (*RP*, p. 30). He was not 'in a mood of bull-dog pugnacity', and was not even prepared 'as an individual, to say that we ought to be fighting the Germans at all':

> But the patterns interested me, and the German pattern interested me almost as much as the British, though, finding myself on this side of the Channel, I can be forgiven for hoping that our pattern would prevail ... And it was easy, with Shakespeare's help, to rationalise that desire, and give it support.[24]

Knight's allegiance was highly ambivalent: he could have supported the 'German pattern' if he had happened to be on the other side of the Channel. Only with 'Shakespeare's help' could he justify his loyalty to Britain and mobilization of the public. The German propaganda machine promoted Nazi ideology with ruthless efficiency, while the 'old cry of democracy against tyranny, right enough as far as it goes, does not go far enough'. The British cause was sadly lacking in 'necessary radiations', as it was not, 'to a superficial view, either more efficient or more attractive':

> The difference is that between a work of great literature, say *Hamlet* or *Paradise Lost*, and a best-seller. Both the German and the Russian programmes are, in their fashion, best-sellers, whereas our own system holds the great dignity and richer worth of some noble classic. (*RP*, pp. 12–13)

Classic literature was hard to sell to the public, but Britain needed to maintain its lofty standards, for 'unless we do that we put across nothing of any real value at all' (*RP*, p. 13). While democracy 'cannot satisfy the royalty of the individual soul and keep alight the superman-faith', the British Crown was 'a mystic, super-personal symbol' potent enough to preserve the nation 'from the dangers of dictatorship, bureaucracy, and the herd-instinct' (*RP*, p. 17). Shakespeare's English kings were therefore an ideal vehicle for Britain's public relations: they were not only 'noble' and 'classic' but also romantic and glamorous. Knight explained:

> His [i.e., Shakespeare's] fondness for kings and dukes is one with his fondness for lovers. The equating of kingship with successful love you get in the Sonnets; and it is, indeed, a universal association. Aristocratic themes are used partly as the cinema to-day shows the heroine in a fine dress: and what hard worker, having paid for a seat, would wish it otherwise?[25]

Shakespearian kings reinforced the established order by adding a touch of Hollywood-style allure to it. The playwright 'exploits dramatically the kingship in every man'.[26] This was also the rationale of 'This Sceptred Isle': by identifying with Shakespeare's warlike kings, Knight's audience would hopefully find their 'own, kingly, selves' noble enough to sacrifice their lives for the nation.

Towards a More Comprehensive Pattern

Knight's strategic use of Shakespeare and his thinly veiled sympathy with fascist nations support his assertion that 'it cannot be said that I was lost in a delirium of flag-waving and jingoism' during the war (*RP*, p. 9). Instead, he was like an intriguing demagogue promoting a cause he did not believe in, as he wrote:

> … though my own personal response remains precisely that of the average male 'intellectual' of our time, and though for all of us the more self-conscious emphasis tends inevitably to fall on 'democracy', on the more feminine and instinctive levels of our community the Crown remains central as ever. Indeed, it appears to be exerting stronger radiations generation by generation. (*RP*, p. 5)

While associating democracy with reason and masculinity on the one hand, and royalism with instinctiveness and femininity on the other, Knight argued that Britain had a 'more subtly inclusive, if temporarily less vital, order' than Germany's unrelenting hero worship or Russia's communism.[27] He would explain Britain's 'inclusiveness' with reference to the surmounting of sexual binarism. In *Neglected Powers* (1971), Knight supported John Cowper Powys's doctrine on 'orgiastic indulgences', by explaining how his own acceptance of such 'dangerous, sex-impelled, instincts' liberated him and facilitated his Shakespeare studies:

> In my own life I recall first a period of sexual frustration, with frantic and futile thoughts and lonely actions related to *normal* sexuality; but this was followed by a more successful release through indulgence in thoroughly *abnormal* fantasies; and it was about then, according to my recollection, that the literary patterns of my Shakespearian interpretations began suddenly to unfurl.[28]

Knight did not explain the exact meaning of 'normal' and 'abnormal', but what mattered was his embrace of the two antitheses, whatever they were. Britain similarly tolerated and encompassed differences, sexual or otherwise, and was therefore superior to Germany. In *Christ and Nietzsche*, the scholar compared Nazi Germany to Marlowe, and Britain to Shakespeare, as regards their sexual propensities. Germany and Marlowe shared a 'strong masculine idealism' and 'a strong homosexual strain', Knight argued, noting 'how widespread is homosexuality in the German psyche'. Masculinity and homosexuality are often 'capable of the finest idealistic and, within limits, creative expression', but they may 'nevertheless also be closely related to brutal military indulgence and sadistic excess against masculine objectives'.[29]

Meanwhile, the Shakespearian, and British, practice was 'far more permeated by the gentler principle'. Shakespeare was himself 'fired by a homosexual love', but his artistic balances were 'always correctly maintained, with integration rather than a one-way relaxation'. Britain's strength was this 'Shakespearian synthesis of the feminine and the virile'.[30] Knight considered the playwright to be not only bisexual but also transsexual. Following Wyndham Lewis's argument that Shakespeare was 'a sort of feminine genius' who had been 'turned into a female at an early age', Knight believed that this 'reversal of sex' would explain 'much of the perfection of the plays'.[31] The 'Shakespearian synthesis' was the prototype of the British constitution even in areas beyond sexuality:

> As in Shakespeare warrior idealisation and its obverse of ironic criticism, revolutionary fervour and governmental authority, justice and mercy, worldly ambition and religious humility, masculine strength and feminine love, are all balanced, harmonised, and integrated, so our British constitution has room for capitalist initiative as well as socialist reform, for armed

strength as well as pacifist counsel; but our sole final allegiance is to that whole of which all these were parts and whose symbol is the Crown.[32]

In this respect, Knight's 'Royal Propaganda' was a paradox, as the Crown allowed for 'every opposite' and was 'the enemy of all one-way propaganda'. His patriotic campaign was 'really propaganda against propaganda' (*RP*, p. 73). To him, the Crown, of which Shakespeare's kings were theatrical embodiments, was a symbol powerful enough to resolve any political divide and hold the nation together in wartime.

Binary Oppositions and Beyond

The synthesis and unification of opposites underpinned not only Knight's wartime thinking but his literary criticism. As René Wellek observes, Knight kept contrasting 'tempest and music, disorder and order, evil and good, darkness and light, tragic and comic, which are reconciled or rather abolished in immortality, infinity, mystery, the other world of ghosts'. The scholar's dualism resulted in the 'flattening out of any distinctions, the reconciliation of everything with everything, the monotonous conclusion that the world is pervaded by dualisms'.[33] Even more problematically, Knight could not register a third party in the conflict of 'mighty opposites', in either literature or the real world. For instance, he could not imagine that anyone would break free from *both* British royalism *and* German fascism. In the post-war period, when the British Empire was collapsing in the worldwide process of decolonization, he repeated 'the main Shakespearian thesis' (*RP*, p. 44) about the centrality of the Crown and Britain's imperial destiny to audiences in colonial countries. In 1951, he delivered his Shakespeare lecture twice for the British Council during his visit to Jamaica. The talk was also broadcast. He repeated the lecture for the British Council in London 'to overseas visitors' in 1952. On his visit to South Africa later the same year, it was given 'as a public lecture through the University [of Cape Town], and again through the University of the Witwatersrand in Johannesburg and the University of Pretoria'. He had been warned that a lecture 'containing any suggestion of British imperialism' might be 'unsympathetically received at Pretoria' but 'the true nature of my theme being so wide in scope' and 'South African audiences so courteous', he gave the lecture anyway. According to him, the audience's reception 'justified my choice' (*RP*, p. 45) and proved the universality of the Crown and the British Empire. In all probability, however, the positive reaction of the colonial people owed more to their courteousness than to the appeal of the scholar's royalism.

Both during and after the war, Knight's patriotic activities were overtly inconsequential – no one seems to have taken them seriously – but his 'Royal Propaganda' serves as a salutary warning even today about the danger of dualism in political discourse as well as in literary criticism, especially when one of the two parties purports to include the other and to be therefore all-encompassing and universal.

Figure 21   Adrian Lester as Henry V in the National Theatre's 2003 production,
directed by Nicholas Hytner (photograph by Tristram Kenton
and reproduced by permission of eyevine).

CHAPTER 21

Shakespeare's Desert Camouflage

Ramona Wray

Since 9/11, a striking number of Shakespeare productions have appropri-ated the distinctive colours of desert camouflage. The print – marked by faded tones and an overall impression of dry and earthy environs – has become almost the standard choice for productions of *Macbeth*, *Othello*, and *Henry V*. Yet there has been little, if any, discussion of desert camou-flage as a costuming decision. Indeed, its presence is rarely remarked on by reviewers. The trend might be seen to originate in the historically pre-scient production of *Henry V* (dir. Nicholas Hytner, 2003) at the National Theatre.[1] Here, the actors appeared in head-to-toe desert camouflage at a time when, to cite the rehearsal diary, 'the nation' stood 'edgily on the brink of invasion'.[2] In the archival image this essay focuses on (Figure 21), the suggestiveness of the costuming is richly apparent. Wearing camouflage head-to-toe, Henry is established not as king but as soldier. Gym-honed and muscular, with teeth bared and weapon brandished, this Henry is, first and foremost, a military commander embedded in the world of his identi-cally dressed and kitted out troops. Their shared print – swirling brown, yellow, and green blots and spots against a pale sand background – is con-gruent with a contemporary military campaign. Indeed, the production diary notes that the design team found it difficult to source the distinctive desert fatigues required because they had been bought up by the British Army 'to replenish … dwindling stocks'.[3] As the British Army struggled to uniform its troops for Iraq, then, Henry's Agincourt camp appeared resplendent and ready for desert operations.

§

According to Tim Newark, Quentin Newark, and J. F. Borsarello, 'patterned camouflage began in the First World War as a method of dis-guising ships, aircraft, tanks and artillery'.[4] The colours first selected – variations on dun green and brown – matched the muddy trenches around which combat took place, although it was not long before additional hues ('contrasting splodges of black') were added to uniforms so as to confuse the outlines of a weapon or soldier identified at a distance.[5] A later development, the desert camouflage pattern, was introduced by the US armed forces to accord with the arid and less elevated battlefields of the Gulf. In deciding upon the palette, 'soil samples from parts of the Middle East, namely Saudi Arabia and Kuwait, were used as testing locations' before a suitable colour assemblage was finalized.[6] Judged more compatible with desert war zones, the resultant beige, light green, yellow, and brown mix replaced the earlier six-colour 'chocolate chip camouflage', and darker patterns quickly began to look periodized and 'vintage'. If all objects function, to appropriate Ludmilla Jordanova's words, as a 'convenient shorthand' bestowing meaning and significance, then this patterned fabric declares nothing less than the 'War on Terror' (the now defunct term coined by the Bush administration that signals the international military campaign waged in the aftermath of 9/11, including the Iraq War and the War in Afghanistan).[7] The historical change in colour – from sombre green, brown, and black to lighter beige, green, yellow, and brown – indicates both a definitive shift in global geographies and a transformation in the ways in which warfare is executed and imagined. And, in the wake of what turned out to be a highly successful *Henry V*, many critics, including Catherine Silverstone, would note the ties between this production and 'contemporary acts of warfare, especially with respect to the production and framing of traumatic images'.[8] Desert camouflage captures the ways in which productions refract contemporary understandings of global conflict, and this essay argues that camouflage costuming ignites a nexus of Shakespearean meanings around the brutality of the protagonist, war-crimes, post-traumatic stress disorder (PTSD), veteran-ship, and spectacular violence.

§

As the twenty-first century unfolded, directors began subscribing to 'desert camo' with varying degrees of visibility and engagement. Among the many exemplary productions, some stand out. The 2013 National Theatre production of *Othello*, which director Nicholas Hytner discusses in an interview with the volume editors in Chapter 22, was distinctive for featuring smart, light green combat collars and darker green undergarments as part of the representation of the military camp in Cyprus. Upper-arm badges indicated 'Venetian' affiliations, while officers transformed into desert personnel entered and exited with scarfs and backpacks in a constant activity of ongoing operations. The entire cast, including Desdemona (Olivia Vinall) and Emilia (Lyndsey Marshal), appeared in recognizable desert dress, suggestive both of a siege situation and of the inimical realities of living in a military milieu (as also indicated in the concrete block and portacabin-like structures of the set). This *Othello* set the scene for later productions, including *Othello* (dir. Iqbal Kahn) at the Royal Shakespeare Company in 2015 (discussed in Chapter 26), in which a key conceit was that both Othello and Iago were played by black actors (Hugh Quarshie and Lucian Msamati, respectively). Over and above casting, however, the production's most powerful impression inhered in its direct invocation of contemporary militarism, as intimated in scenes of the torture of hooded captives (a drill and blowtorch being the offensive instruments). Interestingly, this production, rather than using the specific desert camouflage pattern, instead distributed its constituent colours – faded yellows, browns, and greens – among individualized uniforms. Hence, Othello's green contrasted with Iago's yellow, a seemingly imperceptible difference that suggested a general desert habitus. More generally in the production, the crumbling and yellowing – vaguely Italian Gothic – contours of the set suggested a conflict of long and dry duration.

Macbeth has also proven itself susceptible to a military reading. Two recent productions have elaborated the war zone through desert costuming. In *Macbeth* (dir. Jonathan Fox) staged by the Ensemble Theatre Company at the New Vic, Santa Barbara, in 2016, the visual emphasis on pale yellow jackets and trousers with generous pockets and similarly hued bulky armour evoked a desert frame of reference. Meanwhile, scenes in which Macbeth (Jamison Jones) stripped off his camouflage to reveal a bloodied body pointed up the failure of the armour to prevent injury, a tabloid scandal in the UK at the time and an issue later investigated as part of the Chilcot inquiry. References to the contemporary conflict in the 'Middle East' were easily picked up in reviews, possibly because this production also appropriated sounds of machine-gun fire and incendiary explosions familiar from US news footage of the Gulf wars.[9] Complementing the resonances of this production was *Macbeth* (dir. Polly Findlay), staged by the Royal Shakespeare Company in 2018. At first sight, this production might seem the exception to the desert camouflage rule. Characters appeared either in casual contemporary dress or (as in the case of Macbeth, played by Christopher Eccleston) in formal military attire, complete with brass buttons and golden epaulets. Where camouflage did feature, as at the start, it was of the black and dark blue variety, reinforcing, in Rachael Nicholas's words, a prevailing darkness: the thrust stage was 'edged … with a thin strip of concealed light, defining a sparse set that receded into a black abyss, creating the sense of a perpetual night that variously framed, concealed and enveloped the play's characters'.[10] Complicating the colour-coded play of meanings was that dark colours marked Macbeth (black body armour) while lighter shades demarcated Macduff (Edward Bennett) and Malcolm (Luke Newberry), the latter in particular appearing in the climactic coronation scene in desert fatigues (with camouflage belt and shoulder straps). The suggestion was that Malcolm's 'Gulf'-identified army represented victory and enlightenment, with Macbeth, accordingly, being associated with anti-western forces and consigned to the gloom and obscurity of defeat.

The immediate effect of this slew of camouflage-centred performances is to bring into focus just how many of Shakespeare's male protagonists are soldiers. There has been a long-established tradition of *not* playing the Shakespearean soldier in combat uniform; in contradistinction, the desert costuming trend draws attention to the ways in which Shakespeare conceived of protagonists such as Henry V, Othello, and Macbeth as military professionals. Directing further attention to Shakespeare's fictionalization of the soldier-protagonist is a series of related decisions around props, blocking, and movement. In these productions, care is taken to provide authentic weaponry as a means of making costumes appear congruent with props. And performers are now routinely given military training to go with the camouflage look. The National Theatre production of *Henry V* (2003) suggests itself again here. To cite the rehearsal diary, Richard Smedley, a 'military adviser', was appointed to familiarize the cast with 'commands, procedures … [and] manoeuvres'.[11] 'Weapons' introduced included semi-automatic rifles, magazines, and knives, with the effect that lines between a rehearsal space and a training ground began to dislimn.[12] In the National Theatre's 2013 production of *Othello*, a similar level of attention to militaristic specificity was also evident. Major-General Jonathan Shaw was recruited to address the cast, a role he discusses at length in Chapter 25 of this collection. Part of his job was to support the actors in internalizing a world in which all appear in desert camouflage and in which the 'camp', whether mess room or office, is simultaneously battleground and home.[13] On the one hand, this commitment to military specificity required the understanding of interpolations into the script, such as 'Bravo, zero, delta!' On the other hand, the process extended to cast screenings of *Full Metal Jacket* (dir. Stanley Kubrick, 1987) and *Restrepo* (dir. Sebastian Junger and Tim Hetherington, 2010), war dramas and documentaries dealing revealingly with the intersections between training, trauma, and conflict.[14] But it is important to acknowledge that the training undertaken was to match the inhabiting of the costume: physical movement went hand in hand with displays of camouflage in persuasively 'authentic' performances.

As these productions suggest, dress, military identity, and sexuality often form a self-affirming nexus in performance, bringing to mind the romanticized construction of the soldier in the contemporary war film. In fact, *Jarhead* (dir. Sam Mendes, 2005) was referenced during rehearsals for the National Theatre *Othello* (2013), suggesting a cross-fertilizing connection between 'Operation Desert Storm' lance corporal Anthony Swofford (Jake Gyllenhaal), suspicious and disappointed in love, and Venetian general Othello (Hugh Quarshie), driven to amatory distraction in part by the rarefied masculine/military environment in which he lives.[15] Here, 'camo' as costume aligns with a broader orientation in theatre and cinema to insert a heightened sexual charge into Shakespeare's male roles. There can be no doubt that the combination of charismatic male stars (sometimes with Hollywood credentials) costumed in camouflage clothing generates erotic effects: recent productions of *Henry V*, *Othello*, and *Macbeth* inflect the stage, seductively, with the pleasures of athleticized bodies played up throughout. Often, viewers are explicitly invited to spectate on the soldier's bodily beauty, as when, in the Ensemble Theatre's *Macbeth* (2016), for example, the chiselled protagonist removes his camouflage to reveal a sculpted military physique. In this moment, as at others, divestiture and discovery – what the desert camouflage conceals – shape audience involvement.

A focus on the male body connects with the simultaneous discovery of a number of Shakespearean protagonists as veterans. A recurring type is the soldier who has survived conflict, with all the veteran's attendant, and suggestively contemporary, ambitions and anxieties. In the case of several productions, including Kahn's *Othello* and Findlay's *Macbeth*, the titular hero or his associates (in part thanks to older casting decisions) are veterans scarred with the suffering of past experience, even as they are also realized in terms of inflicting horrors on others. As Kate McLoughlin argues, 'Veterans bring the real world into literature; they are figures at the heart of historical events, active agents in the processes of change.'[16] Her observation brings home how narrow the gap is between soldier and veteran in popular consciousness. In addition, it sensitizes us to the afflictions accompanying the state of veteran-ship: in theatre, as in the contemporary world, the veteran is primarily understood in terms of PTSD associations. Recovering the history of PTSD, Martin Barker notes that discourses around the condition serve as a point of consensus between all sides in American politics and facilitate a reading of the US military as victims rather than perpetrators.[17] In the Shakespearean theatre of the early twenty-first century, the representation of the pervasiveness – and repercussions – of PTSD suggests that the condition is one of soldiering's inexorable effects.

military encounters – whether these be the advance of Malcolm's troops at Dunsinane or the siege of Harfleur – assume the complexions of more recent iterations of conflict, such as the battle of Baghdad, the battle of Tora Bora, or the fall of Kabul. This is not only because they are invariably envisioned according to stage business comprised of smoke and conflagration (suggestive of burning oilfields) and thematics of confusion and havoc, but also because they are recalibrated as victory's obverse: they are seen as unwinnable. In the current climate, as Andrew J. Bacevich has argued, the 'actual experience of war after 9/11 [has] demolished all [triumphalist] expectations'.[24] Instead, theatrical productions mirror the view widely held in both popular and military realms that the costs of conflict are out of proportion to the outcome and that there never will be any kind of 'victory' – its very prospect is unrealizable. Traditionally, critics have debated whether adaptations of *Henry V* are pro- or anti-war. In representing a new kind of warfare in the form of dressing protagonists in desert camouflage, theatre in the post-2001 era not only moves beyond these debates but declares their contemporary irrelevance. Envisaging conflict as self-defeat, these productions speak to incompleteness, irresolution, and regret as its only available outcomes.

§

Since the rash of desert 'camo costuming' productions, American forces have finally retreated from Afghanistan and Iraq. Defeat is now complete, and, in its wake, veterans raise new and fresh questions about legitimacy and the reasons for going to war. How will the meanings of the desert camouflage print modify in the light of the withdrawals? How will other interpretations arise from the outcomes of these conflicts? And in what ways will a shift in the fabric's constellation of signifiers translate onto the Shakespearean protagonist? The first production to postdate the retreat from Afghanistan – *Henry V* (dir. Max Webster, 2022) at the Donmar Warehouse – offers some early answers. The large-scale production, screened globally by National Theatre Live, starred Kit Harrington of *Game of Thrones* fame (who imports into the performance the cycles of violence intertextually associated with his breakthrough role). Conjuring Hytner's *Henry V* and the invasion that underpinned its run, the Donmar production coincided with a new European conflict. As Emma Smith notes in her review, 'Russia invaded Ukraine on the day fixed for the press night … by the time the opening was reconvened … video screens of munitions and explosions, civilians donning army fatigues, and the failures of diplomacy were almost unwatchable.'[25]

Confirming its contemporaneity, the production makes the most extensive use yet of desert camouflage. The costuming emerges organically – the Act 2 chorus (Millicent Wong), after first presenting herself in casual clothes, appears in 'camo' trousers. Camouflage then gradually assumes a greater ubiquity until, at the siege of Harfleur, Henry strides onto a gantry in head-to-toe 'camo' amidst a sea of brown, yellow, green, and sand colours. If the production takes desert camo to its most extreme realization, it also pushes a narrative about the pointlessness and irresolute nature of war to its logical end-point – this is a Henry who has no cause for war beyond ego, who leads via intimidation, who is disengaged from the troops he presides over, and who not only orders the prisoners be killed but models killing one himself. There is no attempt to water down Henry's brutality. Peter Kirwan notes the production's 'depiction of war as cynical, a strategy pursued by leaders seeking to consolidate their own authorities ... in which transparent lies are parroted shamelessly in defiance of the recorded testimony of those suffering the consequences'.[26] Camouflage, in this context, takes on grimly dispassionate associations. Henry's costume trappings are little more than a false assembly of heroic postures disguising a hollow protagonist. As a result, camouflage is stripped of any remaining shards of glory, announcing, instead, conditions of self-defeat (for Henry) and regret (which is most forcefully conveyed in the chorus' concluding summation of events). David Loewenstein and Paul Stevens write that, while 'the memory of two world wars, the Cold War, and the savagery of innumerable postcolonial wars ... lives on, both the conventional and new asymmetrical wars of the last two decades have given Shakespeare's perspectives on war a new urgency'.[27] Desert camouflage – as a key theatrical and cultural property – has crystallized this urgency in a series of crucially interlocking performances. Almost two decades on, combat dress remains a potent articulation of modern-day imperialism, one that has proved itself capable of absorbing new and emerging expressions of global conflict. In making visible contemporary war zones, the 'camo' print allies Shakespeare to some of the twenty-first century's most discomforting material and ethical realities.

Figure 22   Production photograph from *Henry V* at the National Theatre, 2003,
directed by Nicholas Hytner (photograph by Ivan Kyncl, reproduced by permission of
ArenaPAL).

CHAPTER 22

'May I with Right and Conscience Make This Claim?'

Testing the 'Just War' Tradition in Nicholas Hytner's Henry V (National Theatre, 2003)

Amy Lidster and Sonia Massai (LM) in conversation with Nicholas Hytner

LM: Your chosen object is the dossier, shown in this production photo (see Figure 22), that is carried by the Archbishop of Canterbury (played by William Gaunt) in Act 1 Scene 2, and is ostensibly packed with evidence to prove Henry V's right to the throne of France. Could you tell us about the significance of this object – and this moment – in your production?

The production was planned in early 2002, before there was any explicit stated intention to go to war in Iraq – although it felt likely to happen. Even the events of summer 2002 – when Tony Blair and George W. Bush seemed to be starting to form a military alliance – post-dated the decision to do the play. I wanted to do *Henry V* because I suspected that there might be a demand for a Shakespeare play that discusses war and the reasons and justifications for it, and *Henry V* had never been done by the National, so it was a pragmatic decision as well as a political one. During the time that I was actively preparing the production, working on the designs, and thinking about how to do the play, it became ever more obvious that the UK would be part of the coalition going into Iraq. The day before we went into rehearsal, Bush and Blair announced that they would bypass the UN Security Council and go to war with Iraq. As I have explained elsewhere, 'It would have been perverse not to play *Henry V* as a contemporary text.'[1] Anybody would have realized, approaching the play in the early months of 2003, that the most vivid part of it was not necessarily its depiction of combat, but how combat is justified, how the act of war is explained, and how it is spun throughout the play.

Central to this approach is the role of the Chorus, and how the action of the play increasingly detaches itself from the way the Chorus describes the events represented in it. A commentary on war propaganda is thereby embedded in the play: the Chorus always seems to give the sanitized, official version of history, but the play takes on its own life. The first Chorus speech is about the staging of the story, so the audience is not immediately alerted to the fact that the unfolding events, as represented by Shakespeare, are going to undermine the Chorus. But, as early as Act 1, Scene 2, the Archbishop's deliberately tortuous and boring explanation of the Salic Law sounds a warning. One should always take a step back and wonder why Shakespeare is being boring, because Shakespeare is not a playwright who is accidentally boring! The Archbishop's lines in Act 1, Scene 2 are often heavily cut. Laurence Olivier cut almost all of them and made the rest of his lines sound ridiculous. In 1944, he needed to. In 1944, he had little reason for being interested in self-evident sophistry and equivocation about the justification for the British invasion of Nazi-occupied France. In 2003, there was a substantial part of the UK population that felt it was absolutely *not* necessary to be part of a coalition that was planning to invade Iraq and was extremely sceptical about the way the government spin doctors were justifying the invasion. In my production, the Archbishop of Canterbury's dossier was a deliberate echo of Alistair Campbell's famous dossier, which was based, as it turned out, on false intelligence and was motivated by the repeated attempts of the UK and US leadership to torture international law into a place where it appeared to justify the taking of action in Iraq without UN support.

LM: Going back to the dossier, would you say that you took a gamble in retaining Act 1, Scene 2 almost in its entirety, but that the use of such a suggestive prop helped the audience navigate it?

Most definitely. The dossier was slowly passed around the table as the Archbishop delivered his over-elaborate dissection of an obscure law, which was presumably as obscure and as apparently remote to its original audience as it is to us. The visual impact and associations of a prop that conjured so vividly the current concerns about British involvement in the Iraq War felt like a gift, as far as bringing the play alive was concerned. The audience therefore paid attention to a long, long speech which, by and large, audiences are not interested in listening to. I don't think that the audience expected to get any particular insight into the new Labour government's justification for the Iraq War. The dossier, on the contrary, enabled us to understand an aspect of this play, a law that regulated monarchical succession in France, which might otherwise have remained totally obscure.

LM: Would you go even further and argue that this moment in your production gave your audience some sense of agency at a time when they may have felt powerless in the face of decisions that contravened international law and bypassed institutions set up after the Second World War specifically to establish basic 'rules of engagement' in military conflict?

In all honesty, I don't think it did. I think when audiences find in a play from the past a vivid parallel with their own experience, what they draw from it is a sense of solidarity with past generations. It's one of the reasons why audiences return to the classics. But I'm not sure that the sense of solidarity we feel with those who watched *Henry V* more than four hundred years ago galvanizes us into action. I am sure that there were audience members in the Olivier Theatre who felt that the Iraq War was necessary, and that Saddam Hussein could not go unchecked, as I am sure that there were others who were enraged by it. For those who came already suspicious of government spin, I think the excitement stemmed from the realization that the play is capacious enough and ambivalent enough to have already noticed, four hundred years ago, that political leaders will do anything and say anything to rally a nation around military action – even when the justification for war is dubious. Which is not to say that Olivier's 1944 production was wrong, or that anybody else who directed the play as a jingoistic call to arms was wrong, because the play is plainly excited by the idea of a successful English war leader beating the French. At the same time though, the play is also extremely sceptical about what you have to do to gather a nation behind you and to take on a dubious military campaign. In 2004, we staged David Hare's *Stuff Happens*, a documentary play about the build-up to the war in Iraq and this production enraged a lot of people. The most surprising aspect of this play was the suggestion that Bush was an intelligent man and a very skilled political operator, and that Blair had rings run around him. The difference between watching *Stuff Happens* and *Henry V* rested primarily on the fact that, while the former was chiefly aimed at inviting the audience to think differently and specifically about the war in Iraq, the latter established a connection with earlier generations of theatregoers and, crucially, in the last act, asked them to think about what it would be like being the French.

LM: Do you think that Adrian Lester's charisma and his popularity with British audiences undercut the potential for sympathy towards the French that Shakespeare builds into the last act – or, more generally, the play's commitment to debunking the 'spin' that surrounds Henry's decision to go to war?

Adrian has real grace. Since he played Rosalind in Declan Donnellan's all-male production of *As You Like It* for Cheek by Jowl, he's also shown that he is very comfortable with that within him which is feminine and not aggressive. I thought that Adrian brought grace, humour, introspection, and ease to Henry V, and that his Henry worked as a counterpoint to the production's scepticism about why and how the war happened. This juxtaposition is in line with how the play represents war and Henry as a war leader. *Henry V* gets excited at the idea of a successful English war leader. In fact, it gets terribly excited by the figure of the last heroic king of England – and in this respect, the play is very much of its own time. But, as I have explained earlier, it also deconstructs that idea and critiques the cynical self-interest that drives the Archbishop of Canterbury and then Henry to go to war. Having said that, I must admit that I received more letters about the fact that Adrian Lester was playing Henry V, and Adrian Lester wasn't white, than about the play's politics. In those days, the National Theatre audience still contained a small hard core of people who were more bothered by this casting decision than by the production's deliberate allusions to the Iraq War. I did, though, get feedback on the production from Blair himself. I do not think he had seen either *Henry V* or *Stuff Happens*, but when I met him at some government reception a year or so later, he said with a big, warm smile on his face, 'well you've been giving us a very hard time, haven't you?' Then he added, 'and that is your job; it is your job to do that.' To be fair on Blair, I think he probably believed what he said, but it was also an extremely disarming way of reducing my role to that of a court jester.

LM: *Pace* Blair, would you say that your production in fact played a role in shaping public opinion about the Iraq War?
I do not believe that the theatre changes minds very often, let alone changes policy or the way people vote. At most it catalyses views and opinions that audiences bring with them – especially to productions that speak to their historical moment and circumstances. This is particularly true of plays like *Henry V* that place the experience of being at war centre stage. Shakespeare was writing for an audience many of whom had been soldiers – and if they hadn't been soldiers, they had family members who had been soldiers. Contemporary audiences in Western Europe and in North America are unusual, when compared to earlier ones over the last four hundred years, in having had no first-hand experience of combat. Olivier was in the Fleet Air Arm; but since the Second World War, those of us who direct, perform, or watch representations of war in Shakespeare tend to be familiar with conflict only through the media. Staging a war play therefore brings with it a sense

of fraud. Staging ancient or early modern warfare with swords, broadswords, and rapiers can feel entirely ornamental, like ballet. Staging contemporary warfare is also challenging. I have only once handled a firearm. I suspect most actors who come on stage with a gun in their hands have little experience with guns either. We did appoint an NCO [Non-Commissioned Officer] to drill the actors and train them. But we were conscious that there is a long tradition of actors, particularly film actors, going to boot camp for a couple of weeks and believing they have been through an entire conflict. Ronald Reagan seemed to think he had fought in the Second World War and the only thing he had done was put on a uniform on a Hollywood sound stage!

LM: And yet another significant intervention in your production – your decision to have Henry's soldiers refuse to carry out his order to execute their prisoners of war in Act 4 – effectively foregrounded the disaffection on the part of soldiers sent to fight wars that may lack legal justification or popular support.

We were conscious of the fact that there were young men and women who had joined the army and were out there in Iraq putting their lives at risk. Henry's exchange with Michael Williams – one of the three soldiers Henry meets, while walking around his camp in disguise, on the night before the battle of Agincourt – resonated powerfully with the sense of disenchantment and disorientation that vexed our armed forces during the Iraq War. It felt very important to me that the production recognized their courage, but also their lack of agency. In retrospect, one might call it sentimental, but the refusal by Henry's soldiers to carry out the order to kill their prisoners was designed to give them back some level of agency.

LM: Was your decision to have Henry personally execute Bardolph on stage also intended to expose the king's brutality, not only against the French but also against his own soldiers?

There were aspects of this production that I know were a lie. In the context of a contemporary campaign, it would simply not be possible for Henry to execute Bardolph in front of his troops. Saddam Hussein might have done, or Gaddafi, but it constitutes a war crime that would not be perpetrated by an officer at any level of the British or the US Army – or any European army.

LM: So why did you add Bardolph's summary execution to your production?

Because it was an extremely vivid stage correlative for what the play suggests is happening there – namely Henry's denial of any sense of allegiance with the men he revelled with before becoming king. We were not staging the two *Henry IV* plays, so the audience had not watched Prince Hal become King Henry V and had not experienced the relationship that Bardolph had with him. I felt this moment in the play needed something extra to make it as brutal as it always is if you are watching these plays as part of a cycle.

LM: How did you deal with the wooing of Katherine, princess of France? Audiences typically look to the scene for some kind of redemption and light relief.

None of us were persuaded of the scene's charm. If you see it from Katherine's point of view, the romance goes sour: the victor of Agincourt is insisting not just that the daughter of the vanquished king marries him, but that she tells him she loves him: 'in loving me you should love the friend of France, for I love France so well that I will not part with a village of it. I will have it all mine' (5.2.160–62). Henry's heavy humour was lost on Felicité du Jeu, who played Katherine. She accepted him only on compulsion. The scene was one of the clearest examples of how *Henry V*, like all Shakespeare's plays, changes with time. I've seen many actors – Olivier and Branagh included – play it as a kind of romantic counterpoint to the brutality of the war that precedes it, and the text entirely supports them. It's a mark of the way Shakespeare works that it also supports a totally contrary reading. Henry V – romantic hero or arranger of forced marriage? Both. Henry V – hero or war-criminal? Both.

Figure 23   Lieutenant-Colonel Tim Collins, commanding officer of the Royal Irish Regiment, on the eve of the invasion of Iraq, March 2003 (photograph by Giles Penfound; image courtesy of the National Army Museum, London (NAM.2005-01-67-13)).

CHAPTER 23

Henry V *and the Invasion of Iraq*

Tim Collins

I was hugely surprised to receive an official-looking letter in the abandoned sports stadium in Al Amarah, Iraq in mid-April 2003. The high-quality paper was inscribed with a congratulatory note for a speech I had made – and promptly forgotten – to my battlegroup, the Royal Irish Regiment (R Irish), which is captured in this photograph by WO2 (Warrant Officer) Giles Penfound (Figure 23).[1] Dated 6 April 2003, the letter was from a place called 'Birkhall' and apparently signed by someone called 'Manny'. At least that's what it looked like to me. It was in fact a letter from the then-Prince Charles, who now holds the same office as Henry V, whose speech before Agincourt, spoken through the quill of William Shakespeare two hundred years later, is often compared to the words I spoke to the R Irish Battlegroup in Kuwait on 19 March 2003, immediately before we crossed the border of Iraq as a part of the US-led coalition in the liberation of Iraq.[2] Together, this photograph and letter testify to the significance of this moment on the eve of conflict.

In the letter, Prince Charles praises the tenor of the speech and emphasizes, by underlining the word 'profoundly', how moved he was by my words. His response was yet another huge surprise to me. Since delivering the speech, which I had felt was necessary as we embarked on a historical and notoriously controversial venture, it had been in the headlines across the world. In some cases it had incited admiration; in narrow, dark corners at the top of the British Army, fear, jealousy, and loathing. However, as the commanding officer of a battlegroup engaged in battle, quarantined by war from the world of 24-hour news, I was blissfully unaware of it all.

Leading soldiers in battle is a rare and terrible privilege and merci-fully rare in our modern age. My command, 1st Battalion The Royal Irish Regiment,[3] stood on the brink of history, as a war that would transform the Middle East and arguably the modern world was about to begin. Mine was a fully manned battalion with an additional company of Gurkhas – sent as reinforcements at the beginning of my command, now an additional fourth rifle company against the normal three of every other battalion present. And that is the most important point. We had not always been fully manned. When I had taken command two years earlier, we had been at less than half strength. Over the following two years we had recruited, predominantly in Ireland (to the annoyance of the experts in the Army Recruiting group), to achieve full strength. But, in doing so, we now had a very young group of men, many of whom had never been out of Ireland, even for a holiday, before joining the army and who now stood ready to kill and be killed in the sandy wastes of a foreign war – a war that no one would honestly say they completely understood.

My realization was that these fresh young men, with a few veterans, would shortly cross into another country and fight its army with the aim of liberating the people there from the dictator Saddam Hussein. I knew that they would be ordered to take human life – something forbidden by God's law – and that (as far as I knew at the time), for some, this conflict would mark the end of their young lives. I was also very aware that, as a regiment, we represented Ireland, both Northern Ireland, an integral part of the United Kingdom, and the neutral Irish Republic, represented by a large contingent of officers and men, as well as men of several other different nationalities. Having recruited and brought these men to this place, I was responsible for them. Something needed to be said.

I also had the knowledge that these soldiers would need to call on more than courage in the coming weeks and months and that I would need to appeal to their very conscience and self-respect for them to achieve what was needed. And so, I delivered a talk to them that came mostly from the shoulder, as it were, but also from the heart. I was there as an Irish chieftain, entrusted with the precious lives of many other men and women. We would have to work together if we were even partially to succeed. Additionally, it was my clear understanding that we, the British Army, were not on any war of conquest. This was a liberation, no matter what motivated the politicians to side with the USA and their championing of the so-called 'war on terror' on the questionable evidence available at the time about the presence of weapons of mass destruction in Iraq. The Iraqis were our allies; Saddam *was* the enemy.

My sense of responsibility was intensified by the fact that this battalion had the highest numbers of relatives in the British Army – eight sets of fathers and sons (some with two sons) stood ready to cross the line, as well as countless brothers, cousins, and relatives by marriage. My Regimental Sergeant Major had two brothers and five nephews there on the day. If we took large casualties as we crossed the border into Iraq, as the regiment had in the past at Waterloo, Stormberg in South Africa, the Somme, Monte Cassino, and the Imjin River in Korea, a darkness for another generation would descend over homes and families of Ireland despite the fact that, historically and uniquely in the British Isles, the Irish, all to a man, have been volunteers, never conscripts.

The content of my speech was a mixture of emotions, experience, and historical knowledge. I had served in the first Gulf War as a Troop Commander in B Squadron 22 SAS (as well as numerous other conflicts that must remain unmentioned because classified). But it was the moral element of the speech that I felt was crucial. I am often asked if I was influenced by Shakespeare, and especially by *Henry V*. The answer is 'yes and no'. But for the essence of what I had to say, the answer is definitively 'yes'.

In *Henry V*, Shakespeare places dramatic emphasis on a couple of tricky situations. Both at Harfleur and at Agincourt, the odds are against the English. Harfleur sees a stalled attack on the city walls. As the momentum of the assault dissipates, Henry steps forward to rally his men with an appeal to their very stock: 'Once more unto the breach, dear friends, once more' (3.1.1). When I spoke to my men I said,

> Remember … that if you harm your regiment or its history by over-enthusiasm in killing, or cowardice, know that it is your family who will suffer. You will be shunned unless your conduct is of the highest order, for your deeds will follow you down through history. We will bring shame on neither our uniforms nor our nation.[4]

To drive the point home, I added, 'Your mothers will be in the queue at the Co-op and won't want you to let them down',[5] meaning that the impact of anyone turning their back on the enemy would be felt more sharply at home. My appeal drew from *Henry V*:

> Dishonour not your mothers. Now attest
> That those whom you called fathers did beget you.
> Be copy now to men of grosser blood,
> And teach them how to war. And you, good yeomen,
> Whose limbs were made in England, show us here
> The mettle of your pasture. Let us swear
> That you are worth your breeding, which I doubt not.   (3.1.22–28)

Later in the play, on the eve of the battle of Agincourt, as Henry surveys the hopelessly outnumbered ranks of the English yeomen and archers, he can see, in the background, the serried and countless ranks of haughty French knights, beautifully adorned and seated on war horses of the finest breeding – hence his decision to appeal to his men's inner courage, sense of duty, and divine predestination. Henry goes on to say that he fears there may be some amongst them who do not wish to fight. He bids them safe passage, as follows:

> Rather proclaim it, Westmorland, through my host
> That he which hath no stomach for this fight
> Let him depart. His passport shall be made,
> And crowns for convoy put into his purse.
> We would not die in that man's company
> That fears his fellowship to die with us.   (4.3.34–39)

However, in the remaining part of his speech, he once more evokes the excitement of being part of this historic enterprise, what some would call the joy of duty:

> We few, we happy few, we band of brothers –
> For he today that sheds his blood with me
> Shall be my brother; be he ne'er so vile
> This day shall gentle his condition –
> And gentlemen in England, now abed,
> Shall think themselves accursed they were not here,
> And hold their manhoods cheap whiles any speaks
> That fought with us upon Saint Crispin's Day.   (4.3.60–67)

Similarly, when I spoke to my soldiers, my emphasis was on how lucky they were to be there and part of that campaign: 'As for ourselves, let's bring everyone home safely and leave Iraq a better place for us having been there.'[6]

Reflecting on the reasons that led me to draw on *Henry V*, I would like to try and explain why parts of the dialogue from this play seemed to lend themselves to being invoked on the day, both because of the way they sound coming from leading commanders and because of the way in which they speak to their soldiers. I am not aware that Shakespeare ever served in an army, yet his familiarity with the ways of a volunteer force is uncanny. George MacDonald Fraser, better known for his series of books, the 'Flashman Papers', relates a strange conversation he had with a hard-bitten platoon sergeant, Sergeant Hutton, in his biographical account of the time he served as a private solider with the Border Regiment in Burma during the Second World War:

> I was lying on my groundsheet … when Sergeant Hutton squatted down beside me.
> 'W'at ye readin', then? W'at's this? 'Enry Vee – bloody 'ell, by William Shekspeer!' He gave me a withering look, and leafed over a page. 'Enter Chorus. O for a muse of fire that wad … Fook me!' He riffled the pages. 'Aye, weel, we'll 'ev a look.' And such is the way of sergeants, he removed it without by-your-leave; that's one that won't be away long, I thought.
> I was wrong. Three days later … Hutton loafed up and tossed *Henry V* down beside me and seated himself on the section grub-box. A silence followed, and I asked if he had liked it. He indicated the book.
> 'Was Shekspeer ivver in th' Army?'
> I said that most scholars thought not, but that there were blanks in his life, so it was possible that, like his friend Ben Jonson, he had served in the Low Countries, or even in Italy. Hutton shook his head.
> 'If 'e wesn't in th' Army, Ah'll stand tappin.'[7] 'E knaws too bloody much aboot it, man.'
> … I suggested hesitantly that the Bard might have picked up a good deal just from talking to military men; Hutton brushed the notion aside.
> 'Nivver! Ye knaw them three – Bates, an' them, talkin' afore the battle? Ye doan't git that frae lissenin' in pubs, son. Naw, 'e's bin theer.'[8]

What scholars of Shakespeare may not realize is the extent to which Shakespeare's 'language of war' in *Henry V* echoes both the idiolect of soldiers expressing their concerns on the eve of battle and the rhetorical power used by their commanding officers to lead them into battle. Also of note is the way in which regional inflections animate the speech of Henry's army who come from different parts of the British Isles, as Sergeant Hutton points out: 'Them fower officers, the Englishman an' the Scotsman an' the Irishman an' the Welshman – Ah mean, 'e's got their chat off, 'esn't 'e? Ye could tell w'ich wez w'ich, widoot bein' told. That Welsh booger!'[9] As Fraser's account suggests, Shakespeare's representation of war in *Henry V*, despite the critique it could be seen to offer, has also resonated strongly with those involved in combat and who prepared to sacrifice their lives.

Shakespeare, as much as military men down through history, seems to have known that freemen and volunteers fight better than conscripts. Freemen motivated by some greater goal fight even better. Napoleon Bonaparte observed that 'moral power is to physical as three parts out of four'.[10] The Duke of Wellington similarly observed that the appearance of Napoleon on the field of battle was worth 40,000 men.[11] Motivating soldiers requires more than words. It is hard training and discipline. It is tough love. Sweat does save blood when training for war. But when the day comes, it is the power with which leaders infuse their words that can alter the course of battle. Shakespeare understood this clearly and so put the words into Henry V's mouth.

What Shakespeare illustrates in *Henry V* is that, in order to motivate and drive fear out of his ranks and into the ranks of the foe, a commander must recognize the importance of rhetoric. As an ancient art of discourse, rhetoric was founded, coincidentally, it is believed, in ancient Mesopotamia, today's Iraq. In ancient Greece, Aristotle identified three persuasive audience appeals, comprising *logos, pathos*, and *ethos*. The five canons of rhetoric or phases of developing a persuasive speech were first codified in classical Rome: invention, arrangement, style, memory, and delivery.

Armies – like (travelling) bands of players in Shakespeare's time – rely on hierarchy, discipline, and comradeship in order to deliver their trade. The stage for which Shakespeare wrote most of his plays had few special effects and no elaborate props, few sound effects and no lighting to bring the audience to ancient Rome, Venice, or a muddy French battlefield. Shakespeare relied on the power of rhetoric and the skill of the players to cast a spell over the audience. He relied on *logos*, the logic of the argument delivered in a clear unambiguous manner; *pathos*, an appeal to the emotions sometimes through the display of suffering or struggle; and *ethos*, an appeal to ethics and morality in order to persuade.

To achieve this effect, a commander first and foremost needs to be supremely self-confident and, in turn, instil that confidence in the troops. In many respects, I was – with hindsight – fortunate. I was able to mould my command the way I wanted it to be, because there was a deep-seated unease at the heart of my command when I took over. As well as being understrength, the battalion had undergone a traumatic experience the previous year during a hostage crisis in Sierra Leone. They had coped extremely well with the experience as it unfolded at the time, but I found on my arrival as commanding officer on 1 January 2001 an extremely low state of morale. Since I had, by coincidence, been part of the Special Forces operation that had rescued the hostage soldiers of 1 R Irish from the hands of the African gang, the soldiers of my battalion believed that I had some inside track, some understanding of the events that were about to unfold.

However, language and appearance were also crucial to me. Whether he was ever a soldier or not, Shakespeare understood, both as a dramatist and as a player, that his writing would need to be interpreted by the actors and conveyed to the audience in such a manner that would grab their attention from the start and carry them along, if the play was to be a commercial success. Language is also crucial to a commanding officer for a different, but related reason. Both the playwright and the commanding officer need to use language *to move* their audiences and their soldiers to respond to the situation they are presented with. What Shakespearean scholars may understand as the power of Shakespeare's language to move audiences *metaphorically*, I understand as its power to move my troops *literally*, even in the face of imminent danger.

By language I mean more specifically the ability to master different idiolects and nuance. Sergeant Hutton grasped this understanding of Shakespeare's use of regional variation when he was in the jungle reading *Henry V*. I had English, Scots, and Welsh under my command, along with Fijians, South Africans, Canadians, and Australians, not to mention thirty-odd US Marines, but I wanted them to cohere as a regiment, to feel part of a tightly knit group of men and women, regardless of their origins. Once accepted into the regiment, they belonged together, and that meant they identified with their badges, symbols, and with cultural aspects that define Irishness, including accent. Having grown up in Belfast, my accent is distinctively Northern Irish. I consciously deployed my accent to deliver this speech to my troops, so that every individual in my regiment would understand that they were different from the hundreds of thousands of American and British soldiers stood ready to cross the border and that their conduct should be of the highest order to defend and identify with the distinction of being Irish or of associating with Irishness. Shakespeare routinely uses language to nuance characterization so that one knows who the Moorish general or the Danish prince are, but one can *still* understand them. Crucially, Sergeant Hutton could tell who was speaking in *Henry V* 'widoot bein' told'.[12]

In my work since leaving the military, I have run a company that trains policemen and soldiers as agent handlers for overseas governments. Their job is to recruit and run members of subversive organizations, be it in Iraq, Afghanistan, or Latin America. In Afghanistan, where 50 per cent of our police colleagues and all of the agents were illiterate, language, storytelling, and accents were vital. If we were describing a leading member of a subversive group that we wanted to endear, we would say that he had a Pastun accent with a hint of Farsi, which would conjure up an educated man in the mind of the listener. To say he had the tinny voice of a dancing boy from the tea house would have the opposite effect. A police chief who you might say sounds like a farmer immediately loses his standing in the eyes of the group, as they imagine an uncultured man – even if they have not met him.

Shakespeare's work clearly reflects a talent for capturing the essence of a situation and for presenting it to the audience in such a way that their every sense comes alive to it. Commanders in the army need the undivided and cooperative attention of their command if they are to succeed. That is why I resorted to *Henry V* for my eve-of-battle speech back in 2003, and that's at least partly why Prince Charles found my words had the power to move listeners profoundly. I explain this further in a book I wrote about my time in command:

> I wanted to forge a battalion that could react to my will at an instant and interpret my intent with such flair that they could conceive solutions and methods that would both delight me and add to our collective efforts. I knew that when this [my style of command] caught on it would make the battalion an unstoppable force which could move like a flock of birds and press home and attack with the ferocity of a hurricane finding ways through adversity.[13]

US General Colin Powell, Secretary of State to President Bush, once told me that 'when soldiers stop bringing you their problems you are no longer in command'. He was clear that a commander should engage with the whole range of emotions that are likely to be experienced by his subordinates. And this is where the complex, multiple crossovers with the writings and performance of Shakespeare and his players meet the reality of military life. The dramatic text must be written with *logos*, *pathos*, and *ethos*. Its presentation to an audience relies on invention, arrangement, style, memory, and delivery. And military command is the same – as Napoleon says, a leader's power to move is 'as three parts out of four'.

I cannot believe the contrast now with modern Iraq and the huge optimism and good will that abounded in March 2003. The existence of ISIS, popular Shia militias, and an insidious Iranian presence coupled with rampant corruption would all have been seen as flights of fantasy in 2003 – for us and for the Iraqis. Prince Charles's letter captures that spirit and it is written as if the task would have been achieved in a short time-frame. Down the years, since that fateful decision to cross the border was taken, the mistakes have been legion. But the troops who followed me across that border – as I said at the time 'flowing left and right behind me like a great cloak' – now look back in dismay at the turbulence and unrest, much of which has ended on our very shore in the form of refugees and not a few terrorists. As the slaughter of the prisoners in *Henry V* marred that campaign, the events of the botched occupation of Iraq marred the outcome of our mission. Perhaps we need a Shakespeare of the future to write a screenplay to remind us that we went with the very best of intentions.

Figure 24   Production photograph showing Brookes (Mark Theodore) and Sean
(Daniel Dalton) in *Days of Significance*, directed by Maria Aberg
(photograph by Keith Pattison © Royal Shakespeare Company (RSC 63007)).

CHAPTER 24

Who Pays the Price?

Maria Aberg on Roy Williams's Days of Significance (Royal Shakespeare Company, 2007)

*Amy Lidster and Sonia Massai (LM) in
conversation with Maria Aberg*

LM: Could you tell us about your selected object – this production photograph (Figure 24) – and how it captures your directorial take on Roy Williams's *Days of Significance* and how this play, which loosely draws on *Much Ado About Nothing*, represents the Iraq War?

Days of Significance has a three-act structure. The first act shows a group of friends on a night out in an English market town, just before two of them, Ben and Jamie, set off to fight as soldiers in Iraq. The central act takes place in Basra and is book-ended by video diaries filmed by Ben for Trish, his girlfriend, with its central part showing a raid that goes badly wrong for Ben and his two comrades, Brookes and Sean. The final act moves the action back to England, when Jamie, who has been accused of war crimes, rejoins the original group of friends who are gathered at a wedding reception. This photograph is from the second act and from a moment in the production that conveyed the devastation of war – for soldiers and civilians alike. This moment also epitomizes the confusion between who's the enemy and who's the friend, and how, as a soldier, one acts towards a civilian or a fellow soldier and friend. The desert camouflage (which is also discussed in Chapter 21 in this collection) is immediately recognizable as a shorthand for a new type of combat that often takes place in civilian spaces rather than a battlefield or more traditional 'theatres of war'. This moment summed up what I, Roy Williams, and others felt was complicated about the Iraq War, which, to a great extent, involved very young soldiers for whom this was their first experience of active combat, who might have been trained relatively quickly, and who were in many ways not equipped for the level of military and ethical complexities they faced in Iraq.

LM: Blood is often a key prop in your productions. It was especially prominent in this sequence, as the photograph shows, and in the context of a play that one might say attacks its audience frontally.

Yes, Roy and I decided to make it as real as possible. We wanted to make sure that audiences could not ignore what may be a replica of an image of what was actually taking place in Iraq. We went for straight naturalism.

LM: How does 'straight naturalism' on stage differ from the graphic images that come to us via the media from war zones like Iraq? Does it have a different purpose?

I think the key difference is – even if what you see on TV is ever so graphic – that you don't, as a viewer, breathe the same air as the people who are experiencing or enacting the violence. In the theatre, of course, you can't get away from it. The blood gets to you – and sometimes on you! – because you are in the same physical space.

LM: Why did you want the blood to get to (and on) the audience for this play?

The graphic representation of bodily harm and pain was central to this production. Our primary aim was not to argue for or against the Iraq invasion. That was not the purpose or reason for the production. What we wanted to do – and what we all felt very strongly about – was to point at who paid the price in this country for the controversial decision of going to war. We wanted to show the communities that these young men belonged to – and that are still paying the price. The realistic representation of combat and its consequences, on and off the battlefield, was something that we felt had to be shown and have an absolutely central place in our production.

LM: And blood was not the only type of bodily fluid you made copious use of in this production!

Indeed! People were being sick and pissing all over each other! I think there was something shocking, visceral, and confrontational about the emphasis that both Roy's writing and my directorial approach placed on these young people's experiences. I felt that this approach was crucially important, because I didn't want to sanitize either their experience of war or of life in a contemporary British market town.

LM: The locations of Act 1: Much Noise ('*A Pedestrian square in the middle of a city centre somewhere in the south-east of England*') and

Act 2: On the Side of the Angels (*'Basra, southern Iraq. An alleyway.'*) seem, perhaps unexpectedly, to have much in common.

Yes, there is a pervasive presence of violence connected to the kind of masculinity that we allow and foster in young men at home that has enormous consequences when these same men are sent into armed conflict abroad. For me, there was a direct link between the kind of violence – realized or threatened – that we see in Act 1 and the kind of violence that is created when you radically alter the context in Act 2.

LM: Were there aspects of this production that underscored the connection between these two worlds?

The setting allowed for great tempo and fluidity in all three sections of the production. In the original version performed in Stratford, we had what might be called a season stage, which was designed by Mike Britton for *Days of Significance* and for two other productions, *Pericles* and *The Winter's Tale*, directed by Dominic Cooke for the Complete Works Season. We had very thick corrugated metal on the floor and a ramp extending all the way up to the balcony that was very wide and by which the actors could run on and off. It amplified the kind of physical energy that is already embedded in Roy's writing. We also had a large metal box, slightly tilted on its side, which remained on stage and helped us transition between the two worlds. In the second version that played in London and then went on tour, we paid special attention to how the action transitions from Basra back to England, in the new third act, which was radically revised and expanded. In this revised version of the play, we wanted to zoom out of the tragic and operatic aspect of the wartime events at the end of Act 2, before landing back in a context – the wedding reception in Act 3 – that felt quite domestic. I had conversations with my sound designer, Carolyn Downing, with whom I had worked a few times, about what we could do. I wanted something that could function as a bridge between these two worlds, so she put together a sound effect that mixed a call to prayer with sounds of active combat and a song by Benjamin Britten performed by Peter Pears.

LM: The Stratford version was staged as a promenade production, which reinforced the kind of physical stage language you have just described. Were you able to retain some of the energy of the Stratford staging when the second version played at the Tricycle in London and then on tour?

The promenade configuration at the Swan Theatre in Stratford worked really well, as you can imagine, for the first act, when the characters are out getting drunk. It was also effective in framing and focusing the second act; but the third act in the original version was a series of short scenes that didn't have any specific setting. These scenes were played amongst the audience: we had a very abstract square on the ground, with actors stepping in and out and playing these little scenes of confrontation at the end. So the aesthetic production language itself disintegrated as the world of the characters fell apart. But what we found was that the emotional impact, the adrenaline and the sort of catharsis that you crave after the end of the second act, didn't quite deliver in that version. That prompted us, together, to come up with the idea of a wedding, and to repurpose some of those confrontations from the first version of the play for the wedding setting. But, on the whole, the third act was an entirely new idea and, of course, it was much more powerful to have Jamie's character walk into a wedding in his full uniform, seeing everyone again for the first time after he'd been accused of war crimes.

LM: Would you say that your production attempted to connect with the audience in ways that involved them, or even implicated them, in the events represented in the play?

One way in which we ensured that the audience felt they were directly involved was through a little vestige of the promenade configuration we had used in Stratford. When the second version played in London and then went on tour, we kept the fight that took place right at the start of the show between the characters of Jamie and Dan. In the promenade context, it worked very well because everyone was in modern dress and you couldn't tell who the actors were. When the fight started breaking out, suddenly, amongst the audience, you were in the play before you knew it. It worked really well, so in all venues, including the Tricycle, these two actors had a little scuffle, pre-show, in each venue's bar. They were then taken care of by security staff and escorted out. But then, of course, they returned through the auditorium once the audience was seated and made their way up onto the stage and then the play began. This was an important element that came out of the promenade structure, which we decided to hold onto. It felt important to say, very clearly, that these people are from our world; we are from the *same* world as these young men. This opening also triggered the audience's preconceptions and judgments of the two young men they had already seen in the bar. It was very interesting to observe people's reactions, first, when they thought that these young men had just stumbled in from Kilburn High Street, and then when they realized that it was part of the show. At the Tricycle, we did have someone who came up on stage to try and stop them! It really took audiences quite a long time to understand that they were actors – to a point where one of the actors had to say that the fight was part of the show!

LM: How did audiences in Stratford, London, and across the country respond to this visceral representation of the kind of violence that underpins both civilian life and combat in your production?

In Stratford, I think the audiences felt that they did not recognize or identify closely with these young men. But these men, these boys, live in the same country and we cannot look away from the fact that they are the soldiers who go into war to fight for the British flag. So, I would say the production felt more confrontational in Stratford than it did at the Tricycle. At the Tricycle, the show had a very different energy: it was much more emotionally raw from the company, both because the exchange with the audience felt more powerful and because the third act delivered better than it had done in Stratford.

LM: It must have been quite difficult to present Roy Williams's play in the sort of theatrical language you have just described at a time when the war was still far from reaching any level of temporary, let alone permanent, resolution.

I remember there was one review that accused us of treason, which is completely ridiculous. But – and this was again something we felt very strongly about – we never wanted to criticize the soldiers. We had many conversations about how the production positioned itself in relation to this question, especially when the show went on tour in 2009. There were often older members of the audience – especially at venues attended by communities whose young people had been sent to war in larger numbers than elsewhere – who felt that we were doing a disservice to them through the portrayal in the play. This question gave rise to very interesting conversations, because the company members, by and large, were of the exact same background and social circumstances as the characters in the play. They felt they had a great ownership of the stories and we had fascinating conversations – not just in relation to combat or conflict or the Iraq War – about the depiction of young people on and off stage and how young men and women from lower socio-economic backgrounds are represented in the media. *Days of Significance* felt very alive in ways that not all work does.

LM: Did you at any point feel that the connection with *Much Ado About Nothing* affected how audiences responded to *Days of Significance*? Reviewers picked up on the parallels: the war informs relationships

in both plays, some characters share their names with Shakespeare's characters (Ben and Trish, for example), and both plays end with a wedding, though the atmosphere, even in Shakespeare, is far from festive. Do you think audiences picked up on these parallels at all? And, if so, how did this recognition qualify their response to Roy's play?

The connection was more explicit in Stratford, because *Days of Significance* was staged as part of the Complete Works Season. But once we went on tour, I doubt that people knew or thought about the Shakespeare connection at all. And I don't believe we lost anything by not pushing it harder. If we had put it front and centre, I don't think audiences would have got more out of the production. Quite the opposite. There was a real risk that, if audiences were made directly aware of the connection, they may have come to the show looking for Shakespeare – that is, they may have come for a more 'literary' experience and missed what we valued about the production itself.

LM: Would you then say that the 'Shakespeare connection' was more enabling in securing a platform for the new play and the means for the production to tour, than in adding a layering of interpretation that typically emerges in work that more explicitly acknowledges that connection?

The Shakespeare connection was, as far as I understand it, part of the original commissioning brief from the RSC to Roy Williams. If anything, it served as an imaginative jumping off point for him, as a way of using some of Shakespeare's themes and characters to say something very provocative about the contemporary world. In Stratford, the presentation context provided its own layers of interpretation, as it was part of the Complete Works Festival and presented alongside a number of other contemporary plays that similarly borrowed from Shakespeare. Once the show was travelling around the UK, however, it stood proudly on its own two feet and didn't need that context to make its ideas sing.

Figure 25   Production photograph from *Othello*, directed by Nicholas Hytner at the National Theatre (2013) (photograph by Johan Persson, reproduced by permission of ArenaPAL).

CHAPTER 25

'Mere Prattle, without Practice, Is All His Soldiership'
Shaping the Soldier in Nicholas Hytner's Othello (National Theatre, 2013)

Jonathan Shaw

It had to start with a beer. I was introduced to this delicious Turkish brew, Efes, which you can see in the production photograph from *Othello* at the National Theatre (Figure 25), when I'd been based at St David's Camp on the UN line in Cyprus in 1986. We'd drunk it in preference to the dull, imported British beer. And it was for such touches of military credibility that I was asked by Nicholas Hytner (Nick) to be his military adviser for the production in 2013.

The army and alcohol have such an inevitable and double-edged relationship that if Shakespeare was looking for a tool by which Iago could bring Cassio down, alcohol was surely an obvious choice. For if you believe, as some scholars and readers have done over the centuries, that Shakespeare spent some of his 'missing years' in the army, then I suspect he would have seen the same dynamics in his time as I did in my thirty-two years in the army.[1] Two of these dynamics, in particular, I had to explain to the cast of Hytner's production of *Othello*: violence and command culture. Bored soldiers will fight amongst themselves not for the sake of violence itself but for fun or release, and to settle minor scores – and all within limits, intuitively understood by kids who'd grown up in the backstreets and were familiar with violence. But nothing in the life experience of officers like Cassio, very much the Sloane Ranger cavalry officer of his day, would prepare them for these dynamics. Indeed, when I was a young officer in Aldershot, it was very much the rule that you did not go drinking with the boys downtown; 'the Traf' was for hearing stories about, not for visiting. Indeed, it was not until I was a major running the Parachute Regiment selection that I ever went there, escorted by my fearsome group of SNCO instructors to keep me out of trouble. Cassio would seem to lack the requisite wise counsel from a sergeant major and even the most basic understanding of the rules of the game. He also confesses to Iago that he has a weak drinking head. He unwittingly sets his own trap and walks right into it.

It was a fascinating and educative experience, and a real privilege for me to work with Nick and the actors. But why did it matter to the production? Hytner had already directed *Henry V* in 2003 at the National Theatre, again with Adrian Lester in the lead role. He was aware that, whilst *Othello* might start out as an invasion story (much like *Henry V*), it turns into a very different and much more static scenario after the storm sinks the Turkish fleet and Othello finds himself in charge of a garrison in the sweltering heat of Cyprus. How did that work? What were the dynamics of garrisoning, how does 'command' operate in these circumstances, and what are the stresses and strains? I was recommended to Hytner by his old Cambridge friend Nigel Sheinwald who had been Tony Blair's Foreign Policy Adviser and then Ambassador to the USA. I knew Sheinwald in both of these roles and he primarily knew me from my time as general in charge of the multi-national division (GOC MND(SE)) in Basra, Iraq, a role that combined aspects of both invasion and garrisoning. My Cyprus experience was pure serendipity, but it added to my ability to advise on this production of *Othello*.

And so I came to explain my view on the command culture of operationally experienced soldiers. In simple terms, I described how it is easier to command on operations than in peacetime. Operations give an urgency, a motivation, an overriding reason for orders and obedience; having an enemy disciplines the troops. And of course, as Othello makes plain in his speeches, he is a creature of operations and has been promoted on account of his operational excellence. In a peacetime garrison, your enemy is boredom, particularly in the heat of Cyprus. Command involves that fine judgement of working the troops just hard enough to keep them occupied but not too hard to provoke a revolt. This can be tricky, especially in the heat of the Mediterranean and Middle East. The heat of a Cyprus summer, with endless, tedious guarding duties and the weakest of threats, made being adjutant of 3 PARA in 1986 an intriguing challenge! And alcohol was definitely one of the tools for reducing tension and easing pressure. As Adjutant, my greatest source of intelligence came from the Thursday evening suppers in the Sergeants' mess, which didn't stay sober for long; the loose tongues revealed all I needed to know. And it worked. Both my RSM and myself had been in the Falklands with 3 PARA and the bonds of loyalty created there between the ranks were still strong. We trusted them with drink. They respected the rules of the game. To paraphrase Foucault, power is not a possession, it is a relationship. We had that relationship and so we possessed the power to set the example and instil self-discipline in the troops. It proved an enlightening illustration for the cast.

Nick initially invited me to lunch to discuss the nuts and bolts of invasion and garrisoning, but our lunch overran as we both realized how great the gap was between his civilian perception of army culture and my experience. We arranged another lunch to continue exploring this gap and agreed that I'd talk with Adrian Lester to discuss command. Adrian had by all accounts done a brilliant job as Henry V, but Nick wondered if, as Othello, he might be even better and that my insights into the army might be useful for the full cast in acting out these culturally unfamiliar military roles.

And that posed an interesting question for Nick. The army is a fundamentally tribal organization, and you can cut its tribes in many ways. For instance, I always say that I joined the Parachute Regiment, rather than the army; a wider sense of belonging came with wider responsibility and experience. You can also divide cultures between peacetime and 'on operations'. Which did Nick want his actors to portray? I chose Parachute Regiment operational soldiering to set the patterns of behaviour for the cast. This suited Nick perfectly as he wanted to cast the actors as contemporary soldiers, embarked on an invasion but then garrisoning Cyprus. They were to be soldiers experienced in Iraq and Afghanistan but also, for the older ones, in Northern Ireland, the Balkans, Sierra Leone, and, perhaps, the Falklands. What I learnt briefing the actors was that, when it comes to actors convincing their audience, the most important audience they have to convince is themselves. And so it proved with me: being given the freedom to be totally true to myself and my cultural understanding of soldiering made it much easier for me to be credible in front of the cast. Precisely by not being prescriptive, Nick had got what he wanted. His trust paid dividends.

I was aware that, for most of the cast, the military was a strange and indeed culturally alien organization. Irrespective of actors' personal views, the 'army' that they so often portray in movies bears little resemblance to a 2013 army experienced in Iraq and Afghanistan. One of my motivations for taking on the job was to correct this portrayal, to reveal the intelligence, the humour, and the humanity that underlies what is often seen as a faceless bunch of thugs. For whilst soldiers are unlikely to claim any profound religious sense, I was struck by the self-sacrifice and selflessness that I saw in the Falklands: 'Greater love hath no man than this, that a man lay down his life for his friends' (John 15:13). It was that love I was to try to explain to the cast and manifest in their acting. This was the culture of the 'band of brothers' I'd seen on operations and wanted to see portrayed on the stage. To do that, I tried to explain the way the army was, before explaining what it had evolved to become. I needed to deconstruct why it was perhaps right, certainly understandable, for actors in world war movies to behave the way they did. Hence, in abbreviated form, I had to explain to the cast the evolution of military doctrine and discipline.

Most war films I have seen depict a very class-based hierarchy in which orders go one way and are obeyed. It's heavily control-based. Students of military history will know there are good military reasons for this: the mass conscript armies of both world wars were largely ill-trained and inexperienced. Hence Directive Command, which told people precisely what they were to do, period. This was the official doctrine of the army at the time of the Falklands in 1982. In 1990, the army produced its new doctrine, Mission Command, which focuses on intent – what is to be achieved – more than on the precise actions people should take. Once aware of the intent, army personnel are expected to have the knowledge and experience to do what needs to be done to achieve it. I welcomed this change, as I owed my life to having disobeyed the order of my immediate commander, my company commander, in the Falklands. He was a long way away and had no idea of my situation; and I could see a better way of achieving the intent of my commander two levels up, my Commanding Officer. I lived to tell the tale and pass the experience on to the cast of *Othello*.

Mission Command breeds a completely different relationship between the ranks. Traditionally, command was about an individual being in charge; now it is the mission that is in charge and everyone has a part to play in achieving that mission. If Directive Command is heavily control-based, this is command-based. So why might this distinction be useful for the actors? What they really wanted to know was how to salute properly! So I explained that, whereas under the old system, a salute was a recognition of subordination, of control, now a salute is a mutual symbol of respect, that both parties have a role to play in the achievement of the mission, that the commander knows and respects the subordinate enough to give him the job to do, and the subordinate is proud to have been given the task and wants to get on and do it. The key aspect of the salute is less the actions with the arms and hands, but rather with the eyes – look them in the eye and communicate that mutual trust and respect. This is true command, and it is based on trust, respect, and a shared endeavour. I believe that much of the power of Nick's production of *Othello* resulted from the conviction with which the cast embodied that ideal.

Saluting is about vertical trust, but there is a stronger bond yet: horizontal trust. This is between people who have been in combat together, who trust each other with their lives, who have possibly saved each other's lives. This total trust is occasionally established in civilian life (through activities such as rock climbing or firefighting), but it is institutionalized in the army. The very first piece of tactics you learn in the infantry is called 'fire and manoeuvre'. This involves attacking an enemy position by one party preventing the defenders from firing by shooting at them to keep their head down ('fire'), whilst the other party gets out of cover and runs across open ground for a few yards ('manoeuvre') before taking cover, putting down suppressing fire on the enemy whereupon, roles reversed, the first party gets up in its turn and advances. Every time a person moves, they are placing their lives in the hands of their mate. That is what breeds the total trust of the soldiers in each other. And as I explained in the programme notes to *Othello*, this trust is why Othello believes Iago more than his wife. He has known him far longer. He thinks he understands him far better and he trusts him far more profoundly. Poor Desdemona doesn't stand a chance.

Another thing I did was make sure the actors were dressed properly by bringing in an old soldier of mine, Colour Sergeant Steve Parrott, who had been a Tom (Para private soldier) and served with me on operations. He made sure that each actor shaped their berets just so, adapted their webbing to look lived-in, scrimmed their helmets to make them credible, and held and carried their weapons properly. The transformation on the cast was astounding and they relaxed into their roles. Interestingly, the one actor who didn't comply with this advice was Rory Kinnear. I began by trying to make him appear the experienced 'old sweat' and standard setter that he was meant to be, but after a while I stopped. For I realized that his scruffiness was actually a brilliant embodiment of how life had caught up with him and he had gone to seed – all that was left was the old sweat. His spur for revenge may seem immediately linked to Othello having passed him over for promotion in favour of Cassio; but his hatred is also a classic middle-age disillusion – that life has not turned out how he hoped – and, incapable of blaming himself, he takes it out on any and everyone around him, in relation to actual grievances like Cassio's promotion or imagined slights such as his wife's adultery. To military friends of mine in the audience, his tilted-back beret, unbowed beret ribbon, slovenly clothes, all jarred as unbecoming of an operational sergeant major. To use military jargon, he looked like a fat knacker. But as I said to them, that's the point. I never told Rory to do this. He just intuited that this was the way to externally portray his inner corrosion. Genius! No wonder he won the best actor award that year.

I think a military perspective is crucial for helping us to understand and re-evaluate *Othello* today. Adrian Lester told me that my programme notes offered to him the most radical reinterpretation in 350 years. When I read the play as a schoolboy, I saw Othello as a naive fool, out of his depth, and the evidence on which Iago based his sedition seemed too flimsy to be credible. It was only coming back to the play after a thirty-two-year army career that enabled me to see things in a different light, to realize how compelling Othello's downfall really was from a military perspective.

Othello illustrates the gulf that exists between civilian and military cultures (an idea that is also discussed by Iqbal Khan in Chapter 26). And it is a gap that is growing, as the army shrinks and fewer civilians have connections to those who have served. It is also a gap that the law increasingly doesn't recognize. Military culture is based on the requirements of war, where the individual is subordinate to the mission. In effect, when a soldier signs up for the army, they sign away their right to life and place their trust and well-being in the hands of the army. This denial of self, this institutionalized selflessness is what creates that bond between military people and that sense of shared endeavour and purpose that visitors to military establishments always notice. It is this selfless bond that is vital for combat; but it is a bond that is increasingly under threat of erosion from civilianization.

We have not been officially at war since 1945 – that is, there have been no formal declarations of a state of war – and it was notable in Iraq and Afghanistan how all military deaths were reviewed in a coroner's court and judged by civilian standards. There are many people who argue that this practice is inappropriate, and I am one of them. The right to take risks is a key part of being a soldier. Indeed, risk-taking is an obligation, and it comes with the territory. Soldiers take risks all the time. They go on operations with the kit and training they have, rather than the ideal kit and training for the job. This is the 'can do' attitude without which no army would deploy, let alone fight. Yet to a coroner, this looks like the government sending people to their death without the training and equipment that a responsible employer should guarantee (as in civilian employment law). The risk averseness leads to some strange decisions. The saga of the Snatch Land Rover, a highly manoeuvrable but highly vulnerable mode of transport, received much coverage and adverse comments in coroners' courts and led to them being withdrawn. Yet during my time in command in Basra, the Snatch was the key mode of transport. While the heavily armoured Warriors and Challenger tanks were confined to main roads, the Snatch could manoeuvre through the rabbit warren back streets of Basra to get to their target. We lost forty-one people on my tour, plus over one hundred injured; most of them in the heavily armoured vehicles and only a handful in the Snatch. By far the best way to keep safe is to avoid detection, which the Snatch could do by being unpredictable. The armour, by contrast, was channelled and vulnerable to ever-larger IEDs placed on predictable routes. But the subtlety of this argument, based as it was on risk management, not risk avoidance, was lost to coroners' courts. Risk management is key to military command and decision-making; risk avoidance is incompatible with military life.

Military law is based on the needs of the organization and operations. Civilian law seems to me to be based overwhelmingly on the rights of the individual. And those rights, as defined by law, seem to grow each year. It is clear that the two are incompatible. The more that civilian law is applied in the military, the more the moral basis of fighting soldiers will be undermined. *Othello* offers an extraordinary sixteenth-century illustration of this very twenty-first-century incompatibility. Many civilians watching the play will sympathize with Desdemona's pleading, on Cassio's behalf, to show mercy and forgiveness. Her focus is on the individual, arguing in effect that Cassio is highly talented and that this is his first offence, so surely he warrants another chance. Quite apart from feeding Othello's seed of doubt about the relationship between Cassio and Desdemona, this argument also illustrates the cultural gulf between Othello, a soldier since childhood, and his young civilian bride. For Othello's concern is less with the individual, Cassio, than with the good order and discipline of his own command, for which a clear example needs to be set and within which particularly high standards must be followed by the officers. Othello knows how corrosive a weak response would be to military discipline. Demotion is the right punishment for the organization, which is also reinforced by the soldiers' reaction to Cassio in the play.

The corrosive effect of the blurring of lines hit home to me as it recalled an incident during my command in Basra in 2007. Fifteen RN sailors had been captured by the Iranian Revolutionary Guard in disputed waters. A female stoker was filmed by Iranian TV smoking a cigarette, wearing a head scarf, admitting they were guilty as the Iranians said (they weren't) and pleading that she wanted to get home for her daughter's birthday. Other members of the crew were shown wearing earpods and playing music on patrol. My reaction as a soldier was one of outrage. My soldiers were risking (and losing) their lives on a daily basis and here were sailors being treated like heroes for in effect cooperating with the enemy's propaganda campaign. I wanted to see them court-martialled on return to the UK. Instead, they were greeted like heroes who had suffered injustice at the hands of the Iranians. Chiefs of Staff greeted them on the runway and they were allowed to sell their stories to the press. In effect, they were treated like civilians.

If this production of *Othello* brought home the power of that moral military bond and its vital necessity, then the play will have served the original aim of Greek theatre: to educate the audience. What saddens me is that, as it would seem from what Adrian said, this understanding of the military has been overlooked in theatrical responses to this play for centuries and stands ever-less chance of being understood. With fewer people in society recognizing these military moral bonds, the pressure to civilianize the military will only increase.

An article in the *Financial Times* on 4 October 2021 showed how some people at least appreciate these distinctive aspects of military culture. Under the heading 'The army has skills that government clearly lacks', Andrew Hill argued that the government had failed to generate the 'preparedness, resourcefulness, flexibility, decisiveness' required to cope with crises. My letter in response, published two days later, made exactly this point, namely that it was the military culture of the mission first, not the individual, that was key to these qualities. I concluded, 'It is good to see someone recognize that if you are interested in output rather than self-actualization, the mission not the individual must come first.' Othello embodies this idea(l); to Desdemona, it is a mystery.

For a final validation, I asked Nick if I could bring an old Royal Marine friend of mine who had been my Sergeant Major in a previous incarnation to give the play his once over. If the play was credible to Mick McCarthy, it would do for the NT audience! In the interval, Mick confessed to Nick, in his best Irish Scouse, that 'I tried reading it before I came, but gave up on page one. But seeing it – it all makes sense, I love it.' In fact, Mick's comment echoed exactly what Nick wrote in his programme notes – that he often found reading Shakespeare challenging and watching it sometimes incomprehensible. Mick's endorsement of the play reflected how well Nick had achieved his aim to make Shakespeare accessible to the widest possible audience. And that he found the soldiers credible was an endorsement of my insights on military culture and the actors' portrayal of it.

Nick was also amused by Mick's tales of thirty years in the Marines. Perhaps I steered his stories this way, but it has always amazed me how many of Mick's tales end with a punch up! And, of course, I thought Nick would be interested in how Mick's life experience bore out what I had said, that it so often starts with a beer …

Figure 26   Production photograph from *Othello*, directed by Iqbal Khan
(Royal Shakespeare Company, 2015) (photograph by Keith Pattison
© Royal Shakespeare Company (RSC 163865)).

CHAPTER 26

'Thou Hast Set Me on the Rack'
Torture and Modern Warfare in Iqbal Khan's
Othello (Royal Shakespeare Company, 2015)

Amy Lidster and Sonia Massai (LM) in conversation with Iqbal Khan

LM: Your chosen object is this photograph (Figure 26) from your 2015 production of *Othello* for the Royal Shakespeare Company that shows Othello's soldiers preparing to torture a prisoner of war. Could you tell us about the significance of this moment?

In this scene, three soldiers under Othello's command are closing in on a prisoner of war, who is crouching down in fear, with a bag over his head. The soldiers are wielding their instruments of torture – a drill, a gas torch, and a stapler – and circling the prisoner, as they prepare to use torture to interrogate him. Their aim is to extract the truth from him, by terrorizing him into submission. Othello was visible to the audience, as he stood upstage left, leafing through a file, his body language suggesting a detached, business-like attitude towards his men's use of torture, which was clearly happening under his direct orders and supervision. I chose this moment because I wanted to begin with Othello in his place of work, which is one of war, violence, and trading in political information. In my production, this scene (Act 3 Scene 1) takes place in subterranean spaces underneath a ruined sacred building that is being used as a military site. I didn't want to lock it down to an Islamic world and to suggest that the battle was between Christianity and Islam, so this bombed-out site has both Christian and Islamic architectural elements to it. I did, though, want to inflect it with the context of the Iraq War, the most recent conflict the United Kingdom has been involved with, because it would trigger memories of images and tropes associated with this conflict, including the journalistic reporting around the absolutely grotesque violation of the standards of international law for the treatment of prisoners of war at sites like Abu Ghraib.

Having said that, I did not want my production to map out onto this one specific conflict. I've never been interested in making 'closed theatre' that functions like a three-dimensional essay. I love to open out the experience for an audience, so the semiotic richness of a production triggers a constellation of ideas. I, for example, wanted this moment in the play to be linked to the 'persuasion scene' (Act 3 Scene 3), where Othello himself uses torture to force Iago to corroborate the affair between Desdemona and Cassio that Iago has been hinting at. But I also wanted to link this moment in the play to Desdemona's entrance straight after it. In fact, the torturing of the prisoner of war bleeds into the next sequence, when Desdemona walks in and absent-mindedly picks up the drill that's been left lying on the floor. By having the two sequences overlap, I wanted to show that Othello's world is a dangerous one, which his earlier accounts of military exploits (in Act 1 Scene 3) necessarily leave unmentioned, and not to suggest, as some productions do, that Othello's psyche as a black man taints his relationship with Desdemona even before Iago insinuates that she is unfaithful to him.

LM: Could you tell us more about the rationale that informed this fundamental shift from exploring the ravages of racial prejudice, as productions of *Othello* traditionally do, to your exploration of the ravages of modern warfare that is at the core of your production?
The central concern in this play is about the impossibility or the inadequacy of the rational processes that a human being employs to discover the truth about what's going on in another person's mind. If one's faith is disrupted, then the rational, the purely rational, options available to us become void. Othello's tragedy boils down to the fact that he cannot have the 'ocular proof' (3.3.362). I've therefore always thought that *Othello* is not about the fragile, vulnerable black man, but that his tragedy is linked to an epistemological crisis connected to the nature of his work. The central line in the play for me is in Act 3 Scene 3. After Desdemona's brief appearance, Othello says,

> Excellent wretch! Perdition catch my soul
> But I do love thee; and when I love thee not,
> Chaos is come again.   (3.3.90–92)

What is the chaos that is present in his mind? I think it's more than a doubt about his place as a person of colour in a world dominated by people with different traditions that exclude him. I think it's centred on the nature of his work and the nature of his experience as the leader of this mercenary force. That feels to me like a very modern condition that is specifically very, very problematic psychologically for anyone. The questions that haunt Othello haunt us: what makes up one's systems of loyalty? What makes up one's systems of justice and judgement? Whom is one accountable to? It's a very slippery condition, exemplified by Othello's requirement to engage with dark tasks, including using torture, that are not acknowledged in the public domain. So there's an *unreality* to the actions that happen in the shadows and I felt that I should be bold and that I should show Othello's complicity in it.

LM: How does this reconceptualization of Othello sit with the rest of the play?

I think it is key to the play as a whole. Shakespeare is very good at showing us Othello the military man, who's actually surprisingly urbane in the Venice section in the first act. He is supremely courteous, even though he professes 'Rude am I in my speech / And little blessed with the soft phrase of peace' (1.3.81–82). Venice, in fact, shows a man who has no brutality about him. Even when he is confronted by Brabantio, he chooses not to engage with him and opts for the diplomatic path instead. Of course, just before the play, he's decided to elope with Desdemona. No matter what he says in front of the Senate about how much Brabantio loved him and 'oft invited me, / Still questioned me the story of my life' (1.3.127–28), he obviously knew on some level that his feelings for Desdemona were going to be problematic. I don't think he imagined that there would suddenly be orders for him to go on an expedition to Cyprus and to fight a war, so I think the rest of the play accelerates the pace and problematizes his experience. But obviously he knew. I'm always sceptical of his public utterances. He's very, very skilled, very urbane. The whole of the Venice section sets up 'Othello's music', as his mellifluous rhetoric has been called, and it plays that beautifully and plays it in a burnished way. And then we're in Cyprus and he's triumphing, and the soldiers get drunk and he comes between them; but, again, he intimidates without resorting to violence. He acts decisively and takes Desdemona back to bed. When Act 3 Scene 3 happens, we are therefore completely shocked.

What directors often fail to do, as realizers of Othello's world, is show and share with the audience the experience of coming into Othello's place of work. That's why I decided to replace the musicians whom Cassio hires to bid Othello 'good morrow' – which he does in the hope of being reinstated, after Othello has demoted him for starting a brawl – with the torture sequence in Act 3 Scene 1. The original music scripted into the play is transformed into a call to prayer at dawn, and becomes directly linked to the torture scene. A beautiful moment, which has something sublime about it, is immediately contrasted with something that's absolutely reprehensible in every sense. This is why Othello is so reluctant to have Desdemona go to

Cyprus. His place of work is dangerous. In the torture scene, I wanted to show what the nature of his work is. When he's not with Desdemona, he is engaged in cleaning up and removing friction, and in those necessarily 'invisible' activities that happen in his place of work.

LM: Is Desdemona aware of what happens in Othello's place of work?
When Desdemona enters and picks up the drill, immediately after the torture scene, the memory of that previous scene is still saturating the space that she now unwittingly occupies – and that's the point I wanted to make: her domestic space is fraught with violence. I think what we do when we are watching her at this moment in the play is feel her inexperience. She's emphatically not limited in terms of intelligence or personal strength. Desdemona is in fact *incredibly* potent in Venice. For her to stand up against her father is one thing, but for her to force Othello's hand and the Senate's hand, when *she* decides to follow Othello to Cyprus, is genuinely arresting. Instead, she is limited in terms of her experience, and she's unaware of the fact that she is now in a dangerous, volatile space. It's not that Othello is dangerous and volatile: the space is, and Othello's activities are. She has absolutely no sense that the drill is anything other than a toy and she uses it playfully against Othello, which is, for him, as you can imagine, terrible. And it motivates his lines: 'Excellent wretch! Perdition catch my soul' (3.3.90). My Othello attempts to cleanse his soul and redeem himself through her, but he knows that what he is doing is fraught with vulnerability and fragility.

LM: Are the tragic consequences of Othello's vulnerability redoubled by the fact that Iago was played by Lucian Msamati? Is race, in other words, reinscribed into your production by the unconventional casting of Iago?
Yes, but only to some extent. Iago's betrayal is linked to the nature of the connection between these two men, their shared experiences, and possibly to an assumption of some kind of shared identity. But casting Iago as black has problematic implications. I remember that, when I first announced it, people assumed that I was planning to represent Iago as the self-hating black man, the assumption being that Iago is by definition racist and he's motivated by racial hatred – in other words, he hates Othello, so he must also hate himself. That was never my intention. Quite the opposite! I did show that Iago can make use of white fragility around race, as and when he needs – for example, in the opening scene with Roderigo. He can also assume a kinship with Othello, which Othello begins to lean into more and

more. But much more important to me was their shared history – and not so much the fact that they have fought side by side on the battlefield and are ready to take a bullet for each other, as the fact that they are engaged in shameful, invisible acts of brutality and that there are very, very few people who will understand the chaos that each other has experienced over time. In this respect, both men are inscribed by their otherness: Othello is a 'celebrity Other' and his otherness is, apparently, at the beginning, celebrated; Iago seems to have assimilated and so has had to repress his sense of difference. But their otherness is linked to their military world rather than to their racial identities. Both men share a feeling of dislocation from the society that employs them to do what they do, but refuses to acknowledge it. And this sense of dislocation intensifies their bond.

LM: Would you therefore say that the ultimate act of betrayal can be pinned on the state that hires both men, as opposed to Iago's individual motivation for hating Othello?

Precisely! Othello is primarily betrayed by the state. The nature of what he does makes one wonder about the nature of the contract that binds him to the Venetian state. What is the nature of that contract and, by the same token, the nature of Othello's loyalty to it? The worst thing about what Othello does on behalf of the Venetian state is the implicit assumption that certain lives are to be mourned less than others – are to be valued differently, as Judith Butler suggests in *Bodies That Matter*. Or to put it more crudely, the assumption here is that brown lives are less 'mournable' than other lives. Engaging in wars in this way (and the sort of activities they require) will inevitably tear up any pre-existing systems of value, including 'rules of engagement' associated with earlier models of warfare, perhaps the very wars Othello evokes in his speech to the Senate in Act I. An important part of the new rules of engagement that characterizes modern conflict has to do with limiting the amount of information that those who lead the state pass on to those who fight on their behalf. Those who fight in modern conflict – or 'proxy wars' – have a sense that they might be breaking a small rule, but that more traditional rules of engagement are being protected. You might be the instrument of compromise, but with a view to maintaining the noble contract, as it were. The less information you are given about the global activities, the more likely you are to continue to honour your limited rules of engagement that break those more fundamental, international agreements about how to conduct oneself at times of war.

This is a very central part of the journey that Othello goes on, conveyed by the extensive use I made of files as props in my production. Those files enshrine the rules of engagement, which progressively become more and more complex as the scenes continue. So when Desdemona exits the stage in Act 3 Scene 3 and Othello says, 'Excellent wretch! Perdition catch my soul / But I do love thee; and when I love the not, / Chaos is come again' (3.3.90–2), Iago takes a file and smashes him over the back with it. This is a playful gesture, but, actually, the chaos *is* the file. The audience doesn't need to understand it – there's something there that is playful, but also ever so slightly disturbing, which I think is easily picked up in performance. This gesture marks the end of Othello's idealized, positive, and untroubled sense of who he is and what he does as a commanding officer working for Venice.

LM: Thinking about how audiences responded to this moment in your production, but also about your production more generally, would you say that you were successful in inviting a critical reflection on the new rules of engagement ushered in by conflicts like the Iraq War?

The timing of this production meant that it occurred during the 'aftermath' of the Iraq War. Its immediate context allowed me to problematize the idea that there is anything like a 'just war' and that anybody can unproblematically use phrases like that in our own time. Given the temporal proximity of that conflict and how it had complicated people's ideas about war, I knew that the audiences were absolutely ready for me to challenge and to provoke them. The other thing I could do at the time was to explore how someone's identity can be tainted and compromised by their complicity in an action, whilst also struggling with having a limited agency. That would have been harder to do before the Iraq War. To have made Othello the instigator of torture before the Iraq War would have detracted from the audience's willingness to sympathize with him. I think now we have a much more unstable sense of what wars are and how they should be fought. If there was unproblematic criticism in my production, it was directed at the visible agents of invisible activities, like state-sanctioned torture – that is, at the governments involved in this conflict.

Afterword

Emma Smith

'Piece out our imperfections with your thoughts' (1.0.23). Throughout *Henry V*, the Chorus exhorts its audience to do the work to supplement and round out the inadequacies of theatrical representation. In the introductory scene to the final act of the play, spectators are urged one last time. The Chorus asks our indulgence around those 'things / Which cannot in their huge and proper life / Be here presented' (5.0.4–6). This time, those large matters concern the victorious king's return to London. 'You may imagine him on Blackheath' (5.0.16), encourages the Chorus, who is variously part historian, part embedded war reporter, and part spin-doctor. 'In the quick forge and working-house of thought' (5.0.23), the citizens of London flock to greet him.

The Chorus's vision begins simply enough. Imagine the king, here in familiar London. But it soon freewheels into chronological impossibilities, merging pasts, presents, and futures in a moment of synchronicity. This moment is catalysed by a potent shared idea: the celebrations for the end of war. First those imagined Londoners are likened to the citizens of ancient Rome. The mayor and aldermen are as the 'senators of th'antique Rome, / With the plebians swarming at their heels', who greet Henry as 'their conquering Caesar' (5.0.26–28). But the chronology judders: suddenly the simile is not from the past but from the future: 'Were now the general of our gracious empress, / (As in good time he may) from Ireland coming, / Bringing rebellion broachèd on his sword' (5.0.30–32). The reference is to Elizabeth's favourite general, Robert Devereux, second Earl of Essex, concurrently making a serious diplomatic and military hash of his expedition to quell the Irish rebellion. The comparison fixes the play's first performance in a kind of temporal and military limbo during the summer months of 1599. The Chorus's syntax is hanging, a prophecy without a fulfilment. It anticipates a victory that, as the subsequent centuries of Anglo-Irish history have amply proved, will never come: one historian, writing in the 1960s, saw his own contemporary parallel, calling Elizabeth's Irish wars 'England's Vietnam'.[1]

This topicality is unusual. Shakespeare's dramaturgy is more often allusive rather than explicit, and its comparisons with the present shimmer, almost always uncertain, almost always deniable. *Henry V*'s reference to Elizabeth and to Essex here has been claimed to be 'the only explicit, extradramatic, incontestable reference to a contemporary event anywhere in the [Shakespearean] canon'.[2] Perhaps it's this boldness that so discombobulates the Chorus, who then stammers through some unnecessary plot summary about the Holy Roman Emperor interceding for the defeated France, before whisking Henry awkwardly from his imaginary London triumph 'straight back again to France' (5.0.45). The victory, the adulation, the crowds of relieved well-wishers – be they in Rome in 48 BCE, in the post-Agincourt moment of 1420, amid Elizabeth's Irish wars in 1599, or in any one of the many years in which the play has been performed to echo with contemporary conflicts – is illusory. And although Victorian stage productions loved to add in this scene – one report of Charles Calvert's Manchester production of 1872 noted its unusual attention to these welcoming crowds, including 'groups of anxious women who scan the faces of the returned warriors to distinguish, if possible, a husband, son, or father'[3] – it is surely significant that, for the play, the joyful victory parade is simply a brief sequence of rhetorical tableaux, unsettled by different historical comparisons. The text of the play that is most historically contiguous with the events to which it alludes, the 1600 Quarto *The Chronicle History of Henry the Fift*, does not include this speech at all, and even its topicality is illusory when it reaches print in 1623, almost a quarter-century after its referent.

Two elements of this textual example seemed appropriate for an Afterword to this splendid collection of essays and objects. The first was the Chorus's recognition that theatre itself is a kind of proxy. The stage offers us only a small version of something that cannot ever be fully represented in its 'huge and proper life'. It is thus like the images – the production stills and broadsides and exhibitions and documents that make this book so resonant. Like the objects discussed in this collection, Shakespeare's plays themselves work synecdochally. *Henry V*, a play obsessed with warfare is itself a substitute; representation is synecdoche (the rhetorical figure in which the part represents the whole), as Kenneth Burke noted in his influential *The Grammar of Motives*, a book published in 1945 and with the epigraph *ad bellum purificandum* – towards the purification of war. Synecdoche, both theatrical and in the chapters of this book, works by spinning a specific detail or instantiation into something larger, offering a glimpse of the whole that cannot otherwise be fully entertained. So the Chorus to *Henry V* helps focalize the relationship between specificity and generality that is so crucial to Shakespeare's dramaturgy, to forms of representation on stage and in other synecdochic objects. Further, its temporal amplitude speaks to the ways in which his works have been reimagined in so many subsequent contexts.

The Chorus's chronological mash-up also reveals that Shakespeare's engagement with warfare cuts decisively through the scholarly urge to historicize. Weapons, procedures, theatres of war, the specific global fault lines and ideologies around which opposing armies might muster – these are all specific to a time and place. But, as the essays in this volume reveal over and over again, they also echo across those boundaries. Different ages have polished up Shakespeare's works into different mirrors to their own concerns, but war has a horribly recurrent topicality. There is no end to war, as *Henry V* knows all too well. The play's own moment of triumph is transient. It closes acknowledging the inevitable march of history and the loss of all that Henry had gained through his French wars: its anticlimactic ending registers that war is perennial. Only the dead, George Santayana wrote in 1922, channelling Stoic wisdom, have seen the end of war.[4]

So far, so gloomy. Writing this amid a horrifying European war in the summer of 2022 does not help the feeling of fatalism. But what is compelling about the stories and objects in *Shakespeare at War* is how vivid they are. Just as Shakespeare's own depiction of war offered a stage for a range of human behaviour, rhetoric, and tone, so too the ongoing engagement of the works in wartime contexts is life-affirming: variously satiric, hopeful, poetic, connected, resonant. The objects and analyses collected in this volume, like the associated exhibition, offer numerous potential reworkings of its title: Shakespeare in war, Shakespeare on war, Shakespeare not war, Shakespeare therefore war. The contributors reveal how plural and varied the connections between these fields of inquiry are. *1 Henry IV* opens with the king hopefully announcing the end of conflict: 'No more shall trenching war channel her fields / Nor bruise her flow'rets with the armèd hoofs / Of hostile paces' (1.1.7–9). We know he is bound to be wrong. But, as the Elizabethan soldier-poet Philip Sidney recognized, poetry flourishes 'when the trumpet of Mars [does] sound loudest'.[5] Whatever peace we may wish for in our own time, we acknowledge the ongoing creative partnership of Shakespeare and war.

Notes

Introduction

1 For recent accounts that consider the representation of war in Shakespeare, see Nicholas de Somogyi, *Shakespeare's Theatre of War* (Aldershot: Ashgate, 1998); Simon Barker, *War and Nation in the Theatre of Shakespeare and His Contemporaries* (Edinburgh: Edinburgh University Press, 2007); Paola Pugliatti, *Shakespeare and the Just War Tradition* (Farnham: Ashgate, 2010); Patrick Gray (ed.), *Shakespeare and War*, a special issue of *Critical Survey*, 30:1 (2018); and David Loewenstein and Paul Stevens (eds), *The Cambridge Companion to Shakespeare and War* (Cambridge: Cambridge University Press, 2021). For studies that feature wartime responses to Shakespeare, sometimes with an emphasis on a single conflict, see Ros King and Paul J. C. M. Franssen (eds), *Shakespeare and War* (Basingstoke: Palgrave Macmillan, 2008); Irena R. Makaryk and Marissa McHugh (eds), *Shakespeare and the Second World War: Memory, Culture, Identity* (Toronto: University of Toronto Press, 2012); Monika Smialkowska (ed.), *Shakespeare and the Great War*, a special issue of *Shakespeare*, 10:3 (2014); and Emma Smith (ed.), *Shakespeare and War,* the 2019 issue of *Shakespeare Survey* (72).

2 These conclusions reflect the central argument and methodology developed in Amy Lidster's book-length study *Wartime Shakespeare: Performing Narratives of Conflict* (Cambridge: Cambridge University Press, 2023), the other main output produced along with this collection as part of a Leverhulme-funded research project on 'Wartime Shakespeare' (2018–2021).

3 Zelensky's speech was widely reported in the world press; see, for example, Maureen Dowd, 'Zelensky Answers Hamlet', *The New York Times*, 12 March 2022, www.nytimes.com/2022/03/12/opinion/zelensky-ukraine-russia-biden.html (accessed 24 June 2022). For further uses of *Hamlet* and this soliloquy in Ukraine, see 'To Make Oppression Bitter: Shakespeare Scholars on the Frontline in Ukraine', *To Be or Not to Be* podcast, 15 (7 March 2022), https://tobeornottobe.podbean.com/e/to-make-oppression-bitter-shakespeare-s-scholars-on-the-frontline-of-war-in-ukraine/ (accessed 15 March 2022).

4 From a Tweet posted by Ukraine / Україна @Ukraine, and cross-posted to @10DowningStreet on 15 March 2022.

5 Irena R. Makaryk, 'Performance and Ideology: Shakespeare in 1920 Ukraine', in *Shakespeare in the Worlds of Communism and Socialism*, ed. Irena R. Makaryk and Joseph G. Price (Toronto: University of Toronto Press, 2006), pp. 15–37 (p. 20).

6 Matthew Weaver, 'It is illegal to join fight in Ukraine, Grant Shapps tells UK troops', in *The Guardian*, 9 March 2022, www.theguardian.com/world/2022/mar/09/it-is-to-join-fight-in-ukraine-grant-shapps-tells-uk-troops (accessed 24 June 2022).

7 See also *HyperHamlet*, a corpus of references to and quotations from *Hamlet*, www.hyperhamlet.unibas.ch (accessed 25 June 2022).

Chapter 1 'The Truth for Which We Are Fighting'

1 Quotations are from this scribal copy held at the Huntington Library (LA 123). Pagination to this copy is given in brackets in the main text. A digital copy of Garrick's holograph manuscript, entitled 'A Dialogue between an Actor and a Critic by way of Prologue to the English Opera call'd The Tempest', is available at https://openlibrary.org/books/OL25668791M/A_dialogue_between_an_actor_and_a_critic_by_way_of_prologue_to_the_English_opera_call%27d_The_tempest.

2 Even the most sustained critical study of Garrick's opera barely mentions the 'Dialogue' and concludes that, other than 'hav[ing] the merit of brevity, … the opera was a failure, and … Garrick did not relish being mentioned in connection with it'. See George Winchester Stone, Jr, 'Shakespeare's *Tempest* at Drury Lane during Garrick's Management', *Shakespeare Quarterly* 7 (1956), 1–7 (p. 5).

3 This view is still dominant. See, for example, David Francis Taylor: 'Garrick … deployed his *Tempest* to draw the cultural and political battle lines, and to reinvigorate the analogy between Prospero's island and a bellicose, war-ready Britain', in his 'The Disenchanted Island: A Political History of *The Tempest*, 1760–1830', *Shakespeare Quarterly* 63 (2012), 487–517 (p. 492).

4 All quotations from Garrick's opera refer to *The Tempest, an Opera, Taken from Shakespear. As It Was Performed at the Theatre-Royal in Drury-Lane. The Songs from Shakepsear, Dryden, &c. The Music Composed by Mr. Smith* (London: J. and R. Tonson, 1756).

5 All quotations are from John Dryden and William Davenant, *The Tempest, Or The Enchanted Island. A Comedy. As It Is Now Acted at His Highness the Duke of York's Theatre* (London: Henry Herringman, 1670).

6 Paul Franssen, 'Canute or Neptune? The Dominion of the Seas and Two Versions of *The Tempest*', *Cahiers Élisabéthains* 57:1 (2000), 79–94 (p. 81).

7 Gavin Foster, 'Ignoring *The Tempest*: Pepys, Dryden, and the Politics of Spectating in 1667', *Huntington Library Quarterly* 63:1–2 (2000), 5–22 (esp. pp. 8–9).

8 Copies of both prints can be accessed at www.royalacademy.org.uk/art-artists/work-of-art/the-invasion-plate-1-france and www.royalacademy.org.uk/art-artists/work-of-art/the-invasion-plate-2-england-1.

9 Dryden and Davenant were the first to reassign Miranda's speech 'Abhorrèd slave, / Which any print of goodness wilt not take, / …' (3.2.351–62) to Prospero because they found the language too harsh and abusive to be spoken by a virtuous young woman. Later editors and theatre directors followed suit and continued to ascribe this speech to Prospero well into the twentieth century.

10 Linda Colley, *Britons: Forging the Nation, 1707–1837* (New Haven, CT: Yale University Press, 1992), p. 105. Colley's views on the unifying effect of the Seven Years' War on current configurations of British identity have proved controversial and are still being debated. See, for example, Stephen Conway, 'War and National Identity in the Mid-Eighteenth-Century British Isles', *The English Historical Review* 116 (2001), 863–93. But the significance of her analysis of the effect of the growing Empire on the national consciousness remains unchallenged.

11 Though the Azores were by then under Portuguese possession, the British, as well as other European nations, had commercial ventures there and often used their ports to replenish their provisions while crossing the Atlantic.

12 Jonathan Crimmins, 'Reconciliation in David Garrick's *Harlequin's Invasion* and *Cymbeline*', *Studies in English Literature 1500–1900*, 59:3 (2019), 559–79 (p. 561).

Chapter 2   The Seven Years' War (1756–1763) and Garrick's Shakespearean Nationalism

1 David Garrick, *Harlequin's Invasion*, in *The Plays of David Garrick*, ed. Harry William Pedicord and Frederick Louis Bergmann, 7 vols (Carbondale: Southern Illinois University Press, 1980), I, 1.1.48–49.

2 John O'Brien, *Harlequin Britain: Pantomime and Entertainment, 1690–1760* (Baltimore: Johns Hopkins University Press, 2004), p. 222.

3 Garrick, *Harlequin's Invasion*, 1.1.41, 43.

4 O'Brien, *Harlequin Britain*, p. 135.

5 William Hawkins, 'Prologue', *Cymbeline a Tragedy, altered from Shakespeare* (Norwich: Cornmarket Press, 1969 [facsimile]), p. ix.

6 Hawkins, 'Prologue', p. ix.

7 Howard D. Weinbrot, 'Enlightenment Canon Wars: Anglo-French Views of Literary Greatness', *ELH* 60:1 (1993), 79–100 (p. 90).

8 Frans De Bruyn, 'Shakespeare, Voltaire, and the Seven Years' War: Literary Criticism as Cultural Battlefield', in *The Culture of the Seven Years' War: Empire, Identity, and the Arts in the Eighteenth-Century Atlantic World*, ed. De Bruyn and Shaun Regan (Toronto: University of Toronto Press, 2014), pp. 147–68 (p. 158).

9 Jonathan Crimmins, 'Reconciliation in David Garrick's *Harlequin's Invasion* and *Cymbeline*', *Studies in English Literature* 59:3 (2019), 559–79.

10 Garrick, *Harlequin's Invasion*, 1.1.1–2.

11 Carl Schmitt, *The Concept of the Political*, trans. George Schwab (New Brunswick, NJ: Rutgers University Press, 1976), p. 26.

12 Western continues: 'Anyone, therefore, who wished to shine in national or county politics needed to do everything that could reasonably be expected of him to forward it and avoid giving any grounds for the accusation that any lack of progress was due to his neglect'. In J. R. Western, *The English Militia in the Eighteenth Century: The Story of a Political Issue, 1660–1802* (London: Routledge & Kegan Paul, 1965), p. 146.

13 Garrick, *Harlequin's Invasion*, 1.1.7. For more on how theft in the regular army contributed to the discourse surrounding the Militia Acts, see Matthew McCormack, *Embodying the Militia in Georgian England* (Oxford: Oxford University Press, 2015), pp. 33–53.

14 E. J. Hobsbawm, *Nations and Nationalism since 1780: Programme, Myth, Reality* (Cambridge: Cambridge University Press, 1990), p. 33.

15 San Marino, Huntington Library, John Larpent Plays, MS LA 166, p. 3.

16 MS LA 166, p. 1.

17 Ibid.

18 Garrick, *Harlequin's Invasion*, 2.2.4–5.

19 Ibid., 2.2.6–7.

20 Ibid., 2.2.32.

21 Ibid., 2.2.44.50, 56.

22 Ibid., 2.2.44.56, 63, 64–65.

23 Ibid., 2.2.44.71–73.

24 MS LA 166, p. 4.

25 Garrick, *Harlequin's Invasion*, 2.2.21–24.

26 Ibid., 1.1.1, 51.

27 Ibid., *Harlequin's Invasion*, 3.2.121–22.

28 O'Brien, *Harlequin Britain*, p. 221.

29 Carl Schmitt, *The Crisis of Parliamentary Democracy*, trans. Ellen Kennedy (Cambridge, MA: MIT Press, 1985), p. 68.

30 O'Brien, *Harlequin Britain*, p. 220.

31 Garrick, *Harlequin's Invasion*, 1.1.52, 55.

32 George Winchester Stone, Jr, *The London Stage, 1660–1800: A Calendar of Plays, Entertainments & Afterpieces*, Part 4, *1747–76* (Carbondale: Southern Illinois University Press, 1962), p. 765.

33 Stone, *The London Stage*, p. 766.

Chapter 3   Revolutionary Shakespeare

1 Kenneth Silverman, *A Cultural History of the American Revolution: Painting, Music, Literature and the Theatre in the Colonies and the United States from the Treaty of Paris to the Inauguration of George Washington, 1763–1789* (New York: Crowell, 1976), p. 147.

2 Ibid., p. 148.

3 'Advertisement for the 1770 Performance of Julius Caesar', *Pennsylvania Journal*, 31 May 1770, p. 3.

4 Silverman, *A Cultural History*, p. 82.

5 Bernard Bailyn, *The Ideological Origins of the American Revolution* (Cambridge, MA: Harvard University Press, 1968), p. 23.

6 For example, in ancient Rome, Liberty was often depicted as a woman grasping a pike topped with a *pileus*, the cap of a freed slave. This feminized Liberty was a ubiquitous image of the Revolution, as were the Liberty Cap and Liberty Pole. And American military leaders, especially George Washington and General Israel Putnam, were explicitly likened to Cincinnatus, the Roman leader who famously put aside the plough to take up arms for Rome, returning to his farm when Rome was safe.

7 'An act to prevent stage-plays and other theatrical entertainments', *Boston Evening Post*, 23 April 1750, p. 4.

8 Odai Johnson, *Absence and Memory in Colonial American Theatre: Fiorelli's Plaster* (Basingstoke: Palgrave Macmillan, 2006), p. 41.

9 William Dunlap, *A History of American Theatre from Its Origins to 1832* (Urbana: University of Illinois Press, 2005 [1832]), p. 23.

10 David D. Mays, 'The Achievements of the Douglass Company in North America: 1758–1774', *Theatre Survey* 23 (1982), 144–45.

11 Odai Johnson, *London in a Box: Englishness and Theatre in Revolutionary America* (Iowa City: University of Iowa Press, 2017).

12 Ibid., p. 61.

13 Ibid., p. 9.

14 T. H. Breen, *American Insurgents, American Patriots: The Revolution of the People* (New York: Hill and Wang, 2010), p. 42.

15 Richard L. Bushman, *The Refinement of America: Persons, Houses, Cities* (New York: Random House, 1992).

16 Ibid., p. 193.

17 Johnson, *London in a Box*, p. 9.

18 Bailyn, *The Ideological Origins*, p. 44.

19 'John Adams to Abigail Adams, 14 April 1776', *Founders Online*, National Archives, https://founders.archives.gov/documents/Adams/04-01-02-0248.

20 Alan Taylor, *American Revolutions: A Continental History, 1750–1804* (New York: Norton, 2016), p. 94.

21 'Letter from John Adams to Abigail Adams, 20 September 1774', *Adams Family Papers: An Electronic Archive*, Massachusetts Historical Society, www.masshist.org/digitaladams/archive/doc?id=L17740920ja.

22 Carol Berkin, *Revolutionary Mothers: Women in the Struggle for America's Independence* (New York: Knopf, 2005), p. 13.

23 Odai Johnson and William J. Burling, with James A. Coombs, *The Colonial American Stage, 1665–1774: A Documentary Calendar* (Madison, NJ: Fairleigh Dickinson University Press, 2001), p. 249.

24 Bruce McConachie, 'American Theatre in Context, from the Beginnings to 1870', in *The Cambridge History of American Theatre: Volume One – Beginnings*

to 1870, ed. Don B. Wilmeth and Christopher Bigsby (Cambridge: Cambridge University Press, 1998), pp. 111–81 (p. 127).

25 The dating of this event is suggested by Paul Leicester Ford, *Washington and the Theatre* (New York: B. Franklin, 1970), p. 44.

26 Quoted in Ford, *Washington and the Theatre*, p. 44.

27 Worthington Chauncey Ford, *The Writings of George Washington* (New York: G. P. Putnam, 1890), p. 4n.

28 Daniel O'Quinn, 'Half-History, or the Function of Cato at the Present Time', *Eighteenth-Century Fiction* 27 (2015), 479–507 (p. 494).

29 *Journals of the Continental Congress, 1774–1789*, ed. Worthington C. Ford et al., 17 vols (Washington, DC, 1904–37), XII, p. 1018.

Chapter 4   *Hamlet* Mobilized

1 See Isaac Cruikshank, 'The Empress's wish or Boney puzzled!!' (London, 1810).

2 For Woodward's practices, see Simon Heneage, 'Woodward, George Murgatroyd (1760?–1809)', *ODNB*, online edn, September 2004, https://doi.org/10.1093/ref:odnb/29943 (accessed 18 June 2022).

3 See, for example, the broadside 'Shakespeare's Ghost!' (London, [1803?]), which compiled a series of quotations from plays including *Henry V* and *King John* into a single address to Britons that rallied them 'TO ARMS' for 'ENGLAND! and KING GEORGE'.

4 'Bonaparte's Soliloquy at Calais: A Parody', *The Monthly Visitor and New Family Magazine*, 5 (September 1803), pp. 86–87.

5 For Ackermann's networks, see Timothy Clayton, 'The London Printsellers and the Export of English Graphic Prints', in *Loyal Subversion? Caricatures from the Personal Union between England and Hanover (1714–1837)*, ed. Anorthe Kremers and Elisabeth Reich (Göttingen: Vandenhoeck & Ruprecht, 2014), pp. 140–62.

6 Christian Deuling, 'Aesthetics and Politics in the Journal *London und Paris* (1798–1815)', in *(Re-)Writing the Radical: Enlightenment, Revolution and Cultural Transfer in 1790s Germany, Britain and France*, ed. Maike Oergel (Berlin: De Gruyter, 2012), pp. 102–18.

7 'Bonaparte's Soliloquy at Calais', *London und Paris*, 12:5 (1803), 78–82 (p. 79): 'Nicht ohne Spitze und Anzüglichkeit, aber doch immer noch mit einiger Feinheit behandelt ist folgender Monolog, der vor kurzem in mehreren Englischen Zeitungsblättern stand und eine Parodie auf das berühmte Selbstgespräch Hamlets' ('Not without sharp wit and innuendo, but still treated with some subtlety is the following monologue, which recently appeared in several English newspapers and contains a parody of Hamlet's famous soliloquy'; translation mine).

8 Digital versions of these two graphic satires can be found through Yale University Library Digital Collections: 'Maniac-raving's', https://collections.library.yale.edu/catalog/11858810 and 'The flying sword run mad', https://collections

.library.yale.edu/catalog/11858809. From Beinecke Rare Book and Manuscript Library, Auchincloss Gillray v. 5. See also Christiane Banerji and Diana Donald, *Gillray Observed: The Earliest Account of His Caricatures in 'London und Paris'* (Cambridge: Cambridge University Press, 1999), pp. 10–14.

9 Deuling, 'Aesthetics and Politics', p. 108.

10 Jonathan Bate, *Shakespearean Constitutions: Politics, Theatre, Criticism 1730–1830* (Oxford: Clarendon Press, 1989), p. 70.

11 'To the Printer of the Georgia Gazette: A Parody on Shakespear', *Georgia Gazette*, 1 March 1769, p. 3; 'The Pausing American Loyalist: A Parody on the Soliloquy of Hamlet', *Middlesex Journal and Evening Advertiser*, 30 January 1776, p. 4.

12 Samuel Taylor Coleridge, *Omniana*, 2 vols (London, 1812), I, p. 208.

13 Bate, *Shakespearean Constitutions*, p. 107.

14 David Francis Taylor, *The Politics of Parody: A Literary History of Caricature, 1760–1830* (New Haven, CT and London: Yale University Press, 2018), p. 16.

15 Ibid., pp. 113–19.

16 Ibid., ch. 7.

17 For the 'legibility' of graphic satire, see ibid., p. 32.

18 *The Times*, 31 August 1803, p. 2.

19 *The Quebec Mercury*, 1.51, 23 December 1805.

20 'Buonaparte's Soliloquy on the Cliff at Boulogne', *The Times*, 11 September 1805, p. 3, and *The Spirit of the Public Journals for 1805* (London, 1806), IX, pp. 308–9.

21 *The Anti-Gallican* (London, 1804), p. 3.

22 'Bonaparte's Soliloquy: A Parody on Hamlet's Soliloquy', in *The Anti-Gallican*, pp. 259–60.

23 See Bate, *Shakespearean Constitutions*, pp. 111–21.

24 Thomas Ford ('Master Shallow'), 'Parodies of Shakspeare', *The Gentleman's Magazine* (August 1803), pp. 760–61.

25 Bate, *Shakespearean Constitutions*, pp. 112–14.

26 Joseph Cozens, '"The Blackest Perjury": Desertion, Military Justice, and Popular Politics in England, 1803–1805', *Labour History Review*, 79:3 (2014), 255–80 (p. 255).

27 'Assault on His Majesty', *The Star*, 31 October 1795, p. 4.

Chapter 5   Shakespeare, the North-West Passage, and the Russian War

1 William T. Mumford, 'Private Journal of an Expedition to the Arctic Regions to ascertain the fate of Sir John Franklin, and his Crew, under the Command of Captain Sir Edward Belcher, KCB, Captain of Her Majesty's Ships Assistance Resolute Pioneer Intrepid and North Star in the years 1852–3–4 by W. J. Mumford, late of HMS Resolute', Ottawa, Library and Archives Canada, microfilm reel H016662.

2 Revd Edward Parry (ed.), *Memoirs of Rear-Admiral Sir W. Edward Parry, KT, FRS, etc., Lieut-Governor of Greenwich Hospital by His Son, The Rev. Edward Parry, M.A.* (London: Longman, Brown, Green, Longmans, and Roberts, 1857), p. 60.

3 Winfried Baumgart, *The Crimean War, 1853–1856*, 2nd edn (London: Bloomsbury, 2020 [1998]), p. xi, asserts that the ramifications of this 'general war' extended to many other countries, including America and even Australia. In human terms, it was also the costliest of wars between 1815 and 1914. See David M. Goldfrank, *The Origins of the Crimean War*, 2nd edn (New York and London: Routledge, 2013), p. 290.

4 Peter Duckers, *The Crimean War at Sea: The Naval Campaigns against Russia, 1854–56* (Barnsley: Pen & Sword Maritime, 2011), p. xv.

5 Hew Strachan, 'General Editor's Preface', in Winfried Baumgart, *The Crimean War, 1853–1856*, 2nd edn (London: Bloomsbury, 2020), p. 1.

6 Goldfrank, *The Origins of the Crimean War*, p. 48.

7 Orlando Figes, *The Crimean War: A History* (New York: Picador, 2010), p. 70. See also John H. Gleason, *The Genesis of Russophobia in Great Britain* (Cambridge: Cambridge University Press, 1950).

8 Baumgart, *The Crimean War, 1853–1856*, p. 17.

9 Goldfrank, *The Origins of the Crimean War*, p. 262.

10 Figes, *The Crimean War*, p. 78. On the influence of the press, see Kingsley Martin, *The Triumph of Lord Palmerston: A Study of Public Opinion in England before the Crimean War*, 2nd edn (London: Hutchinson, 1963).

11 Figes, *The Crimean War*, p. 147.

12 Clive Ponting, *The Crimean War: The Truth behind the Myth* (London: Chatto and Windus, 2004), p. 35. Indeed, for the first five months of the war, the Baltic was the scene of the only real fighting between the allies and Russia.

13 John Sweetman, *The Crimean War* (London and New York: Routledge, 2013), p. 90.

14 Duckers, *The Crimean War at Sea*, p. 79.

15 Baumgart, *The Crimean War, 1853–1856*, p. 197.

16 Ponting, *The Crimean War*, p. 136.

17 Sherard Osborn, *Stray Leaves from an Arctic Journal; or, Eighteen Months in the Polar Regions, in Search of Sir John Franklin's Expedition, in the Years, 1850–1851* (London: Longman, Brown, Green, 1852), p. 133.

18 Sherard Osborn (ed.), *The Discovery of the North-West Passage by HMS 'Investigator': Capt. R. McClure, 1850, 1851, 1852, 1853* (Edmonton: Hurtig, 1969), p. 144. Royal birthdays were marked with special gestures that included firing royal salutes.

19 Émile-Frédéric de Bray, 'Journal de bord de l'enseigne de vaisseau Émile-Frédéric de Bray à bord de la frégate anglaise "La Résolue". Expédition polaire de 1852–1853 envoyée à la recherche de sir John Franklin', Cambridge, Scott Polar Research Institute (SPRI), MS 864-1, p. 185. A typed copy of the lost original.

20 See Alon Confino, 'Collective Memory and Cultural History: Problems of Method', *The American Historical Review* 102:5 (1997), 1386–1403 (p. 1398).

21 *Memoirs of Lieutenant Joseph René Bellot, Chevalier of the Legion of Honour, Member of the Geographical Societies of London and Paris, Etc.; With His Journal of a Voyage in the Polar Seas, in Search of Sir John Franklin*, 2 vols (London: Hurst and Blackett, 1855), I, p. 139.

22 George McDougall, *The Eventful Voyage of H. M. Discovery Ship 'Resolute' to the Arctic Regions in Search of Sir John Franklin and the Missing Crews of H. M. Discovery Ships 'Erebus' and 'Terror', 1852, 1853, 1854* (London: Longman, Brown, Green, Longmans, and Roberts, 1857), p. 345.

23 Mumford, 'Private Journal', entry for 25 November 1853.

24 This version printed on silk is now in Greenwich, National Maritime Museum Caird Library and Archives, TXT0091.

25 McDougall, *The Eventful Voyage*, pp. 344–45.

26 De Bray, 'Journal de bord', p. 185.

27 Richard Roche, 'Journal on board the *HMS Resolute*', Greenwich, National Maritime Museum Caird Library and Archives, JOD 249, entry for 14 November–5 December 1853.

28 'Prologue', in Mumford, 'Private Journal', unpaginated, loose page.

29 Ibid.

30 On Anderson, see Glenn M. Stein, *Discovering the North-West Passage: The Four-Year Arctic Odyssey of HMS Investigator and the McClure Expedition* (Jefferson, NC: McFarland, 2015), p. 272.

31 De Bray, 'Journal de bord', p. 185 (my translation).

32 Gillian Russell, *The Theatres of War* (Oxford: Oxford University Press, 1995), p. 141.

33 Such was the case with Richard Collinson's treatment of his crew. See William Barr, *Arctic Hell-Ship: The Voyage of the HMS Enterprise 1850–1855* (Edmonton: University of Alberta Press, 2007).

34 De Bray, 'Journal de bord', p. 185

35 Mumford, 'Private Journal', entry for 26 August 1854.

36 Ibid., entry for 6 October 1854.

37 Martin W. Sandler, *Resolute: The Epic Search for the Northwest Passage and John Franklin, and the Discovery of the Queen's Ghost Ship* (New York: Sterling, 2006), p. 236.

38 Theatricals and musicals were also performed in the Crimea during the siege of Sevastopol. The Fourth Division of the British Army's repertoire of farces at their 'Theatre Royal' generally mirrored that of their naval compatriots. See, for example, Douglas Arthur Reid, *Memoirs of the Crimean War, January 1855 to June 1856* (London: St. Catherine Press, 1911), pp. 145–46. I have not (yet) discovered any mention of a Shakespeare play.

Chapter 6   'Now for Our Irish Wars'

1 Robyn Asleson, 'Sant, James (1820–1916)', *ODNB*, online edn, September 2010, https://doi.org/10.1093/ref:odnb/64291 (accessed 20 June 2022).

2 *Freeman's Journal*, 5 February 1778, p. 289; *Hibernian Magazine*, January 1778, p. 62. For an analysis of the production in its greater context, see Helen M. Burke, 'Samuel Whyte and the Politics of Eighteenth-Century Irish Private Theatricals', in Moyra Haslett ed. *Irish Literature in Transition, 1700–1780* (Cambridge: Cambridge University Press, 2020), pp. 129–47.

3 *Freeman's Journal*, 24 January 1778, p. 272.

4 *Hibernian Magazine*, January 1778, p. 62.

5 A Northern Whig [Theobald Wolfe Tone], *An Argument on behalf of the Catholics of Ireland* (Dublin: P. Byrne, 1791), p. 47.

6 For these details and a general account of Davitt's career, see Carla King, *Michael Davitt* (Dublin: Historical Association of Ireland, 1999).

7 See Andrew Murphy, *Shakespeare for the People: Working-class Readers 1800–1900* (Cambridge: Cambridge University Press, 2008).

8 J. J. Lee, 'Michael Davitt: An Appraisal', in *Michael Davitt: New Perspectives*, ed. Fintan Lane and Andrew G. Newby (Dublin: Irish Academic Press, 2009), p. 31.

9 King, *Davitt*, p. 31. This comment relates to a stint in prison in 1881, when Davitt was well treated. In 1870, he had been sentenced to penal servitude and suffered a much harsher regime.

10 W. B. Yeats, *Autobiographies*, ed. William O'Donnell et al. (New York: Scribner, 1999), p. 269.

11 *Irish Independent*, 31 May 1906, p. 5. The article was published immediately after Davitt's death.

12 *Freeman's Journal*, 19 May 1870, p. 4.

13 Michael Davitt, *Leaves from a Prison Diary, or Lectures to a 'Solitary' Audience*, ed. T. W. Moody (Shannon: Irish University Press, 1972), p. 164.

14 Ibid.

15 Edward Dowden papers, Trinity College Dublin, TCD MS 3715/9, letter from Dowden to John Todhunter, 25 December 1876.

16 Darrell Figgis, *Shakespeare: A Study* (London: J. M. Dent, 1911).

17 Desmond Ryan, *Remembering Sion: A Chronicle of Storm and Quiet* (London: Arthur Barker, 1934), p. 159.

18 Wilbraham Fitzjohn Trench, *Shakespeare's Hamlet: A New Commentary with a Chapter on First Principles* (London: John Murray, 1913).

19 'Shakespeare's Brutus in Ireland: Professor Trench's Lecture', *Irish Times*, 16 January 1917, p. 3 (all quotations from the lecture are from this article).

Chapter 7   Shakespeare and the Survival of Middle England

1 *The Sphere*, 7 December 1914, pp. 22–23.

2 The speech in full occurs at 2.1.31–68.

3 See 'Voices of the First World War: The Shot That Led to War', podcast and article, Imperial War Museum, www.iwm.org.uk/history/voices-of-the-first-world-war-the-shot-that-led-to-war.

4   *The Graphic*, 22 April 1916.
5   *The Graphic*, 23 February 1918.
6   Charles Whibley, 'Political Portraits', *Illustrated London News*, 2 March 1918.
7   *The Graphic*, 22 April 1916.

Chapter 8   Ellen Terry Stars at the Shakespeare Hut

1   Letter from Ellen Terry to Maud Warrender, dated September 1917 and reproduced in Maud Warrender, *My First Sixty Years* (London: Cassell, 1933), p. 232.
2   For further exploration of Terry and Craig's involvement in the Hut performances, see Ailsa Grant Ferguson, 'Performing Femininity', in her *The Shakespeare Hut: A Story of Performance, Memory and Identity* (London: Arden Shakespeare, 2019).
3   Katharine Cockin, 'Introduction: Ellen Terry and Her Circle – Formal Introductions and Informal Encounters', in *Ellen Terry: Spheres of Influence*, ed. Katharine Cockin (London: Routledge, 2011), p. 1.
4   Ellen Terry and Edith Craig Archive, National Trust held at the British Library, Loan MS 125/25/2/Ellen Terry Archive/ET/D438.
5   Katharine Cockin, *Edith Craig (1869–1947): Dramatic Lives* (London: Cassell, 1998), p. 123. On the Women's Theatre project pre-war, see Naomi Paxton, *Stage Rights! The Actresses' Franchise League, Activism and Politics 1908–58* (Manchester: Manchester University Press, 2018), ch. 5.
6   Margaret Chute, 'The Eighteenpenny Hotel: A Description of the Shakespeare Hut', *The Graphic*, 16 December 1916, p. 772.
7   Postcard from the Shakespeare Hut, depicting 'The Dormitory Passage', undated, author's private collection.
8   Chute, 'The Eighteenpenny Hotel', p. 772; letter from Gertrude Forbes-Robertson to Edith Craig, 26 April 1917, Ellen Terry and Edith Craig Archive, National Trust, held at the British Library, Loan MS 125/1/6/Z3258/Letter.
9   The thoughts of soldier Private Gordon Stowell on seeing the Shakespeare Hut stage in 1916, as described by Maurice Willson Disher in his *The Last Romantic: The Authorized Biography of Sir John Martin Harvey* (London: Hutchinson, 1948), p. 252.
10 Gordon Williams, *British Theatre in the Great War: A Re-evaluation* (London and New York: Continuum, 2003), pp. 248–49.
11 'Clubman's Notebook: Fallen Actors and Musicians', in *Pall Mall Gazette*, 15 December 1917, p. 3.
12 See Edmund G. C. King, '"A Priceless Book to Have Out Here": Soldiers Reading Shakespeare in the First World War', *Shakespeare* 10:3 (2014), 230–44.
13 Ibid., p. 242.
14 Francis Oswald Bennett, *A Canterbury Tale: The Autobiography of Dr. Francis Bennett* (Oxford: Oxford University Press, 1980), p. 49.
15 Bennett, pp. 89–90.

16 The programme informs us that the actors were drawn from a troupe of teenaged girls from Miss Italia Conte's theatre school.

17 Fabia Drake, *Blind Fortune* (London: Kimber, 1978), pp. 36–37.

18 Drake, *Blind Fortune*, pp. 36–37.

19 Drake, *Blind Fortune*, p. 37.

20 'Ellen Terry at the Grand Opera House', *Evening Post*, 87:139, June 1914, p. 2.

21 On the intersection of Australian ANZAC and Shakespeare, see Philip Mead, 'Lest We Forget: Shakespeare Tercentenary Commemoration in Sydney and London, 1916', in *Celebrating Shakespeare: Commemoration and Cultural Memory*, ed. Coppélia Kahn and Clara Calvo (Cambridge: Cambridge University Press, 2015), pp. 225–44. For further exploration of New Zealand ANZAC and Shakespeare, see Ferguson, 'Performing Englishness: The Shakespeare Hut for Anzacs', in *The Shakespeare Hut*.

22 Katherine E. Kerry, 'The Aftervoice of Ellen Terry', in *Ellen Terry*, ed. Cockin, pp. 65–76 (p. 76).

23 'Dame Ellen Terry's 80th Birthday', *Belfast Telegraph*, 27 February 1928, p. 9.

Chapter 9   The 1916 Shakespeare Tercentenary at № 1 Camp in Calais

1 Hind's letter states that he sent the press cuttings and the leaflets to the librarian. It does not explain the provenance of *The Cambridge Magazine* article and the playbill. All documents are in the Shakespeare Birthplace Trust archive, OSP70.3/1916.

2 See, among others, Werner Habicht, 'Shakespeare Celebrations in Times of War', *Shakespeare Quarterly* 52:4 (2001), 441–55; Clara Calvo, 'Fighting Over Shakespeare: Commemorating the 1916 Tercentenary in Wartime', *Critical Survey* 24:3 (2012), 48–72; and Matthew C. Hendley, 'Cultural Mobilization and British Responses to Cultural Transfer in Total War: The Shakespeare Tercentenary of 1916', *First World War Studies* 3:1 (2012), 25–49.

3 Ton Hoenselaars, 'Great War and Shakespeare: Somewhere in France, 1914–1919', *Actes des congrès de la Société française Shakespeare* 33 (2015), 1–12 (p. 4).

4 Ibid., p. 5.

5 Alan Sinfield, *Faultlines: Cultural Materialism and the Politics of Dissident Reading* (Berkeley and Los Angeles: University of California Press, 1992), pp. 129–30.

6 Claire McEachern, '*Henry V* and the Paradox of the Body Politic', *Shakespeare Quarterly* 45:1 (1994), 33–56 (pp. 53, 51).

7 Jordi Coral, '"Maiden Walls That War Hath Never Entered": Rape and Post-Chivalric Military Culture in Shakespeare's *Henry V*', *College Literature* 44:3 (2017), 404–35 (pp. 406, 413–14).

8 For the early modern period, see Jean E. Howard and Phyllis Rackin, *Engendering a Nation: A Feminist Account of Shakespeare's English Histories* (London and New York: Routledge, 1997).

9   See Deborah Thom, *Nice Girls and Rude Girls: Women Workers in World War I* (London: Tauris, 1998).

10 Katherine Eggert, 'Nostalgia and the Not Yet Dead Queen: Refusing Female Rule in *Henry V*', *ELH* 61:3 (1994), 523–50 (p. 531).

11 Ibid. See also Coral, 'Maiden Walls That War Hath Never Entered', pp. 412–13.

12 Howard and Rackin, *Engendering a Nation*, p. 4. See also Coral, 'Maiden Walls That War Hath Never Entered', p. 408; McEachern, '*Henry V* and the Paradox of the Body Politic', p. 47.

13 Italics in original.

14 Coral, 'Maiden Walls That War Hath Never Entered', p. 408.

15 Howard and Rackin, *Engendering a Nation*, p. 6. See also Eggert, 'Nostalgia and the Not Yet Dead Queen', pp. 531–32; McEachern, '*Henry V* and the Paradox of the Body Politic', p. 54.

16 Howard and Rackin, *Engendering a Nation*, p. 187.

17 Ibid., p. 188.

18 Ibid., pp. 201, 206. Howard and Rackin demonstrate that women appeared on battlefields in Shakespeare's earlier history plays and in the historical records of premodern warfare (pp. 201–4).

19 Ibid., p. 200.

20 For the FANY's history, see Janet Lee, *War Girls: The First Aid Nursing Yeomanry in the First World War* (Manchester: Manchester University Press, 2005); and Juliette Pattinson, *Women of War: Gender, Modernity and the First Aid Nursing Yeomanry* (Manchester: Manchester University Press, 2020). The organization still exists, as the First Aid Nursing Yeomanry (Princes Royal's Volunteer Corps). I am grateful to Commander Kate Brazier, Jessica Lakin, and Lynette Beardwood for their kind assistance with this research.

21 Pattinson, *Women of War*, p. 13.

22 Ibid., p. 7.

23 Pat Beauchamp, *Fanny Goes to War* (London: John Murray, 1919), p. 156. In the book, Beauchamp refers to herself as P. B. Waddell, the name under which she appears in the Calais event's playbill.

24 Ibid., pp. 156–57.

25 Lee, *War Girls*, pp. 12–13.

26 Ibid., p. 13.

27 Ibid.

28 See ibid., pp. 40–1; Pattinson, *Women of War*, pp. 1–2, 56–66.

29 Lee, *War Girls*, p. 4.

30 See Susan R. Grayzel, *Women's Identities at War: Gender, Motherhood, and Politics in Britain and France during the First World War* (Chapel Hill: University of North Carolina Press, 1999).

31 'Cambridge at Calais. How the Shakespeare Tercentenary Was Celebrated', *Cambridge Magazine*, 3 June 1916, p. 513.

32 Ibid.

33 Ibid.

34 Ibid.

35 Ibid.

36 Ibid.

37 B[eryl] Hutchinson, Typescript Recollections, Leeds University Library, Liddle Collection, LIDDLE/WW1/WO/057, p. 15. The paragraph also mentions the *Twelfth Night* scenes, singing, and dancing.

38 Beauchamp, *Fanny Goes to War*, pp. 93–97, 147–48, 212–15.

Chapter 10   Shakespeare Does His Bit for the War Effort

1 Financial support for research behind this chapter has been provided by Research Project PGC2018-095632-B-I00, 'Shakespeare and the Twentieth-Century: Global Afterlives and Cultural Memory', awarded by the Spanish Research Agency (AEI) and FEDER.

2 Buchel was often employed by Sir Herbert Beerbohm Tree to paint the rich, elaborate settings of his productions and produced advertising posters and programmes for the theatre, as well as illustrations for theatrical magazines.

3 Sidney Lee, 'Introduction', *The Shakespeare Exhibition: Catalogue of Portraits, Views, Playbills, etc.* (London: Grafton Galleries, 1917), pp. 5–8 (p. 5). Subsequent quotations in this paragraph, ibid., pp. 5–6.

4 Harvey's 1916 season at His Majesty's Theatre consisted of *Henry V, Hamlet, Richard III,* and *The Taming of the Shrew.*

5 'Shakespeare Relics', *The Times*, 12 January 1917, p. 9.

6 Ibid., p. 9.

7 'Shakespeare and the Red Cross: A War Fund Exhibition', *The Times*, 20 January 1917, p. 9.

8 Clare Pettitt, 'Shakespeare at the Great Exhibition of 1851', in *Victorian Shakespeare, Vol. 2: Literature and Culture*, ed. Gail Marshall and Adrian Poole (Basingstoke: Palgrave, 2003), pp. 61–83.

9 Robert E. Hunter, *Shakespeare and Stratford-upon-Avon: A Chronicle of the Times* (London: Whittaker, 1864), pp. 164–65. See also Richard Foulkes, *The Shakespeare Tercentenary of 1864* (London: Society for Theatre Research, 1984), pp. 30–31.

10 The impact of this exhibition has been well studied by Marion O'Connor in 'Theatre of the Empire: "Shakespeare's England" at Earl's Court, 1912', in *Shakespeare Reproduced: The Text in Ideology and History*, ed. Marion F. O'Connor and Jean E. Howard (London: Routledge, 1987), pp. 68–98.

11 *The Times*, 12 January 1917, p. 9.

12 Lawrence W. Levine, *Highbrow, Lowbrow: The Emergence of Cultural Hierarchy in America* (Cambridge, MA: Harvard University Press, 1988), p. 146.

13 Ibid., pp. 146–60.

14 Stephen Greenblatt, 'Resonance and Wonder', *Bulletin of the American Academy of Arts and Sciences*, 43 (1900), 11–34 (pp. 19–20).

31 'Das 53. Shakespeare-Jahrbuch', *Frankfurter Zeitung*, 5 February 1918.

32 'Shakespeares persönlichstes Drama', *Frankfurter Zeitung*, 21 December 1918.

33 'Französische Wutausbrüche', *Frankfurter Zeitung*, 8 September 1914.

34 'Salonik', *Frankfurter Zeitung*, 7 January 1916.

35 'Der Reichskanzler über die britischen "Gentlemen"', *Frankfurter Zeitung*, 6 October 1915.

36 'Shakespeare über den Minierkrieg', *Frankfurter Zeitung*, 6 March 1915.

37 'Max Reinhardts Tätigkeit in der Volksbühne', *Berliner Börsen-Zeitung*, 30 May 1918.

Chapter 12   Readers and Rebels

1 Denis Condon, 'From the Stomach to the Front: Projecting the World on Irish Screens in April 1915', *Early Irish Cinema*, 30 April 2015, online, para. 6 of 15, https://earlyirishcinema.com/2015/04/30/from-the-stomach-to-the-front-projecting-the-world-on-irish-screens-in-april-1915/ (accessed 1 November 2021).

2 Ibid., paras. 7–8.

3 'Collapse of Sinn Fein Rising', *The Irish Times*, 28 April 1916, p. 1.

4 See, for example, *An Illustrated Record of the Sinn Fein Revolt in Dublin, April, 1916* (Dublin: Hely's, 1916), p. 31; and Paul Clerkin, '1915—Coliseum Theatre, Henry St., Dublin', *Archiseek*, online, www.archiseek.com/2013/1915-coliseum-theatre-henry-st-dublin/#google_vignette (accessed 1 November 2021).

5 See '1916 Rising Postcards', held by UCD Library Special Collections and available through UCD Digital Library, https://digital.ucd.ie/view/ucdlib:38376 (accessed 1 November 2021).

6 'Coming Events', *The Irish Times*, 17 February 1916, p. 5.

7 Mark Fitzgerald, 'Operas without a Hero: A Comic Trilogy (1876–1879) by Elena Norton and Mary Heyne', in *The Golden Thread: Irish Women Playwrights, Vol. 1 (1716–1992)*, ed. David Clare, Fiona McDonagh, and Justine Nakase (Liverpool: Liverpool University Press, 2021), pp. 107–18.

8 Excellent scholarship explores the extensive links between the Easter Rising and the Irish theatre movement. See, for example, James Moran, *Staging the Easter Rising: 1916 as Theatre* (Cork: Cork University Press, 2005); Clair Wills, *Dublin 1916: The Siege of the GPO* (Cambridge, MA: Harvard University Press, 2009); Andrew Murphy, 'Shakespeare's Rising: Ireland and the 1916 Tercentenary', in *Celebrating Shakespeare: Commemoration and Cultural Memory*, ed. Clara Calvo and Coppélia Kahn (Cambridge: Cambridge University Press, 2015), pp. 161–81; and Willy Maley's superbly nuanced 'Shakespeare, Easter 1916, and the Theatre of the Empire of Great Britain', *Studies in Ethnicity and Nationalism,* 16:2 (2016), 189–205.

9 Frank Ryan, 'Lost Revolution: The Abbey Theatre and 1916', Film, History, and Education Project, Queen's University Belfast, www.qub.ac.uk/sites/frankryan/FilmHistoryEducationProject/LostRevolutionTheAbbeyTheatre1916/ (accessed 1 November 2021); Nelson Ó Ceallaigh Ritschel, 'James Connolly's "Under Which Flag", 1916', *New Hibernia Review*, 2:4 (1998), 54–68.

10 Maley, 'Shakespeare', p. 190.

11 Andrew Murphy, '"Bhíos ag Stratford ar an abhainn": Shakespeare, Douglas Hyde, 1916', in *Shakespeare and the Irish Writer*, ed. Janet Clare and Stephen O'Neill (Dublin: University College Dublin Press, 2010), pp. 51–63.

12 'Martial Law', *The Irish Times*, 27 April 1916, p. 2.

13 'Shakespeare's Plays in Dublin, 1660–1904', NUI Galway, database, www .nuigalway.ie/drama/shakespeare/.

14 Seosamh de Brún, *The 1916 Diaries of an Irish Rebel and a British Soldier*, ed. Mick O'Farrell (Cork: Mercier Press 2014), quoted in Jane Walsh, 'The diary of an Irish rebel fighting in the 1916 Rising', *Irish Central*, 13 April 2016, n. 30.

15 Ibid.

16 De Brún, *The 1916 Diaries*, quoted in Walsh, 'The diary of an Irish rebel'.

17 For more on WTF, see Emer O'Toole, 'Waking the Feminists: Re-imagining the Space of the National Theatre in the Era of the Celtic Phoenix', *Literature Interpretation Theory,* 28:2 (2017), 134–52.

18 For background on this production and to understand how Shakespeare's Globe aimed to contextualize it for spectators, see Danielle Pearson's interview with Caroline Byrne, '"Confronting the Shrew", and Mary McAuliffe's "A Proper Position in the Life of the Nation"', in *The Taming of the Shrew* playbill (London: Shakespeare's Globe Theatre, 2016).

19 For more on these aspects of the 1937 Constitution, see for example Caitriona Beaumont, 'Women, Citizenship and Catholicism in the Irish Free State, 1922–1948', *Women's History Review*, 6:4 (1997), 563–85.

20 Descriptions of the performance refer to *The Taming of the Shrew*, directed by Caroline Byrne, Shakespeare's Globe Theatre, London, 6 August 2016.

21 Declan Kiberd, comments at the public panel discussion 'Ireland 1916: Death of a Literary Revival?', sponsored by the Irish Literary Society, Bloomsbury Hotel, London, 25 January 2016.

Chapter 14   'Now Good or Bad, 'tis but the Chance of War'

1 This note (p. 104) and others by James Joseph Christy are taken from his 1973 PhD dissertation at Stanford University. He interviewed Macowan, so any quotes within quotes should be attributed to the director. The full title of his dissertation is 'Five Twentieth Century Productions of *Troilus and Cressida*' (University Microfilms, Ann Arbor, MI, 1973).

2 Ibid.

3 Francis A. Shirley, 'Introduction', in William Shakespeare, *Troilus and Cressida: Shakespeare in Production* (Cambridge: Cambridge University Press, 2005), p. 25.

4 *Punch*, 12 October 1938, p. 412.

5 Christy, 'Five Twentieth Century Productions', p. 104.

6 W. A. Darlington, 'Modern Dress "Troilus"', *Daily Telegraph and Morning Post*, 22 September 1938, p. 10.

7 *Punch*, 12 October 1938, p. 412.
8 Ibid., p. 412.
9 Ibid., p. 396.
10 Ibid., p. 404.
11 Ibid., p. 406.
12 Beneŝ was President of Czechoslovakia from 1935 to 1938, and again from 1945 to 1948. *Punch*, 12 October 1938, p. 407.
13 Ibid., p. 410.
14 See 'cartoon, *n.*' (2a), *OED*, online (modified December 2022).
15 Philip V. Allingham, rev. Jacqueline Banerjee, '*Punch, or the London Charivari* (1841–1992)–A British Institution', *The Victorian Web*, online, www.victorianweb .org/periodicals/punch/pva44.html (accessed 21 June 2022).
16 Helen Walasek, 'Introduction', *The Best of Punch Cartoons: 2000 Humour Classics* (New York: Overlook Press, 2008), pp. 8–13.
17 I am referring to the definition of this term formulated by Gilles Deleuze and Félix Guattari (eds), in *A Thousand Plateaus: Capitalism and Schizophrenia* (Minneapolis: University of Minnesota Press, 1987), p. 4.
18 Lisa Diedrich, 'Comics and Graphic Narratives', in *The Cambridge Companion to Literature and the Posthuman*, ed. Bruce Clark and Manuela Rossini (Cambridge: Cambridge University Press, 2017), pp. 96–108 (p. 96).
19 Will Eisner, *Comics and Sequential Art: Principles and Practices from the Legendary Cartoonist* (New York: Norton, 2008), p. 39.
20 Quoted in Christy, 'Five Twentieth Century Productions', p. 92.
21 Ivor Brown, 'The Week's Theatre', *The Observer*, 25 September 1938, p. 13.
22 Roger Apfelbaum, *Shakespeare's 'Troilus and Cressida': Textual Problems and Performance Solutions* (Newark: University of Delaware, 2004), p. 44.
23 According to Christy, 'Macowan cut approximately one-third of the entire play and about the same proportion of Thersites' lines, but he more than compensated for the cutting of Thersites by giving him the Prologue, and also having him onstage during the epilogue' ('Five Twentieth Century Productions', p. 98).
24 For example, Tyrone Guthrie's production at the Old Vic in 1956 'adopted the Edwardian Fashion of the German and Austrian empires' in order to highlight the 'selfish elegance' of the upper class 'gaily diverting itself on the brink of momentous change'; see 'Introduction' in William Shakespeare, *Troilus and Cressida*, ed. David Bevington, The Arden Shakespeare, rev. edn (London: Bloomsbury, 2015), p. 104. In Terry Hands' RSC production in 1981, 'the Greeks resembled trench warriors of World War I' (p. 110) and, as recently as 1990, Sam Mendes's version at the RSC Swan Theatre also highlighted Thersites' role, as he, according to Dawson, 'embodied the visual concept of disjunction' as did the entire performance; see *Troilus and Cressida*, ed. Anthony B. Dawson (Cambridge: Cambridge University Press, 2003), p. 119. John Barton brought on Thersites, along with Pandarus, to deliver the epilogue in his versions for the RSC in 1960, just as Macowan had done.
25 'Drama of Despair', *The New Statesman and Nation*, 16L1 (1938), p. 491.

26 *Troilus and Cressida*, ed. Dawson, p. 52.

27 Shirley, 'Introduction', p. 24.

28 Ibid., p. 24.

29 Christy, 'Five Twentieth Century Productions', p. 102.

30 Quoted in ibid., p. 102.

31 Quoted in ibid., p. 103.

32 Matthew Greenfield, 'Fragments of Nationalism in *Troilus and Cressida*', *Shakespeare Quarterly,* 51:2 (2000), 181–200 (pp. 181–82).

33 Ibid., p. 182.

Chapter 15   'Precurse of Feared Events'

1 Irena R. Makaryk, 'Introduction: Theatre, War, Memory, and Culture', in *Shakespeare and the Second World War: Memory, Culture, Identity*, ed. Irena R. Makaryk and Marissa McHugh (Toronto: University of Toronto Press, 2012), pp. 3–21 (p. 3). Makaryk draws on theatre studies, in which influential ideas of 'ghosting' have been formulated by Joseph Roach and Marvin Carlson.

2 Makaryk, 'Introduction', p. 4

3 Today, the performances are part of the annual Shakespeare Festival at Kronborg run by the resident theatre company, 'HamletScenen', and include other plays from the Shakespearean canon. I have written more extensively about Kronborg and its theatre festival elsewhere: see Anne Sophie Refskou, 'Whose Castle Is It Anyway?: Local/Global Negotiations of a Shakespearean Location', *Multicultural Shakespeare,* 15:30 (2017), 121–32, and 'Unhomely Shakespeares: Interculturalism and Diplomacy in Elsinore', in *Shakespeare on European Festival Stages*, ed. Nicoleta Cinpoes, Florence March, and Paul Prescott (London: Bloomsbury Arden Shakespeare, 2022), pp. 195–212.

4 Thompson and Taylor cite Folio-favouring editors Philip Edwards (Cambridge 1985) and G. R. Hibbard (Oxford 1987) and the latter's argument that the lines serve to advertise *Julius Caesar*, written shortly before *Hamlet*. See *Hamlet*, ed. Ann Thompson and Neil Taylor, rev. edn (London: Bloomsbury Arden Shakespeare, 2020).

5 Robert Sawyer, *Shakespeare Between the World Wars: The Anglo-American Sphere* (New York: Palgrave Macmillan, 2019), p. 1.

6 For more on Gründgens's and Göring's visits, see Refskou, 'Whose Castle', pp. 128–29. A detailed description (in Danish) of the visit is found in Hans Bay-Petersen's *En selskabelig invitation – Det Kgl. Teaters gæstespil i Nazi-Tyskland i 1930'erne* (Copenhagen: Multivers, 2007).

7 Bay-Petersen describes a certain anxiety about Hitler's photograph in the programme on the part of the Danish state ministry: *En selskabelig invitation*, pp. 109–10.

8 See for example Clara Calvo, 'Fighting Over Shakespeare: Commemorating the 1916 Tercentenary in Wartime', *Critical Survey,* 24:3 (2012), 48–72.

See also Werner Habicht, 'Shakespeare Celebrations in Times of War', *Shakespeare Quarterly,* 52 (2001), 441–55, and 'Coppélia Kahn, 'Remembering Shakespeare Imperially: The 1916 Tercentenary', *Shakespeare Quarterly,* 52 (2001), 456–78.

9 Refskou, 'Whose Castle', p. 129.
10 Tom Kristensen, 'Prolog til Hamlet, Prince of Denmark', Festspillene paa Kronborg. Theatre programme (1939), pp. 20–22.
11 *Berlingske Aftenavis,* 7 July 1939.
12 Bay-Petersen, *En selskabelig invitation,* p. 105.
13 Until 1947, the British representative in Denmark held the title of 'minister' rather than 'ambassador'.
14 Karen Blixen, *I Danmark. Breve 1931–62. Vol. 1,* ed. Frans Lasson and Tom Engelbrecht (Copenhagen: Gyldendal, 1996), pp. 320–21.

Chapter 16   But What Are We Fighting *For*?

1 John Maynard Keynes, *The General Theory of Employment, Interest and Money* (London: Macmillan, 1978 [1936]), pp. 122–31.
2 Sybil Thorndike and Russell Thorndike, *Lilian Baylis: As I Knew Her* (London: Chapman and Hall, 1938), pp. 68, 150–51.
3 Ibid., p. 74.
4 'Pont' (Graham Laidler), *The British Character* (London: Collins, 1938), pp. 32, 7.
5 Dan Stone, *Responses to Nazism in Britain, 1933–1939: Before War and Holocaust* (Cambridge: Cambridge University Press, 2003), p. 5.
6 Frank Tilsley, *Little Man, This Now* (London: Severn House, 1975 [1940]) p. 164.
7 'Myra Hess's Wartime Concerts', The National Gallery, online, www .nationalgallery.org.uk/about-us/history/the-myra-hess-concerts/myra-hesss-wartime-concerts (accessed 21 June 2022).
8 Quoted in Arts Council, *The First Ten Years: The Eleventh Annual Report of the Arts Council of Great Britain, 1955–1956* (London: Baynard Press, 1956), p. 5.
9 *The Times,* 9 July 1941.
10 Audrey Williamson, *Old Vic Drama* (London: Rockliff), p. 1948.
11 *CEMA,* dir. John Banting and Dylan Thomas (Strand Film Production, 1942), available at https://player.bfi.org.uk/free/film/watch-cema-1942-online.
12 John Maynard Keynes, 'Economic Possibilities for our Grandchildren (1930)', www.econ.yale.edu/smith/econ116a/keynes1.pdf.
13 Anselm Heinrich '"It Is Germany Where He Truly Lives": Nazi Claims on Shakespearean Drama', *New Theatre Quarterly,* 28:3 (2012), 230–42.
14 Arts Council, *1st Annual Report 1945–6* (London: Baynard Press, 1945).
15 'The Victoria Theatre, Burnley 1886–1955', *Burnley Civic Trust Heritage Image Collection,* online, www.bcthic.org/Articles/The_Victoria (accessed 21 June 2022).

Chapter 17 *Henry V* and the Battle of Powerscourt

1 'Battle Scenes at Powerscourt', *Irish Times*, 16 June 1943, p. 1.
2 Ibid.
3 Ibid.
4 Donal MacCarron, *The Irish Defence Forces since 1922* (Oxford: Osprey Publishing, 2004), p. 18; see also Roger Lewis, *The Real Life of Laurence Olivier* (London: Century, 1996), p. 205.
5 'Battle Scenes', *Irish Times*.
6 Ibid.
7 The National Archives (TNA) DO 35/1011/3. W. Bridges-Adams, Letter to R. B. Pugh, 13 August 1941. See also Edward Corse, 'British Propaganda in Neutral Eire after the Fall of France, 1940', *Contemporary British History*, 22:2 (2008), 163–80 (p. 163).
8 Winston Churchill, 'War Situation', Speech in the House of Commons recorded in *Hansard*, vol. 365, cc1205–310 (5 November 1940), https://api .parliament.uk/historic-hansard/commons/1940/nov/05/war-situation (accessed 24 January 2022).
9 Robert Fisk, *In Time of War: Ireland, Ulster and the Price of Neutrality, 1939–1945*, repr. edn (London: Paladin, 1987), pp. 487–96, 378.
10 Donal Ó Drisceoil, *Censorship in Ireland 1939–1945: Neutrality, Politics and Society* (Cork: Cork University Press, 1996), p. 4.
11 Ibid., p. 1.
12 Ruth Artmonsky, *Jack Beddington: The Footnote Man* (London: Artmonsky Arts, 2006), p. 49. See also 'The Shell Guides – A Short History', *The Library Blog* (November 2019), https://libraryblog.lbrut.org.uk/wordpress/2019/08/ shell-guides/ (accessed 24 January 2022).
13 Jack Beddington, Letters to John Betjeman, 20 April, 6 May, and 19 August 1943, in John Betjeman Special Collection (SC015), Box 3, Folder 16, Artmonsky, University of Victoria Library (UVL), Canada. My thanks to John Frederick at UVL. See also Artmonsky, *Beddington*, p. 51 and Robert Cole, *Propaganda, Censorship and Irish Neutrality in the Second World War* (Edinburgh: Edinburgh University Press, 2006), p. 69.
14 Corse, 'British Propaganda', p. 169.
15 The National Archives (TNA), DO 35/1011/3, J. Betjeman, Note to H. Hodson entitled 'Eire', 21 June 1940, p. 3.
16 L. Illingworth, 'No Bases for Britain', *Daily Mail*, 9 November 1940, p. 2.
17 See Carolle J. Carter, *The Shamrock and the Swastika* (Palo Alto, CA: Pacific Books, 1977), pp. 56, 244 (52n), regarding the strengthening of de Valera's position.
18 Corse, 'British Propaganda', p. 170.
19 TNA, INF 1/539, J. Rogers, Letter to Lord Davison, 10 June 1941.
20 TNA, DO 35/1011/3, 'Minutes of a Meeting held on Thursday the 19th of June [1941] to discuss Propaganda in Eire', 21 June 1941.
21 Cole, *Propaganda*, p. 135; and Cole, '"Good Relations": Irish Neutrality and the Propaganda of John Betjeman, 1941–43', *Eire-Ireland*, 30:4 (1996), p. 44.

22 Ó Drisceoil, *Censorship*, p. 149.

23 See Corse, 'British Propaganda', p. 174.

24 Michael Munn, *Lord Larry: The Secret Life of Laurence Olivier* (London: Robson, 2007), pp. 102–26; see also Nicholas J. Cull, *Selling War: The British Propaganda Campaign against American 'Neutrality' in World War II* (Oxford: Oxford University Press, 1996), pp. 80–81.

25 Richard Inverne, 'Henry V in the Cinema: Laurence Olivier's Charismatic Version of History', *The Historian* 127 (2015), 24–29 (p. 27).

26 Laurence Olivier, *Confessions of an Actor: An Autobiography* (New York: Simon and Schuster, 1982), p. 122.

27 Inverne, 'Henry V'.

28 Laurence Olivier, *On Acting* (London: Weidenfeld and Nicolson, 1986), p. 186.

29 Olivier, *Confessions*, p. 123.

30 Kevin Ewert, *Henry V: A Guide to the Text and Its Theatrical Life* (Basingstoke: Palgrave, 2006), p. 117.

31 Jack J. Jorgens, *Shakespeare on Film* (Bloomington and London: Indiana University Press, 1977), pp. 123, 126.

32 Lewis, *Real Life*, p. 138.

33 Anthony Holden, *Olivier* (London: Sphere Books, 1988), p. 212.

34 See also interview with Dallas Bower in Brian MacFarlane, *An Autobiography of British Cinema: As Told by the Filmmakers and Actors Who Made It* (London: Methuen, 1997), pp. 81–82.

35 Holden, *Olivier*, p. 214.

36 '"Moderns" not wanted', *Irish Times*, 3 April 1943, p. 3.

37 'Agincourt Scenes Film', *Irish Times*, 14 April 1943, p. 3.

38 'Big Film to Be Made in Wicklow', *Irish Times*, 17 April 1943, p. 1.

39 Ibid.; and 'Grazing for Film Horses', *Irish Times*, 21 April 1943, p. 3; 'Film Preparations at Powerscourt', *Irish Times*, 27 April 1943, p. 1; '"Henry the Fifth" at Enniskerry', *Irish Times*, 28 April 1943, p. 3.

40 'Agincourt and Powerscourt', *Irish Times*, 22 April 1943, p. 3.

41 'Filming Next Month', *Irish Times*, 30 April 1943, p. 1.

42 'Waterford Horsemen to Take Part in New Film', *Waterford Standard*, 29 May 1943, p. 1; 'Waterford Cavalry Men', *Waterford Standard*, 5 June 1943, p. 2.

43 'Agincourt Battle Film', *Irish Times*, 31 May 1943, p. 3.

44 'Agincourt to Enniskerry', *Irish Times*, 1 June 1943, p. 3.

45 'The Powerscourt Film', *Irish Times*, 10 July 1943, p. 2.

46 Lewis, *Real Life*, pp. 204–5.

47 Ewert, *Henry V*, p. 121.

48 Jorgens, *Shakespeare*, p. 131; Anthony Davies, *Filming Shakespeare's Plays* (Cambridge: Cambridge University Press, 1988), p. 27.

49 For the £80,000 figure, see Cole, 'Good Relations', p. 44; conversion estimated using inflation figures in G. Allen, 'Inflation: The Value of the Pound 1750–2011', House of Commons Library Research Briefing RP12-31, 29 May 2012.

50 'Cloughjordan', *Midland Counties Advertiser*, 5 August 1943, p. 3.
51 'Bray Step-Together Week', *Wicklow People*, 24 July 1943, p. 2.
52 'Taoiseach Visits Enniskerry', *Irish Times*, 20 July 1943, p. 3.
53 Robert C. Woosnam-Savage, 'Olivier's *Henry V* (1944): How a Movie Defined the Image of the Battle of Agincourt for Generations', in *The Battle of Agincourt*, ed. Anne Curry and Malcolm Mercer (New Haven, CT: Yale University Press, 2015), p. 258.
54 Advertisements by Goff's Sales in *Leinster Leader*, 24 July 1943, p. 1, *Wicklow People*, 24 July 1943, p. 1, and *New Ross Standard*, 23 July 1943, p. 1.
55 Advertisement by Goff's Property Sales, *Wicklow People*, 14 August 1943, p. 1.
56 Cole, *Propaganda*, pp. 69, 173.
57 Laurence Olivier, Letter to John Betjeman, 8 December 1944, UVL, SC015, Box 34, Folder 8.

Chapter 18   *Unser Shakespeare* in Nazi Germany

1 Werner Krauss, *Das Schauspiel meines Lebens: Einem Freund erzählt* (Stuttgart: Goverts, 1958), pp. 199–209.
2 This point is made by Ludwig Schnauder, 'The Most Infamous Shakespeare Production in History? *The Merchant of Venice* at Vienna's Burgtheater in 1943', *Shakespeare en Devenir*, 9 (2015), https://shakespeare.edel.univ-poitiers.fr/index.php?id=865 (accessed 30 January 2022).
3 David Edgar, 'Making Drama out of Conflict', in *Conflict Zones*, ed. Carla Dente and Sara Soncini (Pisa: Edizioni ETS, 2004), pp. 31–48.
4 On Nazis and the theatre, see, for example, Glenn Gadberry (ed.), *Theatre in the Third Reich, the Prewar Years: Essays on Theatre in Nazi Germany* (Westport, CT: Greenwood, 1995).
5 Werner Habicht, 'Shakespeare and Theatre Politics in the Third Reich', in *The Play Out of Context: Transferring Plays from Culture to Culture* (Cambridge: Cambridge University Press, 1989), pp. 110–20.
6 See William Abbey and Katharina Havekamp, 'Nazi Performances in the Occupied Territories: The German Theatre in Lille', pp. 262–90 and John London, 'Non-German Drama in the Third Reich', pp. 222–61, both in *Theatre under the Nazis*, ed. John London (Manchester: Manchester University Press, 2000).
7 Herbert Freeden, *Jüdisches Theater in Naziduetschland* (Berlin: Ullstein, 1985).
8 Friederieke Euler, 'Theater Zwischen Anpassung und Widerstand: Die Münchener Kammerspiele im Dritten Reich', in *Bayern in der N-S Zeit*, ed. Martin Broszat and Elke Frölich (Munich: Oldenbourg, 1979), II, pp. 90–173.
9 Quoted in Habicht, 'Shakespeare and Theatre Politics in the Third Reich', pp. 175–77.
10 Rodney Symington, *The Nazi Appropriation of Shakespeare: Cultural Politics in the Third Reich* (Lewiston, NY: Edwin Mellen Press, 2005), pp. 175–77.

11 On Weimar theatre, see Wilhelm Hortmann, *Shakespeare on the German Stage: The Twentieth Century* (Cambridge: Cambridge University Press, 1998), pp. 44–111.

12 Gerwin Strobl, *The Swastika and the Stage: German Theatre and Society* (Cambridge: Cambridge University Press, 2007), pp. 122–29.

13 Ibid., pp. 226–27.

14 Ibid., pp. 119–20, 161–63.

15 Ibid., p. 118.

16 Ibid., pp. 192–95.

17 Hortmann, *Shakespeare on the German Stage*, pp. 117–19, 124–27.

18 Ibid., pp. 127–32.

19 Klaus Mann, *Mephisto* (London: Penguin, 1995 [1936]), ch. 2.

20 Günther Rühle, *Theater in Deutschland, 1887–1945* (Frankfurt: S. Fischer, 2007), pp. 762–63.

21 William Grange, 'Ordained Hands on the Altar of Art: Gründgens, Hilpert, and Fehling in Berlin', in *Theatre in the Third Reich, the Prewar Years: Essays on Theatre in Nazi Germany,* ed. Glenn Gadberry (Westport, CT: Greenwood, 1995), pp. 75–89.

22 See Symington, *Nazi Appropriation*, pp. 175–77, for a list of Shakespeare plays performed during the War.

23 Strobl, *Swastika and the Stage*, p. 153.

24 Ibid., pp. 166–67.

25 Zeno Ackermann, 'Shakespeare Negotiations in the Perpetrator Society: German Productions of *The Merchant of Venice* during the Second World War', in *Shakespeare and the Second World War: Memory, Culture, Identity*, ed. Irena R. Makaryk and Marissa McHugh (Toronto: University of Toronto Press, 2012), pp. 35–62; Andrew G. Bonnell, *Shylock in Germany: Antisemitism and the German Theatre from the Enlightenment to the Nazis* (London: Tauris, 2008).

26 Werner Habicht, 'German Shakespeare, the Third Reich, and the War', in *Shakespeare and the Second World War: Memory, Culture, Identity,* ed. Irena R. Makaryk and Marissa McHugh (Toronto: University of Toronto Press, 2012), pp. 22–34 (p. 23).

27 Alessandra Bassey, 'Shylock and the Nazis: Continuation or Reinvention?', *European Judaism: A Journal for the New Europe*, 51:2 (2018), 151–58.

28 Henry Picker, *Hitler's Tischgespräche in Führerhauptquartier* (Stuttgart: Seewald, 1983), p. 457.

29 Hortmann, *Shakespeare on the German Stage*, pp. 134–37.

30 Thomas Eicher, 'Spielplanstrukturen 1929–1944', in *Theater im 'Dritten Reich': Theaterpolitik, Spielplanstruktur, NS-Dramatik*, ed. Thomas Eicher, Henning Rischbieter, and Barbara Panse (Seelze-Velber: Kallmeyer, 2000), pp. 279–486.

31 Ibid.; Rühle, *Theater in Deutschland*, p. 22.

32 Eicher, 'Spielplanstrukturen 1929–1944', pp. 279–486.

33 Ackermann, 'Shakespeare Negotiations', pp. 35–62.

34 Ibid.

35 Ibid., p. 49.

36 Strobl, *Swastika and the Stage*, p. 120.

37 Carl Zuckmeyer, *Als wär ein Stück von mir: Horen der Freundschaft* (Frankfurt: Bookclub ex Libris, 1966), pp. 67–68.

38 Lothar Müthel, 'Zur Dramaturgie des Kaufmanns von Venedig', *Neues Wiener Tagblatt*, 13 May 1943; Schnauder, 'Most Infamous Shakespeare Production'.

39 Müthel quoted in Schnauder, 'Most Infamous Shakespeare Production'.

40 Ibid.

41 Werner Krauss, *Das Schauspiel meines Lebens: Einem Freud erzählt*, ed. Hans Weigel (Stuttgart: Henry Goverts, 1958), p. 208.

42 Ben Ross Schneider, Jr, 'Granville's "Jew of Venice (1701)": A Close Reading of Shakespeare's "Merchant"', *Restoration: Studies in English Literary Culture, 1660–1700*, 17:2 (1993), 111–34.

Chapter 19 Framing the Jew

1 Julia Pascal, *The Shylock Play* (London: Oberon Books, 2008), p. 27. All in-text citations from the production are from this edition.

2 Callum May, 'Over a quarter of British people "hold anti-Semitic attitudes", study finds', *BBC News Online*, 13 September 2017, www.bbc.co.uk/news/uk-41241353.

3 Bethany Dawson, 'Survey finds 45% of UK adults hold antisemitic views', *The Independent*, 17 January 2021, www.independent.co.uk/news/uk/home-news/antisemitism-barometer-survey-data-jews-yougov-b1788352.html.

4 John Gross, 'Theatre; Shylock and Nazi Propaganda', *The New York Times*, 4 April 1993, www.nytimes.com/1993/04/04/theater/theater-shylock-and-nazi-propaganda.html.

5 'Shakespeare and the Holocaust', *Evening Standard*, 17 September 2007, www.standard.co.uk/culture/theatre/shakespeare-and-the-holocaust-7399319.html.

6 Lyn Gardner, '*The Merchant of Venice* (Arcola, London)', *The Guardian*, 17 September 2007, www.theguardian.com/stage/2007/sep/17/theatre.shakespeare.

7 Kevin A. Quarmby, 'Big Q Reviews: *The Merchant of Venice*, Pascal Theatre Company, Arcola Theatre' (2007), www.academia.edu/42009673/The_Merchant_of_Venice_Pascal_Theatre_Company_Arcola_Theatre_London_2007_.

8 Rivka Jacobson, 'Review: *The Merchant of Venice*, Pascal Theatre Company' (2007), *British Theatre Guide*, www.britishtheatreguide.info/reviews/merchantarcola-rev.

Chapter 20 G. Wilson Knight's 'Royal Propaganda' in 'This Sceptred Isle' (1941)

1 'George Wilson Knight scrapbook' (The Wolfson Centre for Archival Research, Library of Birmingham, S 650.8 F). I wish to thank Paul Taylor, Coordinator

at the Library, for helping me research the item during the coronavirus pandemic, and Michael Bartelle, for creating an excellent digital reproduction of the scrapbook. I also wish to thank my former colleague, Matthew Hanley, for kindly reading and commenting on an early version of this essay.

2 G. Wilson Knight, *A Royal Propaganda, 1956. A narrative account of work devoted to the cause of Great Britain during and after the second world-war* (British Library, 11768.f.13.), p. 27. This item is hereafter cited parenthetically as *RP*. I am grateful to Amy Lidster for digitally reproducing this unpublished typescript in October 2020, when access to library materials was severely limited.

3 The show's promptbook is in the 'George Wilson Knight scrapbook'. Knight's commentaries on the Shakespearian passages are also in *RP*, pp. 24–38.

4 G. Wilson Knight, *The Olive and the Sword: A Study of England's Shakespeare* (London: Oxford University Press, 1944), p. 48. See also Knight's commentary on *Timon of Athens* in the 'George Wilson Knight scrapbook'.

5 G. Wilson Knight, *The Sovereign Flower: On Shakespeare as the Poet of Royalism* (London: Methuen, 1958), p. 87.

6 Michael Taylor, 'G. Wilson Knight', in *Empson, Wilson Knight, Barber, Kott: Great Shakespeareans*, ed. Hugh Grady (London: Continuum, 2012), VIII, pp. 58–89 (p. 72).

7 Knight, *The Olive and the Sword*, p. 3. Knight often used 'England' when contexts required 'Britain'. See Willy Maley, '"This Sceptred Isle": Shakespeare and the British Problem', in *Nation, State and Empire in English Renaissance Literature* (London: Palgrave Macmillan, 2003), pp. 7–30.

8 G. Wilson Knight, *Christ and Nietzsche: An Essay in Poetic Wisdom* (London: Staples Press, 1948), p. 13.

9 'Donald Wolfit – greatest actor since Henry Irving', *Sunday Express*, 27 October 1940, cited in Zoltán Márkus, 'The Lion and the Lamb: *Hamlet* in London during World War II', *Shakespeare Survey 72* (2019), pp. 112–20 (p. 116).

10 Márkus, 'The Lion and the Lamb', p. 116. Márkus observes that the success of 'Lunchtime Shakespeare' was itself a myth, and that people were suspicious of chauvinistic appropriation of Shakespeare (pp. 117–18). Churchill's famous speech, 'Their Finest Hour' (18 June 1940), is available on the International Churchill Society website, https://winstonchurchill.org/resources/speeches/1940-the-finest-hour/their-finest-hour/ (accessed 30 October 2021).

11 'Westminster Theatre', *The Times*, 23 July 1941, p. 6.

12 Donald Wolfit, 'Dared to put on Shakespeare in bombed London', *Sunday Express*, 27 October 1940, cited in Márkus, 'The Lion and the Lamb', p. 116.

13 Márkus, 'The Lion and the Lamb', p. 117.

14 Ibid., p. 116.

15 Janet Clare observes that, to Knight, *Hamlet* was 'a parable of England's supposed abhorrence of warfare', in '*Hamlet* and Modernism: T. S. Eliot and G. Wilson Knight', in *Shakespeare and European Politics*, ed. Dirk Delabastita, Jozef De Vos, and Paul J. C. M. Franssen (Newark, DE: University of Delaware Press, 2008), pp. 234–43 (p. 240).

16 Knight, *Christ and Nietzsche*, p. 13. Knight started to write this book in 1940 though he could not publish it until after the war.

17 G. Wilson Knight, *The Wheel of Fire: Essays in Interpretation of Shakespeare's Sombre Tragedies* (London: Oxford University Press, 1930). Knight explains his spatial interpretation in the first chapter (pp. 1–18).

18 Knight, *The Wheel of Fire*, p. 3. René Wellek regards Knight primarily as a 'new Romantic', in *A History of Modern Criticism: 1750–1950*, 8 vols (New Haven, CT: Yale University Press, 1955–92), V, pp. 128–38; Hugh Grady emphasizes Knight's affinities with Modernist aesthetics, in *The Modernist Shakespeare: Critical Texts in a Material World* (Oxford: Clarendon Press, 1991), pp. 86–112; Michael Taylor sees him as a transitional figure, in 'G. Wilson Knight', pp. 58–89.

19 G. Wilson Knight, *Shakespearian Dimensions* (Brighton: Harvester Press, 1984), p. xiii.

20 Northrop Frye, 'The Search for Acceptable Words', *Daedalus,* 102:2 (1973), 11–26 (p. 17).

21 Knight, *The Wheel of Fire*, pp. 36–37.

22 Knight, *Atlantic Crossing: An Autobiographical Design* (London: J. M. Dent, 1939), pp. 327–28.

23 Knight, 'Four Pillars of Wisdom', cited in *RP*, pp. 11–12; *Neglected Powers: Essays on Nineteenth and Twentieth Century Literature* (New York: Barnes and Noble, 1971), p. 111.

24 Knight, 'Four Pillars of Wisdom', pp. 4–5.

25 G. Wilson Knight, *The Burning Oracle: Studies in the Poetry of Action* (London: Oxford University Press, 1939), p. 41.

26 Knight, *The Burning Oracle*, p. 41.

27 Knight, *Christ and Nietzsche*, p. 14.

28 Knight, *Neglected Powers*, p. 30 (italics original).

29 Knight, *Christ and Nietzsche*, p. 46.

30 Ibid.

31 G. Wilson Knight, *The Mutual Flame: On Shakespeare's 'Sonnets' and 'The Phoenix and the Turtle'* (London: Methuen, 1962), p. 30.

32 Knight, *The Olive and the Sword*, p. 89

33 Wellek, *A History*, V, p. 132.

Chapter 21 Shakespeare's Desert Camouflage

1 For a comprehensive discussion of this production, see Abigail Rokison-Woodall, *Shakespeare in the Theatre: Nicholas Hytner* (London and New York: Bloomsbury, 2017), pp. 107–19.

2 Peter Reynolds and Lee White, *A Rehearsal Diary: 'Henry V' at the National* (London: NT Education, 2003), p. 1.

3 Reynolds and White, *Diary*, p. 2.

4 Tim Newark, Quentin Newark, and J. F. Borsarello, *Brassey's Book of Camouflage* (London: Brassey's Limited, 1996), p. 15.

5   Newark, Newark, and Borsarello, *Camouflage*, p. 15.
6   'Desert Camouflage Uniform', https://en.wikipedia.org/wiki/Desert_Camouflage_Uniform (accessed 16 January 2022).
7   Ludmilla Jordanova, *The Look of the Past: Visual and Material Evidence in Historical Practice* (Cambridge: Cambridge University Press, 2012), p. xxi. In 2009, the phrase was quietly dropped by the Obama administration.
8   Catherine Silverstone, *Shakespeare, Trauma and Contemporary Performance* (London and New York: Routledge, 2011), p. 110.
9   See Austin Nachbur, '*Macbeth*: The Ensemble Theatre Company', *The Horizon*, 10 April 2016, https://oldhorizon.westmont.edu (accessed 18 January 2022).
10 Rachael Nicholas, Review of *Macbeth* (dir. Polly Findlay, 2018), *Shakespeare Bulletin*, 38:3 (2020), 502.
11 Reynolds and White, *Diary*, p. 25.
12 Ibid., p. 31.
13 Natasha Dixon, *National Theatre Collection: 'Othello' – Rehearsal Insights* (London and New York: Bloomsbury, 2013), pp. 3, 8.
14 Ibid., pp. 7, 8.
15 Ibid., p. 5.
16 Kate McLoughlin, *Veteran Poetics: British Literature in the Age of Mass Warfare, 1790–2015* (Cambridge: Cambridge University Press, 2018), p. 1.
17 Martin Barker, '"America Hurting": Making Movies About Iraq', in *Screens of Terror: Representations of War and Terrorism in Film and Television since 9/11*, ed. Philip Hammond (Bury St Edmunds: Abramis, 2011), pp. 37–50 (p. 39).
18 Dixon, *'Othello'*, p. 24.
19 Ibid.
20 Jenny Hughes, *Performance in a Time of Terror: Critical Mimesis and the Age of Uncertainty* (Manchester: Manchester University Press, 2011), p. 9.
21 Lois Potter, 'Shakespeare Performed: English and American Richards, Edwards and Henries', *Shakespeare Quarterly*, 55:4 (2004), 450–61 (p. 454).
22 See Robert C. Doyle, *The Enemy in Our Hands: America's Treatment of Enemy Prisoners of War from the Revolution to the War on Terror* (Lexington: University Press of Kentucky, 2010), pp. 292–349.
23 See 'The Director's Cut: Interviews with Kenneth Branagh, Edward Hall, Nicholas Hytner and Michael Boyd', in *'Henry V': The RSC Shakespeare*, ed. Jonathan Bate and Eric Rasmussen (Basingstoke: Macmillan, 2010), p. 180.
24 Andrew J. Bacevich, *The New American Militarism: How Americans Are Seduced by War* (Oxford: Oxford University Press, 2013), p. 233.
25 Emma Smith, 'Wrong-footed by events: Shakespeare's "lovely bully"', in the unpredictable present', *Times Literary Supplement*, 11 March 2022, p. 14.
26 Peter Kirwan, 'National Theatre Live: *Henry V*', 23 April 2022, https://blogs.nottingham.ac.uk/bardathon/2022/04/23/henry-v-donmar-warehouse-broadway-cinema-via-nt-live/(accessed 25 April 2022).
27 David Loewenstein and Paul Stevens, 'Preface', in *The Cambridge Companion to Shakespeare and War*, ed. David Loewenstein and Paul Stevens (Cambridge: Cambridge University Press, 2021), pp. xiii–xvi (p. xiii).

Chapter 22 'May I with Right and Conscience Make This Claim?'

1 Nicholas Hytner, *Balancing Acts: Behind the Scenes at the National Theatre* (London: Jonathan Cape, 2017), p. 53.

Chapter 23 *Henry V* and the Invasion of Iraq

1 Comprising men of the 1st Battalion The Royal Irish Regiment (R Irish), Gurkha Rifles, Household Cavalry, Royal Artillery, The Royal Engineers, Royal Electrical and Mechanical Engineers, and a detachment of US Marines, which included 1,500 men and four women.

2 The speech was taken down by *Mail on Sunday* journalist Sarah Oliver and circulated widely in news media. See 'UK troops told: Be just and strong', *BBC News*, online, 20 March 2003, http://news.bbc.co.uk/1/hi/uk/2866581.stm (accessed 25 June 2022).

3 Whilst Northern Ireland represents 3 per cent of the UK population, the British Army is 5 per cent Irish.

4 Tim Collins, *Rules of Engagement: A Life in Conflict* (London: Headline, 2005), p. 160.

5 Not recorded at the time by Sarah Oliver, but quoted by Kenneth Branagh in the BBC's *10 Days to War: Our Business Is North*, aired on 19 March 2008.

6 Collins, *Rules of Engagement*, p. 160.

7 Cumbrian slang for 'totally amazed'.

8 George MacDonald Fraser, *Quartered Safe Out Here* (London: Harper Collins, 2000 [1993]), pp. 190–92.

9 Ibid., p. 192.

10 Napoleon makes this remark in his 'Observations on Spanish Affairs' ('Observations sur les affaires d'Espagne'), written in the palace of Saint Cloud on 27 August 1808 to his brother, Joseph, King of Spain. See *Correspondance de Napoléon Ier publiée par ordre de l'Empereur Napoléon III*, vol. 17 (Paris, 1865), pp. 545–49 (p. 549).

11 From J. W. Ward to Miss Berry, Paris, 11 May 1814, in *Extracts from the Journals and Correspondence of Miss Berry … 1783–1852*, ed. Lady Theresa Lewis, 3 vols (London: Longman, 1856), III, p. 16.

12 Fraser, *Quartered Safe Out Here,* p. 192.

13 Collins, *Rules of Engagement,* p. 34.

Chapter 25 'Mere Prattle, without Practice, Is All His Soldiership'

1 William John Thoms, 'Was Shakespeare Ever a Soldier?', in *Three Notelets on Shakespeare* (London: John Russell Smith, 1865), pp. 115–36; Duff Cooper, *Sergeant Shakespeare* (London: Hart-Davis, 1949).

Afterword

1 R. B. Outhwaite, 'Dearth, the English Crown, and the "Crisis of the 1590s"', in *The European Crisis of the 1590s: Essays in Comparative History*, ed. Peter Clark (London: George Allen and Unwin, 1985), p. 16.
2 Gary Taylor (ed.), *The Oxford Shakespeare: Henry V* (Oxford: Oxford University Press, 1984), p. 7.
3 Emma Smith (ed.), *Shakespeare in Production: King Henry V* (Cambridge: Cambridge University Press, 2002), p. 33.
4 George Santayana, *Soliloquies in England, and Later Soliloquies* (New York: Charles Scribner's Sons, 1922), p. 102.
5 Philip Sidney, 'The Defence of Poesy', in *The Oxford Authors Sir Philip Sidney*, ed. Katherine Duncan-Jones (Oxford: Oxford University Press, 1989), p. 242.

Index

Index